Going Up, Going Down

The Aliyah of an Innocent
Israel, 1973–1977

Maggie Goren

"The ability to believe is our outstanding quality, and only art adequately translates it into reality. But when we assuage our need for faith with an ideology, we court disaster."

Gerhard Richter (Notes, 1988)

aliyah n. immigration to the Holy Land [from Hebrew, literally: act of going up, ascent]

Collins English Dictionary, 3rd Edition, 1991

First published in 2011 on behalf of the author by
Scotforth Books, Carnegie House,
Chatsworth Road, Lancaster LA1 4SL.

ISBN 13: 978-1-904244-65-3

Printed in the UK by Blissetts

Contents

To the memory of Palo, a man of wicked
and huge humour and his wonderful wife,
Aviva, for their enduring friendship, constant help and
love before, during and after our brief stay in Israel.

Also for 'little' Adam, killed in action in Lebanon,
August 2006, aged 21.

And with love for Non, Adam, Matti,
Ben and Dan.

Foreword

Everyone has stories to tell about significant times in their lives. In adding a few more words to that expanding and limitless heap, I hope to share for a brief moment something of my own experience of the exciting, funny and sad madness of a life lived for a while in a mad country that has suffered and regrettably caused suffering ~ the fate of all nations across time. The story covers a short period of four years only when I lived in Israel and cuts across that nation's own short history of sixty years. The brevity of my stay is the tale's shaping spirit. We left before the complete collapse of political goodwill.

Lovers, detractors and critics of this historically new nation are inevitably confronted with older histories, present conflicts and a whole swathe of emotional, intellectual, academic and religious points of view. How one sees Israel today, which invites so much controversy, obviously depends largely on who we are; where and when we were born and our personal experiences.

I was born in London two years before the outbreak of the Second World War. My civil servant father was a pacifist and agnostic and my mother, fortunately for me perhaps, a wife who worked hard at home bringing up her three children until well into their teens. She had briefly worked in an office and been a Church of England Sunday School teacher before, at the tender age of seventeen, she met and shortly afterwards married my father.

Father ceased to be a choirboy when, as he said, he began to recognise the meaning of words hitherto spoken or sung automatically. *"Harold be thy name"* is not perhaps an original joke but was, as he told us, the sort of repetitious misunderstanding of his rote learning. My grandfather had fought from the early days in the First World War and was killed in the last few months when my father was only six years of age and one of three brothers, with one on the way, in a working class family. Those circumstances, when my father reached an age to think for himself, no doubt played a key role in his coming to doubt the existence of a loving God and in his decision in his youthful years to give up both the choir and the church. It happened to many at that time. I grew up in a caring, thoughtful and argumentative household where talking was the thing and thinking for yourself encouraged as we children advanced into well chosen secondary education.

In my account of life in a small village in Israel half way between Haifa and Nazareth from 1973 to 1977, the politics are mainly local and religion remains background material only. But since I believe totally in the fundamentally shared qualities in being human across every physical or religious boundary ~ as Shylock famously said *"if you prick us, do we not bleed? "* ~ I can only hope these qualities pop out of the print to override any prejudice, ambivalence or even malice aforethought. I would like instead to think that being simply and complexly human is what lights up a small corner that was other people's lives from another place, in another time and with a little wit and less wisdom lights up a corner which is ours today ~ and entertains. The characters, real enough, who appear in my pages do so because of my affection for them and with my deep gratitude for being who they were in our brief encounter and for constantly reminding me that we all laugh and cry at much the same things.

Maggie Goren
April 2011

How to 'Become' an Immigrant

It was the 10th June, 1967, and the Six Day War in Israel was over, in less than a week indeed. My priorities on that day were much the same as they had been before the war began and for several years while I had been working in the BBC Television Newsroom at Alexandra Palace, typing the news of that war and a number of others. I was looking for a father. Not my own, but a prospective father for my unborn children.

You might imagine that there would be plenty of opportunities to successfully conclude my search in the bustling world of 'live' TV News with editors, journalists, cameramen, crew, 'old Uncle Tom C and all' daily popping in and out from around the country and across the globe. And that is without including the permanent newsreaders employed not only for their suitable accents and serious presentation but also to encourage a core of female fans who might adore the old-school type Bob Dougall, fancy the chirpy ex-naval officer Richard Baker or simply fall in love with heart-throb Michael Aspel.

Affairs or simple sexual flings were not quite as common as they might be today when condomised, one-night stands are just part of the party or any scene. And, indeed, I probably thought then that such careless mating is not the worthiest way in which to introduce new life onto the planet, despite living my halcyon days in the 'fab' sixties. Some serious thinking should surely go into that project as a first step to protecting the progeny. I imagined then that I was trying to be 'responsible', well sort of.

Bearing a child, though, was definitely in my mind. Thinking about the real consequences of that action or emigrating to foreign parts was not. Indeed, I had already emigrated once to Australia for ten pounds and returned after three years convinced that despite the call of the wild, or at least the wide open spaces, my heart belonged to Europe. Daddy was also pleased that I returned.

This adventure had taken place in the early sixties when I should have been smoking pot and running around in bare feet with flowers in my hair. Somehow I missed the great love-ins while I was juggling with a 2nd World War .303 jungle carbine given to me unexpectedly as a birthday present from my current lover, a wild, travelin' man. The gun was for practice-shooting in the outback and occasionally hitting a rabbit. The rabbits, I should add, had recovered from that dreadful '*myxi*' disease and were reproducing again at a great rate. Maybe it was that which sparked the urge in me in my mid-twenties to get on with the job. The travelin' man, French by nationality and Communist by political inclination, was not interested in adding to a grossly over-populated world or in giving up the travelling. So by 1963 I guessed it was time to give him up and return to the Old Country.

I was already thirty when the Six Day War ended with the Newsroom jubilantly watching film footage of Egypt's fighter planes being bombed very early in the morning on their own airfield and put out of action before they could take off. That was an Israel attacked from all quarters and under siege ~ the underdog the British love so much. How the world changes and the dogs in it.

I had not been without suitors during my six years at Ally Pally, some suitable, some not, but fatherhood was either not on their agenda with me or on mine with them. Heigh ho, thought I, as plans refused to progress and time marched on. But I began to realize that anxiety was the worst way to come at getting a plan together, or even getting pregnant. So I decided to relax, sit it out

mind. I was left berating him for his lack of care at such an
nt time in both our lives and wondering why he looked so
d, despite his obvious joy and amazement when holding his
son who weighed just over five pounds.

lly decided that Arni was not cut out for the physical
of giving birth even at one removed, especially as he had
y brought me a book to read, *Teach Yourself Hebrew*,
as enduring the final stages of labour. But Arni did turn
a very practical Dad, not being in the least squeamish at
nappies and bathing the baby. But to return to dear old
le, after being patched and touched up she was sold to
iastic young man who wanted to go on safari across the
sert. I only hope he made it!

doubting my sanity in contemplating a partnership with
wild man, our Register Officer marriage took place six
er in Harrow, where we had bought a little end-terrace
best man was Arni's jolly office colleague from Guyana
n Forbes, married to a pleasant English girl. I remember
rticularly because of his namesake Orson Welles, a much
but no doubt as nimble on his feet for all that, as was our
was a natural dancer with bags of rhythm. My best friend,
ron of honour and she held the murmuring baby Adam
ter Office, causing some consternation and laughter in
area, hosting three marriage parties, when she looked
ss at me to ask whether baby needed a bottle yet.

pared and set out the wedding breakfast and chilled
gne at home ready for our return from the ceremony
and a few friends. Having forgotten to slowly defrost
time to cook it, I'd had to leave it in a bath of salty
urs on the wedding eve and get it hastily dressed,
eady to carve before making the rest of the food for
day. This little effort, alongside sorting out my mini-
ing outfit, feeding and dressing the baby, finding my
and laying the table, was all that was left for me to do
g morning. What luxury!

and forget all about it for a while, more or less. A few months later,
a young man knocked at my bed-sit door in a rather weird state. By
that I do not mean he was wearing flowers in his hair or smoking
the weed, as some in the house might. Rather his thick, dark hair
seemed to be spattered with green highlights smelling of verdigris,
his hands were shaking and his face covered in black streaks. He
looked for all the world like a soldier camouflaged for the jungle.
He held a box of matches in a slightly trembling fist.

Today one might immediately think of terrorists but then it
seemed to me that the only terrified person nearby was this unfor-
tunate fellow. I gathered, through an unfamiliar foreign accent and
much arm waving, that the man had recently fought in the Six Day
War and had not been scared at all but that on this night he had
been frankly overcome with fear. Naturally I asked him in, despite
the hair, sat him down with a coffee and discovered that he had
nearly succeeded in blowing up our geyser in the only bathroom in
the large house. Having never seen such a monster machine before,
and using little common-sense, this recent arrival to London decided
to tackle it stage by stage, for he realized it had to be lit to heat the
water. Excellent initial reasoning. It did not occur to him, however,
to ask for help in the lighting of it. He was, after all, a fully qualified
engineer and an 'officer and gentleman' of the Artillery.

Ours was a coin operated boiler and my unexpected guest had
found the requisite pence and put them in the slot. This of course
allowed the gas to be turned on. Without any matches to hand
he opened the gas, turning the pilot light as indicated into the
cylinder and then left the bathroom to find some matches. After
several minutes searching in his room along the corridor he found
the matchbox, returned to the bathroom and put a lighted match
to the boiler. The explosion which ensued certainly cleaned out
the old boiler and deposited much of the coppery silt on the young
man's head and streaked his face with soot. It was in this sad state
that this new tenant knocked on my door for sympathy and practical advice in getting a bath, which he now needed more surely
than he had before.

The language problem was quite difficult to overcome as my visitor, it transpired later, had no way of pronouncing the awful English 'th' and therefore when he explained that he needed a *bus*, I naturally asked him where he wanted to go and if he wanted to take a bath first. "I must get *bus*," he repeated, and wanted to know *if there was upstairs…and water*. Again, at complete cross purposes and totally bemused by the conversation, I explained that all the buses in our area were double-deckers and none were open-topped so you didn't get rained upon. Once again I asked where he wanted to go. Clearly he understood nothing and looking at me with some desperation said "*Pleez* come to *bus room* with me." The penny suddenly dropped and I was unable to contain my laughter but he followed me rather diffidently to the bathroom where I cleaned up the mess and showed him how to light the geyser, amazingly still operational, and run a *bus*. Well, I actually ran the first *bus* for him and still giggling returned to my little flat. Now, as it happened, that *bus* was the first stage on the road to emigration.

The second stage came after the clean-up and a return visit when I noticed that the 'chimney sweep' had turned into a rather handsome, quite charmingly funny and enthusiastic Israeli engineer, who had a permit to work for a while in London and hoped to take a Masters degree in Concrete Technology at Imperial College. It occurred to me that building a concrete bunker to cope with unexpected explosions might indeed prove useful but, then again, a degree in plumbing perhaps even more useful.

The third stage followed when our first son was on the way and we were having a pre-marital honeymoon touring Spain and Portugal in an old Ford Thames van called *Ermintrude*. We had converted *Ermintrude* to a motor-caravan by installing a hand-made, fold-down double bed, an old telly case to house blankets, a little sink and cooker unit and a bench seat and table. After losing the first gear in the first week, we were steeply approaching the high view point of Puerto de Palares in the Cordillera of Northern Spain when my resourceful or panicky engineer, depending on your viewpoint, suddenly steered the van round across the road

and braked hard. We were then facing
mountain route we had just climbed up.
ment he shifted the gears and made th
road to the summit viewing area, zig-za
quite understood the purpose of this ma
feared he would not make the summit
nowhere else to go gear-wise.

Without a prior explanation for th
kittens at that point but was fortunatel

It was somewhere in the greener No
parked in a quiet spot on a slope of
Arni was jacking up *Ermintrude* with
the tea leaves out of the door before
said, "What do you think about marr

"Quite a nice idea," I replied, "and
me to marry you?"

"Hmm" was all he answered and
ders. Nothing further was said on
managed to drive a couple of hundr
direction to Oporto and the neare
gear and with some broken springs.

Ermintrude was repaired and
rides and visits to fantastic, out-o
with diesel instead of petrol on on
England and the baby was born a
weeks early.

After affording us that unforg
sold following a too close enco
roundabout near Bushey, Herts.
maternity home to make an ac
when the collision occurred. N
the time and I, with no idea o
upset that he did not appear fo
even when he finally arrived did
of upsetting me at a delicate ti

the mal
importa
distracte
tiny first
I fina
business
previous
when I w
out to be
changing
Ermintrude
an enthus
Sahara de
Despite
a second
months la
house. Ou
called Ors
his name p
larger man
Orson who
Jo, was ma
at the Regi
the receptio
straight acro
I had pr
the champa
with family
the turkey i
water for h
roasted and
serving on th
skirted wedd
husband's tie
on the weddi

Whether or not tea leaves and turkeys provide good omens, we had a second son two years later and only then was the idea mooted that I might like to emigrate to Israel, lock, stock and two bouncing babies. I asked my Irish neighbour, Helen Burke, what she thought of this. The Burkes were a lovely family and she tearfully told me, "Sure we'll all miss ye, but we'll be back to Ireland ourselves shortly and could ye please help us to get our stuff to Waterloo Station."

These honest folk couldn't afford to hire a van, so Arni set off on two practice refugee runs; tables, bedding and boxes roped to the roof of our old Austin A40 and spilling out of the windows. On the first run, two bright-eyed, little ginger-haired boys and their mother were balanced precariously on heaps of belongings in the back of the car. They would remain with the luggage at the station and wait for Dad to come back with the rest of it on the second run. Where there's a will! Well, they made it to Cork where they happily settled in a village outside the town and as far as I know, and God willing, are still thereabouts today. We kept in touch for many years.

During his first five years in England my husband became infatuated not only with antique chairs, and a few larger pieces we could barely afford from the Railway Shop, a house clearance business by a bridge over the tracks in Harrow Weald, but also with vintage cars. First Arni bought a derelict, wooden 3-wheeler Morgan from the Forest of Dean which went nowhere after it was unloaded from a trailer and parked at my parent's country cottage in the Cotswolds, much to my father's consternation. That was sold on at a loss. Finally he bought a vintage Rolls Royce which needed and got a complete engine reconstruction by a marvelous engineer working from a garage in his back garden, at a price we could not afford but somehow did. We called her Rosie. My husband also found a little caravan at a bargain price which also needed some attention. He apparently had in his mind the sacrilegious idea of towing it behind Rosie, after fixing a tow-bar to her chassis! "How could he?" ...I can hear the RR Enthusiasts scream.

It was our intention to make a leisurely three-week journey across France and into Italy, savouring the delights of countryside, art and architecture on the way, and then take the boat from Napoli to Haifa with Rosie, caravan, children *et al* on board. The rest of the furniture, nearly antique or otherwise was to be shipped by door-to-door container service.

There were a few hurdles yet to cross. Firstly the final stage to becoming a new immigrant to the State of Israel. This involved searches, paperwork, interviews and final granting of immigrant status for me, the non-Jewish wife of an Israeli born and bred citizen. This did not give me citizenship, simply concessions as a new immigrant intending to settle permanently in Israel. Our two sons automatically received the nationality of their father. The prime concession for Arni was that I could be the registered owner of a car which could be imported free of tax. The only difficulty was that I needed not only to be the owner but to hold a driver's licence. To that point in my life in 1973, I had only driven a scooter of 150cc and my licence did not cover a car, let alone an antique. I had to take a test. By this time Arni had organized everything, including boat tickets for the second week in May for the Napoli to Haifa run. I had time only to have fifteen driving lessons and had to pass the test, otherwise Rosie and the rest of the family were going nowhere. My husband had not countenanced failure. I wondered at that stage where my reading of the tea leaves had gone wrong or how I had managed to convince him that I was 'superwoman'.

The test took place in Harrow Weald and I was fortunate or not to have a big, taciturn Welshman, physical qualities not normally associated with that race, who was retiring from service that very day. Was I the first or the last? He was sternly intimidating. I wondered whether he envisaged going out with a bang or a whimper and laughed to myself despite feeling sick.

I imagined I had completed my 3-point turn without hitting the kerb but was unprepared for the elderly woman who decided to cross the main road in the middle of town at lights that were green.

I hit the brakes, without looking in the rear vision mirror, and she stepped back onto the pavement, whereupon I started shakily to check my gears and move off. At the same time the lady, deciding I had been waiting for her, stepped off the pavement again, with a little hesitation and no regard whatsoever for the lights which were still green. Once more I lightly braked to avoid a collision with her, never mind a vehicle about to run into me from behind, and sensed the lights were about to go amber. I gave up, thinking 'what the hell, it's too late now' and revving up in first made it to the left around the corner as my tester, and I, had indicated I should. He had said nothing throughout the incident and shortly afterwards told me to turn right into the Test station. I did not know if I was visibly shaking by then but was certainly inwardly shaking and unable to judge whether bang or whimper covered my own situation, never mind his. I hardly remember reciting anything of the Highway Code to my retiring Welsh examiner.

My husband had asked me to phone him at work to let him know the driving test result. "Well," he said in eager anticipation, "you passed?"

I was upset, not only by the whole experience but by the fact that our immediate future had been left dependent solely on me while he sat happily doodling at his drawing board. I felt that I did not deserve to be put in such a position and was silent for a moment. I then said, "What do you think?" He read this as proof of the fact that I had failed and I could almost see him crumbling with disappointment and anxiety on the other end of the phone.

"Oh, dear," he said very quietly and sighed very loudly.

"It's OK, I passed," I shouted down the phone before slamming it back on the receiver. The return call was ignored but we did open a bottle of wine that night and eagerly go over our travel itinerary with glad hearts and great expectations.

Chocks Away – More or Less

The day in April 1973 came when Arni said goodbye to the friends and colleagues with whom he had worked at a Consulting Engineering firm in Wembley and after the container men had carefully packed all that we owned for shipping to the Port of Haifa. The container was full. How, we wondered, had we accumulated so much in three short years?

The fond farewells, however, had to be played out. It was agreed that we would spend our last long weekend with the family in their lovely country cottage not far from Stratford-upon-Avon. Our firstborn, Adam, was just three years old and his young brother, Matti, aged eleven months. They were in for a fairly comfortable ride in our superbly, but originally, upholstered 1933 Rolls Royce. We had only had enough money to properly restore the engine, having to leave the hugely expensive business of restoration of the buff leather interior, its beautiful wood and metal work and the black chassis to a later date…when we got rich, if. The model had been designed to be chauffeur driven. It was therefore divided into a commodious, walnut veneered and upholstered passenger area separated from the driving cab by a partition ingeniously containing two comfortable, upholstered foldaway seats. Above this was a glass partition which could be shaded with faded oatmeal silk blinds, if one had no desire to see or speak to the driver. Alternatively the glass could be opened for communication. The sumptuous back seat was deep and beautifully sprung.

In front of that was a floor space of almost three feet to the partition where a carry-cot could comfortably sit.

Having sold the little old Austin A40, affixed a tow-bar to Rosie and hitched the caravan behind her, we set off for the Cotswolds, Arni in the driver's seat, mother and kids wallowing in the classy comfort of the separate compartment. Following a short trial run, this was the first major journey Rosie had faced with the caravan in tow. The leisurely jaunt down the old A41 went without a hitch but certainly attracted the curiosity of folk in the towns and villages through which we passed during the two and a half hours it took to reach the village of Winderton, a hint of things to come. On arriving we were greeted affectionately but, one felt, with a little sadness. My parents were worried about their grandchildren going to live in a troublesome part of the world.

My elder brother with his wife and three young children were coming to see us off from their home in Leicester, arriving on the Saturday evening. They were expected to appear at around 5pm but it was already gone 7pm before we received a phone-call from the emergency unit of a hospital in Rugby an hour or more away. The message was that my brother had hit something on the Fosse Way, injured his leg and damaged the car, a Volkswagen camper van. Everybody else was alright but following treatment requiring him to use crutches it was necessary for Arni to go and pick them all up from the hospital. So Rosie set forth on her first mission of mercy and brought the family of five safely home.

During the day Adam had been playing on his own and managed to topple a small but rather heavy, free-standing radiator onto his foot, which promptly swelled up. My father bathed and bandaged it and found a thick sock to put on the foot which would not go into his shoe. Sadly there was another young person in the family who needed crutches on a permanent basis. This was Jackie, my brother's daughter, who'd had a motor-muscular problem from birth.

The family, not without humour, decided that the auspicious occasion of our departure required photographic coverage and one picture was taken in front of Rosie of three persons supported on crutches! We hoped that this would not be an omen for the rest of our three-week journey through France and Italy to our port of departure for the Holy Land. It was already becoming a crusade.

I suppose with all the emotion and tension of that occasion, my mother stalwartly cooking a bacon and egg breakfast for sixteen people, we rather hurriedly stuffed the little cupboards of our caravan with the last minute tins and packets we had been given and had probably not stowed them all away with due care. While Arni had been a member of the Rolls Royce Enthusiasts' Club, neither of us had ever had any contact with a Caravan Club let alone a caravan. Hence, perhaps, a swift learning curve as we tried to swing majestically out of the gate at the bottom of the farmer's drive leading from the cottage onto the lane with a very acute right hand bend to negotiate. I was busily waving my tearful farewells out of the window when the van suddenly locked as we attempted to get through the gate and turn sharply right. With this sudden halt came the sound of cupboards flying open and the crashing of tins onto the floor.

We stepped out of Rosie for a moment to inspect and adjust matters in the caravan and suddenly saw various members of the family flying down the hundred yards of the track to see what had happened, my father at the helm and my brother quite fast on crutches in the rear. Naturally there was a lot of tut-tutting and apprehensions expressed about our getting as far as the coast of England, let alone the coast of Italy. We laughed a little nervously, gritting our teeth to hide the embarrassment of such an ignomin-ious exit following an heroic farewell. The tow bar adjusted, we waved goodbye again and were finally on our way on Tuesday 24th April, 1973.

Excitement was high and I do not remember the road between our point of departure and arrival at Newhaven but it was a lovely sunny day and I do recall driving onto the Cross Channel ferry with a nervous Arni getting the RR safely on board and into its appointed spot in the hold, where he wished but was not allowed to stay with it. We disembarked at the unearthly hour of one o'clock in the morning of the 25th in Dieppe, when a very tired and rather irritable family rolled off the boat to park for the rest of the night somewhere on the seafront. Now the caravan did not sport a loo, which meant we had to find public lavatories in towns and if we were not on a camping site then it was necessary to organize ourselves as campers must. We carried a potty with us for the children but not for the adults. Somehow we chased for an hour around Dieppe in the bright, misty morning trying desperately to find a public lavatory. It was finally located just a few yards from where we had been parked. Well, it wasn't the first time we'd buzzed off in the wrong direction and would not be the last. So it was a slow take-off that day but just after noon we headed for Rouen.

I should at this juncture point out that our trip across France and down through Italy to Naples had been carefully choreographed along a route compatible with seeing much of the unforgettable architecture and art that had been featured in Kenneth Clark's wonderful 'Civilisation' series on TV. The book had been read and notes made of the all the places that we might include in a three week trip along a route taking us across central France, down to Lyons and Grenoble towards Briançon and across the only mountain pass into the North West of Italy open at that time of the year, the Col du Lauteret at Montgenèvre. Having descended from the Alps we would skirt Turin and turn towards the coast at Genoa, thence to Pisa and Florence to meet friends before continuing towards Rome and Naples. Neither of us had traveled that route, been to Italy or seen any of those places before and certainly not in a Rolls Royce of any age. That was the plan.

I was looking forward to seeing the Cathedral of Rouen made famous by the eerie colours in the ethereal paintings of Monet. Traffic and parking was a problem but a local guide kindly gave us good directions to ensure we found a place off the main street and pointed us in the direction of the Cathedral. The Gothic building loomed tall and large with its great grey façade and huge rose window set off by the pink of a beautiful flowering cherry in full bloom in its foreground.

After a quick visit we left to do some necessary shopping and take it back to the car, where we were greeted by a couple of young reporters enthralled with the Rolls. They wanted pictures of the car in front of the Cathedral so we asked them to hop into the vehicle, to their huge delight, and they directed us back to the ancient building where we were asked to park our vintage vehicle with its tow in a no parking zone on an extremely busy thoroughfare. They quickly took their photos and we weren't booked despite the fact that we were soon snarling up the lunchtime traffic. Our journalists surely painted out our shabby little caravan, which was always a major part of the parking problem!

It was now 2pm and none of us had eaten except Matti, or Bubble as I called him, who had somehow found some chocolate while we were busy talking and was not only smothered in it but was crawling all over the back seat with his little sticky fingers. Adam was whining with hunger. It was time to leave the town and find somewhere quiet to have a late lunch of charcuterie, cheeses, fresh bread and wine. Feeling so much better, we motored on down to Nonancourt and arrived at dusk in a camp site by the river Eure with lovely hot showers which we immediately used, Adam with his Dad and Bubble with me. I then made a quick beef stew in the pressure cooker which we ate with relish before all tumbling early into bed to make up for lost sleep.

From Rouen we traveled to our second awe-inspiring landmark, the Cathedral of Chartres. On arriving in the town, with its quaintly dressed lace-makers selling their work on the cobbled hill in front of the Cathedral, we were able to park near that magnificent and unique building. What can one say? Its size, grandeur and amazing structure simply took our breath away. Its sculptured portals of elegant, sophisticated figures with gentle faces full of compassion were so unexpected in a medieval cathedral. Its great flying buttresses to support the inner columns and arches were astounding. The cool space inside was immense, lit up by the sun shining through its one hundred and seventy wonderful and deeply vivid stained-glass windows. If those early Gothic builders had had it in mind to reach heaven across a wide Romanesque space supported on immensely tall, elegant Gothic arches, they had been well on the way to succeeding. We stood there looking upwards to an enormous height with our mouths disrespectfully open. Such a pile. Such an architectural and artisan achievement. Such testimony to faith in a God.

We left Chartres to cross the light orange-brown, ploughed earth of the region. This was wheat country where fields met the road with no hedges or verges as we entered the Cloiret district. Eventually we found one field with a wide, uncultivated grass verge edged with a clump of tall blackthorn bushes covered in white blossom. We pulled off on a track and parked behind the bushes for the night. After feeding the kids and putting them to bed we tucked into a quiet dinner for two of tender veal escallopes with lemon wedges, salad and fresh French bread, followed by a purée of apricots and cream, biscuits and French soft cheese. Very tasty, very romantic, except that I suddenly felt the bright flame of the gas mantle under a glass already accidentally cracked, needed turning down for a softer lighting effect to lend a more romantic atmosphere before serving coffee and a little liqueur. Arni, in an effort to please me, managed somehow to push holes in the cotton mantle in the process. We had no spare mantles ~ so the light was out and we had to go to bed without the coffee and liqueur, without reading ... or talking a great deal. Ah me, what silly trifles can blight the best intentions, the most romantic moments. Someone up there was trying to tell me something or was immoderately laughing.

The next morning shone bright and clear. We continued across country to Pithiviers, later a famed centre for natural 'as-you-like-it' childbirth, and on to Montargis where a fellow offered me serious money for Arni's little treasure ~ not the baby! I told him, "no way José...Jean...Jacques...Rosie is not for sale." We bought more bread and cheeses... oooh...and missed our turning to Doucy and found ourselves on the Route National 7. We got off that as quickly as possible only to find ourselves in Toucy! The countryside was taking another shape. The fields were smaller and there were plenty of woods. The villages looked as though they had been lost in time, having a feudal air about them. There were great disintegrating houses with wrought iron balconies and rusting wrought iron balustrades on semi-circular sweeps of weed strewn steps up to old and decrepit large, carved wooden front doors.

The terrain was now more suited to dairy than arable production and gently rolled upwards towards Clamecy and then got steeper still. We continued towards Chateau Chinon and at seven o'clock turned off on a side road that led to a camp site at St. Péreuse. It was in the grounds of an old, dilapidated Manor House. There were chickens and a dog running loose and the place was managed by a farmer and his wife. We were the only campers. We set up the caravan in the shade of a huge cypress tree and firs, beyond which a grassy area was alive with bright yellow buttercups. This out of the way site did, however, provide hot showers and a marvellous view across the hillocky, verdant, scenery. It was so pleasant that we decided to stay another night and visit Chateau Chinon the next day.

It was raining at noon as we motored into the town of Chateau Chinon, perched high above the knobbly landscape. We found a modest restaurant and had a typical local set meal of radishes with paté and ham, escallopes de veau with little roast potatoes and a lovely green salad, accompanied by an excellent red wine and then a choice of cheeses and fruit, followed by coffee with cognac ~ all for just over one pound each. Well, Mr. Clark…simple, maybe, civilised …yes! There was a viewing point above the town from which we scanned an impressive geographical area; green, wooded pregnant bumps and little valleys thrown up by God knows what cataclysmic and ancient past when our world was spat out.

The next day we wanted to get away early but there had been a great downpour during the night and Rosie's electrics had got wet. Arni took a cloth to her plugs and with bonnet open allowed her to dry out in the morning sun. We left before noon and rode down to Autun from where we intended to take the main route to Macon via Nolay and Chalon. Instead we found ourselves on a beautiful secondary road winding through sleepy old villages with castles perched precariously atop hillocks overlooking a natural wine country with its vineyards firmly in bud. We were then headed in the direction of another remarkable landmark, Cluny. As we passed through the pretty town of Buxy, the pale afternoon sun shone again on a remarkable Burgundian landscape of gentle, vineyard-clad slopes, emerald green fields and the soft, brick-pink tiles and sandy stonework of the old villages with their Romanesque churches. We arrived in Cluny at two o'clock.

Luckily we were able to park in the old square right in front of the ruins of the Abbey, the flanking walls of its grounds topped here and there with little pink Romanesque turrets. We joined a small group being given a tour of the ruins and learned that this famous Romanesque Abbey, built in the 11th and 12th centuries by the Benedictine monks and added to in the Gothic period, had once been a magnificent building by any standards then or now, the largest stone monument in the world. It had been an amazing 187 m. long, the nave 180 m. with a four-sided aisle crossed by eleven spans and sixty-eight pillars. There had been two transepts of unequal length crossing the nave and towers from which two fantastic spires had reached into the skies. Only one remained, gracefully attaining its needle peak at about 30 m.

The Abbey had been wittingly and joyfully destroyed and its stone largely sold off to merchants following the French Revolution and the Age of Enlightenment, when men said goodbye to God and hello to Reason. Something told me that you cannot destroy the spirit of such an inspired place by simply removing the stones. After the new *humanism* had taken over, the Benedictine monks who had flourished in Cluny over several centuries had then dispersed far and wide throughout Europe, spreading their influence in the promotion of peace and humanity. Something spiritual definitely remained in the atmosphere clinging to Cluny, 'enlightenment' or no, in the peace and gentleness of its surroundings.

We left Cluny for Macon and the fields on either side were

dressed as for a bride, the lush green adorned by the pink and white blossom of apple and cherry orchards. On leaving this lovely countryside behind we made for the auto-route down to Lyons, which we hastened through as quickly as possible, ignoring the grubbiness of the industrialized area. We intended to get well out onto the road towards Grenoble and the foothills of the Alps before finding somewhere to camp. It was dusk as we started to climb out of the flat valley and at 7pm Arni turned off the road down a tiny lane just after La Combe. This only led to a couple of old farmhouses. A farmer and his wife appeared and after a chat and smiling at the children they very kindly offered us their farm courtyard in which to park overnight, which we thankfully did.

It was now Monday 30th April and we had been on the road for six days but not without sustaining a little damage to the caravan. One of the long springs of the van had broken, so that it was riding all on one side, as it were. The farmer did no more the next day than get out his welding equipment and cut three new leaves for our spring from the spring of an old, abandoned hay cart. Arni then managed to re-instate this part lying under the van, precariously jacked up for the purpose.

The couple were charming, in their fifties and with two grandchildren in nearby La Combe. They were trying to 'modernize' their three-hundred years' old farmhouse. They would take no payment either for letting us stay overnight or for providing us with a new spring but Arni was hauled in to share a pernod at the kitchen table before we left and to make the best of conversation with his non-existent French. There was much gesticulating and considerable laughter which I heard as I took the children for a short walk up the lane. Although I was not there to translate, it became obvious that goodwill, kind hearts and hearty laughter speak their own language. We were ready for the road again and after salutations all round were told that we must come back again next year.

After a few kilometers we were facing the height and grandeur of the snow-capped Alps and wondered how Rosie would fare getting up and over those mountains. We shopped in Grenoble before setting off for the foothills after lunch on a perfect afternoon. There was no wind, the sun was hot and the sky was a clear, deep blue.

We began the gentle climb to Bourg D'Oisans before making a steeper ascent for 18 kms; a steady but continuous gradient with many bends in the road, sometimes hugging the rock and sometimes looking precipitously down on the drop side into the valleys below. There were a few parapets and barriers of metal or stone but not many. As we faced one sharp bend Adam asked his father if we were going to drive in the sky. I know how he felt but I assured him this was not where we were going. But you certainly had to keep your eye constantly on the road and remember the lights before you entered the occasional short tunnels. At one point we passed a huge dam several hundred feet below us. We were on a flat stretch at that point and got out to look at the massive structure with just a little basin of water glinting in the sun far below. This time Adam said he didn't want to go into the water! For a very small child this scenery must have appeared gigantic and frightening

We set off climbing again and I clung with grim death to Rosie's silky plaited straps as poor Arni gently steered the old girl up and up and round the bends. I suffer from vertigo. Was Arni also holding his breath, I wondered? We were silent. The trees up there were not yet in leaf and even the pines looked brown and yet looming ahead of us was another thousand meters to climb before we reached the Col du Lauteret. This pass was open daily for twelve hours between 7am and 7pm in April.

At about a third of the way up this alpine ascent Rosie began to get disgruntled, showing off by cutting out the petrol feed through some piece of her automated equipment called the Autovac. This meant, if we were not to grind to a halt on a steep incline or dangerous bend, that Arni had to keep pumping the accelerator and changing down ~ well there's only so far down that you can change to ~ and I began to feel his frustration and nervousness, the old caravan bobbing along behind us and not liking sudden halts. So despite being a perfect day, it was not an easy one, especially at one point when we met a giant petrol tanker as we were going through a curved rock tunnel. This created an impasse. Both drivers braked hard simultaneously and stopped. The tanker was too long to carry on around the curve without making a wider loop onto our side of the road. In the end the tanker driver had to back some way and get closer to the nearside tunnel wall as we edged as close as possible to the rock on our side and somehow just managed to squeeze past one another.

The snow-capped peaks of Montgenèvre were in sight about twelve kilometers away as the road began finally to wind down towards Briançon, where we parked with great relief and Arni took a look at poor Rosie's Autovac. By then we had motored up to a height of more than six hundred meters or two thousand feet, as I prefer to think of it, on a constantly winding alpine road. It had taken us three and a half hours to drive less than fifty kilometers from Grenoble to Briançon. But it was worth it. Those distant peaks we had stared up at from the plain were now spread around us like the stiff and glittering meringue on a pie. It was awe-inspiring. Sad to say there was no welcoming inn in Briançon. We were chased from one place to another, quite literally in one case by a large lady who shouted at us that the season was over! So we motored off again to find our own site not far from the town and about eleven kilometers from the border crossing into Italy.

What we hadn't realized was that April 30th was the eve of May Day and a general holiday. All shops were shut but fortunately we had plenty of food on board and soon found a splendid meadow with a rushing, ice-cold mountain stream bordered by tall pines where we could quietly park and bother no-one. It was as picturesque as any advertisement for ski-ing or sparkling mountain water. We relaxed, surely it was going to be downhill all the way from hereon, surely....no? Despite the glistening snow, the sun shone hot on us as I drew water from the stream to make a well-earned cup of tea for the master, the chauffeur-handy-man and probably the only husband alive who would take a very old lady of forty called Rosie, one much younger lady of nearly the same age and a couple of kids on such a hare-brained spree. We needed no rocking that night.

Borders & Beyond

We woke the next morning to the sun shining in a clear blue sky. It was a perfect site, a perfect May Day and we had slept deeply and recovered from the longest part of our alpine journey. There was now less than 10 kms to climb on a final precipitous route to the Italian border post before our descent into another country. We were in a wide meadowland, if you like, a high, green, shallow basin of pasture way above the plain in which Grenoble had sat, the area encircled by those frosted, glistening peaks which suddenly seemed no more high than 'an elephant's eye'.

We opened the door of the caravan and breathed in the fresh air and could hear the rushing stream down a steep bank a few yards away. We felt the sun hot on our faces. After dressing the children and enjoying a quick breakfast we went off to explore the stream in shorts and tee shirts, the babe in his papoose on Daddy's back. The rushing water spluttered around boulders and large limbs of fir trees which, having come down in the winter winds, were lying tossed here and there across the stream as though a giant had been playing matchsticks. Arni with the babe and Adam clambered upstream while I lay stretched out in the sun listening with my eyes closed to the splashing and gurgling of the fast running, ice-cold water, feeling cleansed by it. There was not another soul in sight although I could hear Adam excitedly laughing and shouting to his Dad, the sound sharp in that clear atmosphere. I sat up and took great draughts of the pure and sweet mountain air, wishing I could store it in my lungs to use at will. A fanciful notion, maybe, but we were in a fanciful place, all of us entranced with this picture postcard spot we had happened upon. It was a wonderful tonic for the travel weary and made us feel bright and glad to be alive.

After a late lunch, it was decided we should put on a little more clothing, hitch up the wagon and start moving. We drove towards the final peaks in late afternoon and began another hair-raising, tortuous climb with sheer drops and many unguarded edges towards Montgenèvre as the mist rolled in and the sun hid behind it. The sky turned grey but vision was still amazingly clear. The ravines and valleys dropping away from the roadside were thickly wooded with deep green pine and fir trees. It was spectacular. But we could only look at it through the windows for there was nowhere to stop. We just willed Rosie, pulling the extra weight behind her, around every hairpin bend, afraid at any moment that she might start coughing. It was the longest few and constantly winding kilometres I had ever travelled and the closest to heaven, if not hell if you took your eyes off the road. But like the aristocratic lady she was in a time of trial, Rosie made it and rolled quietly into the ski resort of Montgenèvre without a moment's fuss. The resort was a damp and cold place that afternoon so we motored straight through to the nearby border post at Claviere, where we pulled up at the little Custom's office.

The Italian customs officer politely asked for our green cards for the vehicles. We only had one for Rosie and were therefore asked to go and organise another card for the caravan in a café a little way down the street. Arni suggested I change some travellers' cheques and get the card at the same time as my language skills were better than his. This gave him a few moments rest, so Adam climbed onto the front seat next to him and I left Bubble tucked up with a bottle on the back seat and went off on my errand. I was in the café filling in forms and paying up when their phone rang. "*Scusi, signora,*" said the lady behind the desk … "it is your blondie bambino in old car…? *They* are saying he cries." At that moment I saw Arni and Adam waving and grinning at me through the window. So they had got bored and left the car with Bubble in it. We rushed up the street to Rosie…but the baby had vanished.

Arni looked quite as grey as the sky but not wishing to panic I was thinking about who 'they' must be and hurried into the little custom's office. And there stood an officer in his uniform, gently rocking Matti in his arms and making little Italian cooing noises at him. "*Grazie, grazie*," was all I could think of to say while I exchanged the green card for the baby. "*Prego*," said the officer and then tutting quietly added "*il bambino alone crying, no good.*" I hung my head in shame.

We bought some bread, milk and wine, the staff of life, and continued on our way down the Valle de Susa, the river Dora running through the valley to Aviliagna. It was a magnificent ride down the Italian side of the Alps. The ancient dwellings built on the steep slopes near the roadside were so different from the modern buildings around Briançon. The little roofs were slate tiled, the old slates laid on in criss-cross patterns, big ones and small ones as they came to hand and heavy enough to hold against wind and snow. The mist had rolled by and a watery sun was now low in the sky, casting its late afternoon light through the soft, wooded or vine-clad slopes. We passed numbers of simple dwellings along the road and one picturesque fortified village on a hill, centuries old, and little farmsteads dotted across the valley and after reaching Susa continued along our first flat road in Italy to Aviliagna. A motorist mis-directed us to the camp site so that it was quite dark when we eventually found it, somewhere near a lake which we couldn't see.

Well, to be fair it was May Day and all the world and his wife had come to this camp site, probably from Turin, with their camper vans, caravans and tents, with their families and friends and children and cats and dogs. They had come in hundreds, I am sure. There seemed not an inch of space left when we arrived. But we were greeted kindly, welcomed and, like letting out the seam of a skirt, a place was found for us to just about squeeze in the van after unhitching it from Rosie around which stood a little gathering of admiring males. Our van was swung into place by several pairs of broad shoulders and strong arms, leaving maybe two feet only between us and our neighbouring campers. It was quite a feat and something which would surely have been forbidden in any campsite in Germany, France and England, not to mention the Netherlands, Belgium and most certainly Switzerland.

The noise of laughing, talking, shouting people, radios full on, the crying of babies, screaming of kids and barking of dogs was something never to be forgotten. It is doubtful whether a more complete contrast could have existed between that site and the silent site of our alpine meadow of the previous night. It seemed no-one wanted to go to bed for lights shone and the music continued well into the early hours. Having hardly slept, we crept away with as little fuss as possible at dawn, a couple of dogs yapping as we quietly manoeuvred the vehicles out of their tight spaces while the children were still asleep. It seemed rather bad-mannered, a little unfriendly after the welcome and help we'd received and it had only cost us fifty-five pence for the night but although as dawn broke we could see the lake and the green hills around it and all the scenic charms of the place, we had felt severely over-numbered.

So we continued on the main route to Turin, lying in its northern plateau, skirting that town to get to Asti and Alessandria. It was a dull, flat drive in a grey, heavy atmosphere but shortly after Alessandria we drove off into a field to have our lunch. All around us were maize and wheat fields dotted with stumps of trees in a wide, flat landscape. It had its own charm. In the afternoon the sun came out and we found ourselves approaching the green hills which rise to about four hundred meters above sea level on the road leading to the coastal port of Genoa. And so, having left the Turinese plateau behind us we began the steep descent towards the coast through breathtakingly beautiful scenery. Villages, all pink and sandy, spilled down the thickly wooded slopes at all angles.

Life is full of contrasts and having passed a huge oil refinery on the outskirts of Genoa, we found ourselves snarled up in an awful rush-hour traffic jam as Genovese workers tried to get home faster than was possible in the circumstances. We were not a welcome addition to that frenzied scene, being simply holidaymakers with a choice of when to travel and with such an old car and caravan how dared we be on the road. We continually felt we were being pushed from behind, willed to get out of the way and indeed had numbers of motorists who could not get past solidly hooting at us. The smell of the exhausts was reaching our heads and the frustrated queues, the dodging in and out was nerve-racking, especially as we didn't know the road lay-outs.

It took us an hour and a half to travel through this small city of a population of under 700,000 and birthplace of Christopher Columbus, who might have sailed to Marseilles in that time with a following wind. We didn't stop in Genoa but took the coast road towards Nervi, Rapallo and La Spezia. After Nervi, the built up area gave way to the natural scenery again and we found ourselves once more on a switch back, a road cut into the side of the hills. This area was where the well-off had their villas with beautiful sloping gardens and where more picturesque villages, houses painted to blend with the landscape ~ umber, cream, pink, soft green ~ tumbled towards rocky shores. The hills seemed randomly pointed with tall, elegant cypress trees.

We climbed from Rocco to Rapallo with magnificent views down the hillsides to the sea and a kilometre from Rapallo we found our camp site, Miraflores, at Santagna Santa Pietro. Apart from being tucked below the crossing of some curving motor-ways, the place was excellent. Nowhere was level on this sloping site but it was grassy and full of wild flowers and apple trees in blossom. The facilities were very clean and beautifully decorated in imaginative, colourful tiling. We met the Italian owners who, after spending thirty years in Peru, had decided to return to Italy when they found they could no longer stand the awful race rela-tions, the inequalities, the corruption in that country. They had started working on Miraflores and had opened it only a month ago. Apart from the drone of lorries throughout the night, it was peaceful enough on site and we slept well.

The next day we jumped into the car and went down to the coast and holiday town nearby of Santa Margherita. The tall, plastered houses which formed a horse-shoe backdrop to the bay and its quayside were again painted in lovely colours; yellows, pale orange, chocolate mousse, brick pinks and so on, most of the shutters in contrasting colours, the wavy cypress gracing the gardens. The season had not yet begun so everywhere was quiet. We walked around the little harbour and had a difficult job stopping Adam from walking up every gangplank to the luxury private launches moored there, his taste for the good life evidently overcoming his fear of the water for he had been afraid to paddle in the sea. We shopped for lunch and dinner, bought a bottle of chianti and sat on a shaded bench where we spread out the picnic and poured out our wine. Bubble was happy with a baby jar of ragout and a chunk of fresh bread to suck on. The sun shone hotly on the sea, dancing with millions of pin-pricks of light.

After motoring in a leisurely way back to the site we did our chores, retrieved the nappies from the line we'd strung up, put the children to bed and started to prepare our supper of a good steak seasoned with peppercorns and garlic, mixed salad, bread and wine. Completely mellowed out we were about to turn in for the night when there was a loud thump on the door. This was Lilian and Norman, a retired English couple travelling across Italy in their Fiat campervan. They had arrived via Geneva and the Mont Blanc tunnel on a six week tour, hoping to get as far as the Calabrian coast before returning home. A very spirited pair, interesting and interested, we were to continue meeting them and enjoying their company all the way to Naples.

Next morning while I cleaned out the van, Arni took the kids for a little walk and met an elderly woman, all wrinkles and smiles, scything the grass. She stopped to talk and seemed fascinated with the children, the blondeness of them, gently touching Adam's curly hair and stroking Bubble's straight and almost white hair. Arni understood she was asking their ages so he scratched them with a stick on a nearby stone and she used the same stick to scratch her age. She was ninety-two, her handshake was firm and when Arni said goodbye and turned to come back she went on scything the grass in a steady rhythm that would have done credit to anyone half her age. He was so sorry he couldn't speak the language to talk to her a little longer.

We left the site at coffee time and continued along the main route towards La Spezia and eventually Pisa, winding as before high up above the sea, sometimes close to the cliffs or further away in a green landscape dotted with houses and villages. As we drove inland we became part of the random, mountainous green hills all around us. Suddenly Norman and Lilian drew up beside us. We stopped for lunch with them and I noticed that the van was leaning again on one side. Another spring had broken! We all set off for the highest viewpoint and stopped to admire the scenery before descending to a village where Arni managed to find a piece of wood for a temporary repair of the broken spring. It was about five o'clock when we arrived in the naval town of La Spezia and seeing a sign for camping we followed it through a road to Lerici on the sea and out of that town until we found the Camping Garden an hour and a half later. Norman and Lilian had arrived at the same site. When the children were in bed and fast asleep we popped into a nearby restaurant within site of the van and enjoyed a wonderful meal of mixed hors d'oeuvres, a sea-food speciality of tasty squid, cuttle fish and muscles, followed by a mixed salad and a slice of country cheese. It was very reasonably priced, equivalent to £5.50p for the two of us including wine and service. We returned to our van for a cognac and more conversation until the early hours in a quiet site shared only with two other campers.

It was now Saturday 5th May and we had another nine days for the Grand Tour before embarking at Naples for our new life. The next morning we met on site a Dutch family doing a six month tour with a baby a few months older than Bubble, who had been all over France, Spain and Portugal and after Italy intended motoring to Greece in their Fiat dormobile. We agreed it was a great life. This was before we met the coast road through Carrara and Massa to Viareggio, an ugly stretch of main road; fifteen miles of beach huts, hotels and neon signs. We passed quickly through this and started along the road to Pisa in flat land around the river Arno. Our first sight of this town was the amazing architecture of the domed roof of the baptistery on the site enclosing the cathedral and 'leaning tower'. We were lucky to be able to park just outside the old stone wall enclosing the cathedral square and very close to the tower, eating our lunch before visiting one of the Seven Wonders of the World.

The leaning campanile, cathedral and baptistery stood in an area of green grass with a little road running down one side of it for limited traffic. We were astounded by this graceful architecture of the middle ages, conceived and built between the 11th and 12th centuries, and the beauty of its shining white marble, its wonderful proportions, sophisticated design and lovely sculptures. In the baptistery we were treated to the echoing sounds of harmonic notes sung by a guardian which are sustained and catch themselves up to make a final heavenly chord, an eerie, beautiful sound, raising faith to a new pinnacle in an inspired building. We opted not to climb the 240 steps of the campanile but lay on the grass gazing up at its height and crazy tilt with respect. The interior of the cathedral also took our breath away with its outstanding gold ceilings, painted dome, lovely frescoes and the incredible, intricate sculpture of Pisano's huge pulpit.

And On Through 'La Bella Italia'

Having taken in as much as we possibly could of the white architectural splendour of Pisa, we left at teatime and made our way out of town on the road to Florence. No signs appeared for camp sites so we turned off the main road after thirty kilometres or so when the landscape was becoming a little more hilly and interesting. Just outside a village we found a piece of sandy waste land where we parked the van overlooking a small valley and across to three little hillocks. We were undisturbed and settled down for the night after consuming a pan of spaghetti and home-made sauce and taking a brief snatch of soft, fresh air while looking at a dark velvet sky scattered with stars.

We awoke to a perfect Sunday morning and wandered with the children along the sandy lanes among the little green hillocks. The area was not cultivated but offered a tangled picture of knee-high grasses, old un-pruned olive trees and vines between which grew numbers of wild flowers including orchids and tall, bright blue irises shining in the sunshine. Climbing to a small ridge of one of the hillocks we obtained a splendid view of the plains and mountains between Pisa and Florence, our next exciting cultural stop on a wonderful trip so far. There we had planned to meet Lilian and Norman at a camp site which was well appointed but once again surrounded by autoroutes. We found a note had been left for us at the office to the effect that our friends had decided to look for a nicer site. They returned shortly afterwards and we all set off for the

30

Villa Camerata north of Florence, an old palatial house turned into a hostel with a camping ground in its antique gardens. The gardens were unkempt but beautiful and quiet and, situated well above the city, the only sound greeting us the next morning was birdsong.

We now had to meet our old friends from England, Tovah and George Green, who were staying with their daughter Jan who was studying fine art and rented a flat in the Duomo Square. Tovah's life had taken her from pre-war Berlin in 1938, where she had been part of the underground Social Democratic Party attempting to disseminate anti-Nazi propaganda, to England as a twenty-one-year-old refugee fleeing for her life. She was Jewish, born in Poland but brought up from childhood mainly in a Jewish orphanage in Berlin and educated in a Jewish school since her father had been left with five children for whom he was unable to personally care.

A very English Englishman, George was a brilliant, quiet and philosophical man with a keen wit and equally strong political views as his wife. They met in post-war Germany, to which Tovah had returned as part of the Allied effort to get Germany back on its economic feet under the watchful eye, among other offices, of the international Trades Union movement. George was later to become Assistant General Secretary of the Civil Service Union. They were stimulating company. I had met Tovah at a Schule in Stanmore where Arni had suggested I go to learn modern Hebrew shortly before the exodus and where she was learning it to keep up with one brother she visited in Israel who had survived the Holocaust. Strange as life is, she also had a cousin, Masha, who was a member of Arni's kibbutz.

We left the Rolls parked not too far from the centre of the city and with pushchair and papoose walked past an imposing Synagogue built in the 1870s before coming to the magnificent Renaissance buildings close to the Piazza de Duomo and then those fantastic buildings themselves which form the Cathedral Square. To say impolitely that I was gob-smacked would be an understatement. Neither of us had ever seen anything like it before; the cathedral, the baptistery and Giotto's campanile.

Well, there's a first for everything and this 'first' was nearly as momentous for me as falling in love or giving birth. The structures were amazing but their adornment was out of this world. I know I had seen the 'Civilization' series but nothing compares with standing in front of the real thing, looking in this case at the incredible detail of the geometric and floral patterns of the mosaic cladding in soft green, pink and white marble. The exquisite sculptures, representing this highest point of European artistic endeavour, magically and amazingly achieved that sense of mystery in what it means to be truly human; all that gentleness and compassion ~ in stone.

If being born again could produce another *Renaissance* today of the power and purpose of 14th and 15th century Florence, well Allelujah! Sometimes I think we are on the brink of it but an overwhelming global culture of consumerism and mass production veils the essence of what some very fine artists, poets, architects and composers have to offer us.

To my mind a broad church of self-obsessed 'individualism', which barely acknowledges socio-cultural values, historical perspectives and the importance of basic skills and training has led to an acceptance of mixed metaphors, messages and ability in the arts. The 'anything goes' approach is constantly disseminated through a mass media determined to make 'notoriety' and fame ever more desirable, cheaper at any price and with little respect for the future of the arts.

This is where we broadly seem to be today despite amazing talent that often goes untutored or unnoticed. But no doubt the tide will turn. I may have it wrong and one day distance may lend enchantment, even understanding ~ or was it ever thus? At least in the Medicis' affluent Florence they seemed to know what they prized, what they were aiming for and what incredible skill could produce and it remains there in all its glory to remind us of a remarkable and unique period of artistic focus and achievement in human history ~ daunting in its execution, no matter what we think. Perhaps it is now the turn of our brilliant technocrats to connect more closely with a 'technically ignorant' majority and inspire us in their turn with new aspirations incorporating the same humanity, beauty and compassion!

We took it in turns during our stay to amuse the children or give our untrammelled personal attention to the glories of art and architecture. We stood in awe in front of Ghiberti's bronze sculpted baptistery door, the *Paradise Door* with its gilded panels depicting scenes from the Old Testament. I gazed silently and peacefully on my own at Michelangelo's immensely moving *Piéta* inside the quiet, cool and simple but massive interior space of the cathedral with its huge Brunelleschi dome.

In due course we all went to see Michelangelo's extraordinary *David* in the museum. We visited the powerful Medici Chapel with its lovely painted dome, its wealth of fine art and exquisite, dark inlaid marble floors depicting exotic flowers and animals. We each spent a morning in the Uffizi Gallery overlooking the ancient Ponte Vecchio spanning the green waters of the river Arno. We looked over the city's higgledy-piggledy red tiled roofs from the Piazza Michelangeli above the town on the south bank of the river, at its towers and domes and the sandy stonework of its magnificent buildings glowing in late afternoon sunshine. This city was, I think, the *jewel in the crown* of our Grand Tour, despite other sights of wonder yet to come.

The first evening we visited our friends, parking Rosie in the Piazza and climbing up the narrow winding stairs of the centuries' old apartment to Jan's little room looking out at the Duomo. There was a knock on the door as we were eating a lovely supper Jan had prepared and it was opened to a policeman who had noticed not only a crowd of interested people around Rosie but also that the RR emblem on her bonnet, the silver Flying Lady, was missing. Arni produced this and Jan explained that he had removed it himself to avoid any temptation for others to do so and the officer happily departed after being thanked for his observation and action.

It was agreed that we would meet our friends early next morning to make a fairly long trip across Tuscany to Marche to visit the superb medieval walled town of Urbino, another Lord Clarke highlight and the birthplace of Raphaello. We eventually set off with the children and the Green family at eight o'clock and made our way via Arezzo through increasingly lovely scenery that began to climb up and wind through very steep and hilly countryside, looking over a wide valley to a mountain ridge of the Apennines running southwards on the other side. This was a quiet agricultural area full of small fields on steep slopes either smothered in flowers or in which little round hay stacks stood like cheeses with wedges cut out of them here and there. Everywhere looked lush and green and we continued to climb for another thirty kilometres. On a final ascent looking down on streams and valleys we went around a hairpin bend and suddenly saw Urbino perched on a hill, a majestic medieval town literally shining yellow in the brilliant midday sun. It had taken us four hours to motor there but the trip and its final goal were stunning.

We drove through a tall archway in the outer city wall and were able to park Rosie at Raphael's statue above the centre of the town and walked down the steep old cobbled streets past his birthplace. We soon found ourselves outside the grand Palace of the first Duke of Urbino, that powerful, intellectual and artistic man responsible for the magnificent building which was both elegant and homely, giving you a sense of ease and refinement. His small study had floor to ceiling cupboards ornately decorated in superb marquetry creating an illusion of perspective, a *trompe l'oeille* effect of buildings, doors, windows, furnishings and every aid and tool to learning in wonderful, coloured woods. The work was unique, outstanding and asked to be admired in every detail.

The entire town with its massive walls, turrets, towers and perimeter fortification dominated the surrounding countryside and was surely a safe haven from which its military commanders might assail envious neighbours.

After visiting the Palace we left this amazing town in the afternoon sunshine and made our way back to Florence, dark descending as we drove again through Arezzo with faltering rear lights.

Otherwise once more Rosie had behaved like a lady, giving us all an unforgettable drive through unforgettable scenery to an unbelievable medieval town. We spent five full days wandering around Florence and only on the morning of the sixth day realised we would have to tear ourselves away from not only our friends but this magnificent city if we were to stick to our itinerary and eventually arrive in Naples in good time. It was an emotional departure.

Again we travelled towards Arezzo over some rather bad roads that shook up Rosie and the van and were forced to take the auto-route for nearly 50 kms through Umbria until we were close to the old town of Perugia which we skirted to continue on our way to Assisi where we intended to spend the next night. And there suddenly we saw the town some distance away, a hazy white finger of building high on the largest mountain in the area. We were looking at the huge monastery with its long colonnade of arches erected in the incredible time of twenty-two months in the mid-thirteenth century on the orders, it is believed, of a Franciscan monk, Brother Elia, as a monument to his master, St. Francis, following the death of this man who believed in a life of simplicity, humility and dedication to the poor. An astounding if somewhat inappropriate memorial!

We climbed up to the town and parked outside its gates. From there we could scan the uneven floor of the valley with its little hills on which villages, churches or bell towers were dotted. It was around five o'clock and the warm late sunshine, this time from the western side of the valley, threw a deep yellow light into Assisi. Our first visit was to the Basilica with its upper and lower churches in the one building, with the tomb of St. Francis and the beautiful cloisters of the dead.

There were few visitors and we found ourselves alone in the cloisters with their central garden of grass and shrubs with small trees arching over the space, providing shade and giving sanctuary to a number of birds flying above our heads. It was so peaceful, so serene that we were overcome by a powerful sense of the past and the simplicity of the message of the man whose spirit pervaded that place built after his death. Even the children, tired and fractious as they had been, were quiet, subdued.

We walked through the old town, wandering about the narrow and steep streets unaltered for centuries, admiring the buildings in their lovely pink and white stone and enjoying the view through arches to the valley far below or down steep steps with waterfalls of pale blue wisteria shimmering down the house walls. Only the dozens of little shops trading in ceramics, mostly hand-painted replicas of old designs, and wood carvings and other souvenirs were there to remind us that we were visitors from the twentieth century looking back across seven earlier centuries.

There was a strange, embracing atmosphere in this quiet little town that we had been lucky enough to visit without the crush of tourists. It was hardly surprising, perhaps, that after a peaceful night's sleep in a small site above the town, Arni and I felt compelled to talk in the morning about St. Francis, who had turned fanatically to follow the teaching to the word as well as spirit of Jesus. What was the essential perspective he exemplified within the Judeo-Christian system of belief? It was a quiet discussion in a quiet place which added a new perspective to our thinking. We had both been deeply moved in our visit to the extraordinary old town.

The sky was overcast that morning as we contemplated moving on from Assisi but after a slow start the sun came out and we drove down through the town, drinking in for the last time the atmosphere of this remarkable place flying high above the valley into which we slowly descended. We reached Spolente and then climbed into the hills towards Terni along an excellent road, the landscape around us lush and thickly forested.

Stopping in Terni to shop for lunch, dinner and petrol, Rosie again drew an admiring crowd of men, laughing children and some women more curious than interested. We stole the show from a 1922 Citroen parked along the main street. After lunch we continued in another valley until we reached the turnings to the autoroute and the Via Flamina. We chose the latter and again started an ascent with the hills topped with steeply graded villages and the valleys cultivated and sheltering scattered farmsteads. We reached a high plateau and gazed across landscape that recalled those background landscapes dramatically and firmly depicted by the 16th century Georgione and Titian. The road continued along a ridge so that we were able to look across splendid vistas on either side with the afternoon sun softening the many shades of green, terra-cotta and burnt umber with its subtle light. So this was the inspiration for those Italian house painters.

The Via Flamina runs into Rome to the west of the auto-route but sixty kilometers from the city we had to leave its extremely bumpy surface and take the main motorway and an hour later were entering the outskirts of that great city. Having decided that we had unfortunately to motor through and find a site for the night due to lack of time, we nevertheless were able to park for a little while in the Piazza Ventzio in front of the large, white marble Victor Emanuel memorial with the Colosseum in the background. We sadly could not enter this latter great monument but motored around the Forum and Colosseum before proceeding southwards towards Ostia and just off the south ring road found the large site of Pini de Roma ~ as the name suggests, in a pine grove.

Here we met again a New Zealand family in their huge Ford Convertible Van, a mobile home with sun deck atop, three double beds in three separate compartments, gas stove and oven, fridge, constant hot water, w.c. and shower with a 60 gallon disposal tank and a 100 gallon water tank. This luxury apartment on wheels, bought in the U.K., had central heating, swivel seats for driver and co-driver, and a Ford Dodge V8 engine with power steering. This monster was home for a year to parents plus four children who were travelling the continent of Europe as far as Greece and Turkey and returning to England via Scandinavia. Quite an education for all concerned I would have thought.

It was Sunday 13th May as we headed straight off for Naples, stopping for lunch along the coast just past Terracina. The beaches were virtually deserted, the sand soft and fairly clean. Adam kept well away from the water again but Bubble made a bee-line for it as fast as he could shuffle. A mother and her four children including dark eyed, two-year-old identical twins were sitting on the beach and one of the twins took Bubble's hand and tried to pull him away from the water's edge, crying bitterly and exclaiming over and over "bambino, bambino, il mare". Bubble lapped this up and let the little tot stroke his head and face very gently. It was a really touching scene. I picked Bubble up and held the little one's hand while mother just smiled gently.

Neapolitan Sunday drivers must surely be amongst the worst in the world. They treated the road like a race course, revving up to pass, cutting in and always trying their luck. Heads we win, tails we win. Eventually we nosed our entry into smelly Naples up a steep cliff road. The air was thickly polluted but we managed to pick out the sign for the Citta di Napoli camp site where we'd promised to meet our friends the Fletchers. The large site, looking like a grubby ghost town, was full of empty caravans and we were about to leave when our friends appeared so we did no more than park ourselves and make a cup of tea. They at least had managed two days in Rome.

We had to try and phone the shipping company to check on arrival and departure and Arni went off in search of a public telephone but didn't find one. His attention in any case was caught up by other matters near the site entrance which was off a clear, straight strip of main road leading to the city and which appeared to be a street of ill repute. The girls were getting busy at that time and to demonstrate their wares had to light themselves up for passing motorists to get a good view of them. Since there were no street lamps they did this by setting fire to old lorry tyres on the pavements, creating a long, slow, black burn which gave off the most disgusting acrid smoke imaginable ~ not exactly Chanel No. 5 gals! Other ladies of the night were hanging out in every dimension from beat-up, once snazzy cars. We moved back into the site as far away from the road and prevailing wind as possible and retired after sharing a good bottle of chianti and chat with our friends, glad we had finally made it to the port of departure.

Arni got hold of the Zim Line the next morning only to find that the boat would be delayed by eight hours and so our friends who had wanted to wave us off decided to set off for Calabria. We negotiated further awful driving to get over the bumpy old main roads to find where the port and central post office were and returned to the site, glad to get out of the mayhem for a while. We planned to return to the port around four o'clock, a big mistake, and park at the quayside until the boat arrived. At this time we met the worst traffic jam ever, far worse than Genoa and made more unpleasant by the need to enter a three-lane tunnel, just before reaching the city centre, with end of the line trams stopping at its exit and where six lanes of traffic converged from across a large square upon the tunnel from the opposite direction. It surely can't be like that today! It took us one and a quarter hours to do a fifteen minute journey amidst the worst hooting and fumes we had ever experienced. We finally parked on the quayside at half-past five and went off with the children to Telephone House to contact the parents. We were told it would take one hour to connect that call! Having explained to the operator we were sailing in ten minutes, we miraculously found ourselves on the line straight away to my delighted parents.

It was half past six by the time we got back to Rosie and the van with another bottle of chianti to brave the long wait. We waited in comfort, had dinner and changed the children for bed. The boat arrived at half past eight and another half hour went by before customs and Zim Line began checking our tickets and passports. Surprise, surprise, we were one of only two English families travelling via the offices of the London Jewish Agency who were not on the Italian Agency list. Eventually, after a lot of shouting and argument we were pushed through the crowd onto the boat and finally got the kids to bed after ten o'clock. They and we were exhausted.

After embarkation Arni had to negotiate and supervise, with further shouting, the raising of Rosie in a huge net hoisted above the hand rails and then lowered onto the deck where she was to be chocked and stabilised for the two nights and two days journey to the Port of Haifa. Had Arni known about this 'loading system' maybe he would have travelled all the way overland just like the Crusaders. And why not? It might have been simpler. The boat, a relatively small one, not your regular Channel ferry size even, was chock-a-block with immigrants, tourists, commercial travellers and anybody else you care to mention, so Rosie had to be guarded much of the time, or so Arni thought. Not a space to drop a pin in. But finally, finally we set sail under a clear night sky with a gentle breeze to a home-coming for Arni and a new home for me and the children in a totally foreign land. Indeed, indeed!

Pass the Port – if You Can!

Having disembarked ourselves, Rosie and the caravan at the port of Haifa at 6am on the 18th May, 1973 we were greeted by Arni's parents, Yisrael and Klara, with mother-in-law somewhat dismayed that our vehicle was such an old affair and not worth showing off. But Klara tried to put a brave face on it as she and Yis waited patiently for us to clear immigration and customs as the sun rose higher in the sky with a steady rise in the temperature. It was indeed the beginning of a very hot day, reaching 38° before noon. The children had hardly slept, what with the noisy mooring procedure and port activity in the early hours and were by now thirsty, over-heated and extremely tired and miserable. Being smothered by an exhibition of grandmotherly love just at that moment set them both howling which did not exactly please 'grandma'.

Arni quickly found out that the container had arrived and was in store before we attached the caravan and all boarded Rosie to head for our new home a dozen miles away. On reaching our rented accommodation in the village of Ramat Yishai we were effusively greeted by our new landlady, Mrs Larish, a woman with a saccharine smile and less than frank manner. She was short and stocky, in her sixties, dressed like a townie and belonged, we felt, closer to the suburbs of Golders Green than a once pioneering outpost of *HaEmeq*, the Valley. Strangely, mother-in-law and Mrs Larish seemed to be speaking a common language, which I nevertheless found difficult to follow. It was more the essence of the conversation than the words which impacted on me.

The house, however, was a dream. Solidly built in stone and sitting within a fringe of tall pine trees with a fantastic garden at the rear full of fruit trees, I saw endless potential in this house which we had been promised before we left England we would be able to buy, if that was our wish. Of course at this point in time we had no furniture but we had the caravan and were able to boil a kettle and make a cup of tea before putting Yis and Klara on the bus home. Mrs Larish was a different kettle of fish and we could not get her out of the place. It was as though she was afraid we might walk off with her property if she left us alone with it. She had not rented it out before.

At last we found ourselves on our own and whooped with joy as we danced around our empty home before taking a leisurely walk to the centre of the village. There we located the post office and general stores, buying fresh milk, groceries and other foodstuffs to keep us going for a couple of days. We naturally introduced ourselves and were introduced to everyone we came across. People were very friendly and helpful.

A phone call to the port of Haifa the next day evaporated our immediate enthusiasm with the news that Customs in Israel demanded that all household containers be emptied at the port for thorough inspection of the contents before being re-packed and delivered. We had paid through the English shipping company for a door-to-door delivery service and told the Port Customs Authority that we had those documents and would bring them to the port.

"It makes no difference" was the reply. "You come tomorrow at 9am and be here to witness the unloading, if you wish ~ those are the rules." The man hung up.

We had employed a recommended and experienced firm of shippers to pack and load the container in London. Obviously no such experienced packers would be on hand to re-pack the container after our precious home contents would have been spilled onto the dockside by port authority workers, possibly causing damage in the process to fragile and well-wrapped objects. This was preposterous, I thought. We were hardly poor immigrants arriving with a few possessions bundled up in rags but, as I had been told, desirable, qualified persons, one of whom was a returning Israel citizen who had left a good life and high standard of living in the UK to start again in this young country crying out for this kind of immigration. I felt hot internally as well as externally and had not yet been in Israel for a full week.

We motored down to Haifa with the children and politely requested to see the Chief of Customs. Having been brusquely denied this privilege, Arni managed at least to find out where the office was of the Assistant Chief of the Port of Haifa. To ensure entry we fairly burst through his door to find a startled Mr. Braun with blunt face and spectacles staring at the four of us with some concern. I was holding Adam by the hand and Bubble was in the papoose, as usual.

"What are you doing in my office?" he asked. "I did not invite you ."

"No," I answered in English, "but neither did we invite your men to unload a container shipped from the U.K for a door-to-door delivery, as per these papers." I put them on his desk in front of him. He ignored our papers but stated that the procedure had been introduced to stop illicit goods being brought into the country. Arni then explained we had paid for the door-to-door service and that we wanted him to organise or give us a written authority to call off the unloading of our container shipped with a full Customs' declaration, underwritten by reliable international shippers. Mr. Braun laughed. "You are joking," he said, "leave my office I have work to do." Arni then picked up the man's phone and said he was phoning the police. At this Mr. Braun jumped up and down, furious that a stranger had not only invaded his office but had the audacity to use his phone. "Get out immediately," he shouted "and if you do not I shall order the port police to throw you out."

43

For the very first time in my life, through both shock and amazement at this unseemly behaviour, lack of common courtesy and civil treatment from a government official, I became hysterical. It may have been the heat as well. I shouted that I could not have imagined anything so shameful as this treatment of new immigrants and started metaphorically waving the union jack, suggesting that never in a month of Sundays would any British customs officials behave so badly towards members of the public as he was doing. "You are obliged," I screamed, "to honour the international shipping agreement in place when we left the UK. If the rules are changed, you are responsible for informing the shipping companies accordingly." I continued loudly to blather on.

Mr. Braun's eyes were popping from his head by this time and he leapt up and left the room saying he was fetching the port police to have us thrown out. Arni looked out of the window and shortly afterwards saw two policemen on bikes turn up and park below the window. Their riders climbed the stairs and entered the room.

By this time the children were crying, I was exhausted and we were told that Mr. Braun would not be returning until we had left. Arni quietly explained the situation to the police and we understood that on no account did they wish to make an issue of the business and would certainly not arrest us. They spoke quietly and suggested we try some other channels. "Did we know someone" for example "who might be able to exert some influence." We did not. We asked the police to inform Mr. Braun that Mr. Goren would be in the port tomorrow morning early and that the container must be left intact until he arrived. Any damage and we would go to the press. He also left a scribbled note to that effect on Braun's desk stating 'my wife is a journalist and works for the BBC'. Having just witnessed a screaming banshee, he might have had doubts about those credentials.

Arni got on the phone at home to the kibbutz and spoke to Klara who immediately said she had a friend whose cousin's husband held an important post at the Port of Haifa. She would call us back. Fifteen minutes later we were given the name of the man to contact ~ Assistant Chief of the Port of Haifa, Mr. Braun, a very nice man, she told us.

Well, in spite of everything, I couldn't help laughing. "Too late," Arni told her, "we've already spoken to your nice Mr. Braun" and started to explain what exactly had taken place in Mr. Braun's office.

"Oi vai voi" Klara replied, "if only you had asked me first."

"Well," I added with my mouth close to the phone, "how could we possibly guess we would have to ask for such a favour?"

"Ttt, tt," Klara clucked, "in Israel you have to know somebody even before you blow your nose …have you forgotten that, my son?…(pause)… you have been away far too long!"

Early the next morning Arni went off to the Port and was there before the container was opened. He then told the two port workers assigned to the task of emptying the contents that he would be standing there examining their handling of every piece of our property and would be insisting that anything unpacked would be re-packed and stowed away carefully, exactly as it had been found before removal. The container was so full that anything less than very careful stacking back would mean they would probably not be able to return all the goods. Arni kept his foot on the tail of the container as they began the job and as each piece was removed shouted, "Slowly….Careful!" After ten minutes of this one of the port workers walked off. An hour later, with little of the contents removed, those items were replaced and the container sealed for despatch to the house. The remaining worker got the paperwork signed stating the inspection had been executed and all was in order. He too had had enough.

The following day the delivery took place and another two men began unloading and bringing the contents into the house. They were supposed to unpack and remove all the packing materials and return them with the container. This they refused to do, insisting they only had to bring the contents into the house. A further argument ensued but to little avail so we began feverishly tearing off all wrapping ourselves and depositing it and the tea-chests back into the container as fast as the men were emptying it. No-one was offered a cup of coffee! It was like Casey's Court but happily, apart from a few small glass or china items that had got broken, there was no major damage to anything except my psyche.

One item alone had gone missing, how, where or when, we had no idea. That was a little nine inch portable television. Well, you might have guessed it and even if it had only cost us a few pounds it was disappointing as it was the only television we owned… an object irresistible to thieves then as now!

We climbed into bed totally exhausted that night, first checking out the baby Matti who'd been asleep on and off in the caravan all day with a high temperature. Following a visit early that morning to the village clinic, before the container arrived and the circus began, we'd been told Bubble was going down with the measles. The nurse was on hand next door if we needed her.

Well, I'd heard about the 'breaking-in' of horses. This filly was fast learning.

Ramat Yishai

Our arrival in Northern Israel had been planned in advance and our wonderful friends, Palo and Aviva who lived in a small town called Tivon on the hills south-east of Haifa, had secured for us the rented property in the nearby village of Ramat Yishai. The square stone house had originally belonged to earlier settlers who had farmed the area.

The settlement of Ramat Yishai had been built on a finger of high land stretching out to overlook the wide and fertile Jezreel Valley. Across the valley at its northernmost sweep was a range of hills known as Mount Carmel. The Carmel fell steeply at its furthest reach into the sea, north-west at the Port of Haifa perched on its height and flanks down to the bay. Our home lay equidistant by road about twelve miles south of Haifa and east to Nazareth. The Jezreel Valley, known biblically as the Plain of Esdraelon, continues south-eastwards towards the famous site of Megiddo where so many battles have taken place in ancient and modern times and which gave its name to the word Armageddon, the last battle … if only.

The Carmel range blocked any view of the Mediterranean on its western slopes but provided a most beautiful, shadowy backdrop for occasional brilliant sunsets, appearing cool, dark green and alive in the summer when the valley between us had become scorched and yellow. I enjoyed looking across to this natural, hilly barrier, which tucked us into a geographical horseshoe and kept the busy world of Haifa, its noisy roads, traffic, smoke and pollution well at bay. In March there were places to visit on the nearside slopes of the hills, smothered in bold blue irises and jazzy scarlet poppies. Northern Israel was awash with flowers in the Spring.

You could smell Ramat Yishai from some little distance if the wind was in the right direction. This was because at the village entrance to the right off the main Nazareth road, and opposing a crumbling old Turkish fort, was a thriving chicken factory called *Of Haemeq*, Chicken of the Valley. Here kosher chickens and turkeys were processed, packed and sold both wholesale and retail. It was a fairly large concern adjacent to a small village and the smell of pre-and-post-disposal of chicken and turkey waste was not pleasant. The kibbutz owners had not wanted it on their territory! We rarely ate the birds ourselves, preferring mutton bought in the Arab quarter of Nazareth or beef from a non-kosher kibbutz. A garage also stood at the junction turn-off which marked a fork in two narrow roads, one leading into the village centre and one along the western edge of the promontory at the farthest end of which a few houses unusually built in stone, including our own, were located. Beyond that point the road ended in a dirt track leading down hill a couple of miles through grapefruit orchards towards Sede Ya'aqov, a farming community or *moshav* in the valley.

Off Ramat Yishai's central road and cross roads, where small businesses including the post office were situated, barely metalled, rough lanes squarely criss-crossed over undulating land which housed the majority of the five or six hundred population in their little agency houses or *shikunim*. Many of these pre-fab type buildings had been extended and improved by their owners over the years. Most still stood in a quarter or half acre of land, now dotted with citrus and other fruit trees but which in 1925 it had been decided might provide a living and new way of life for Jewish immigrants trickling into Palestine at that time from across the world.

When we arrived in May 1973 the united nations were represented in numbers along our sparsely populated road alone. There were earlier generations of Israelis like the respected village elder and horseman of the 'old guard' Avigdor, from tall, blue-eyed Caucasian antecedents. There was a fair-haired and blue-eyed Russian, of medium height, the stocky Alexander Shoshani, also a member of the 'old guard' with his bow-legs to prove it, whose wife Yudit was from Yugoslavia. Their son Danny and daughter Ruti, of their four children, also lived along the street with their families. There was a rather aristocratic Hungarian widow called Etush, Hungarian-Rumanian Muscal, the Yanai family and Shaul's family from Yemen and the family Maman, uniting Eli from a Jewish family amongst many from Algeria who had settled in the land from a previous century, to Canadian wife Ruthie.

These folk and their offspring were our immediate neighbours and good friends. I could add to this list other people across the village whom I personally came to know whose families or themselves had come from Persia, Algeria, Turkey, Iraq, America, Austria, Germany and Poland. I was one of three non-Jewish immigrants at that time, with the Canadian Raza married to Algerian Hagit and a Welshman married to an Anglo-Austrian, Adrienne. The largest single contingent in the village may have been the Ben Lulus who had come from Morocco, producing two, or was it three, sets of twins among their other children and who ran the local general store.

It was salutary and heart-warming to see how people from widely different backgrounds, cultures and nations could happily rub along together in a relatively small community; to see how background differences were automatically accepted despite the normal personal likes or dislikes, irritations or difficulties that might arise between people. It was good to live in a place where most were happy to help each other out, to laugh and sing together, to argue politics together because they were glad to be living in their own land, no longer long or short-term refugees, a land chosen for as many and various reasons as their were individuals. Well, this was the feeling you got.

Of course there was the usual family strife, and indeed a war to come in October 1973 and its aftermath, and the continual, subterranean movement that marks change that nobody recognizes at the time. But shortly after we arrived in May we felt Ramat Yishai was alive then with a sense of purpose, community and well-being that satisfied its mixed population. In this respect it differed considerably from the co-operative farming communities, *moshavs*, where families were commercially linked, or the *kibbutzes* whose memberships were culturally and politically linked and who shared a communal way of life without personal ownership of finance or goods.

There were very few settlements like Ramat Yishai set up in Israel and, as small as it was, it had its own Council and Mayor, elected to represent one of two major national parties, *Mapaam* and *Mapai*, and later *Likud*, as well as providing a clinic, sports area, kindergartens and junior school. It had the joy of being largely self-contained, a mish-mash of individuals who nevertheless shared a common identity in living in one particular place. It was private enough not to promote too much envy, greed or feuding amongst fellow villagers at that stage, for no-one was rich, though some families naturally amassed more than others by fair or foul means. Criticism was usually good humored, open or sardonic, with the usual wit and noisy exchanges of people of different views and political persuasions. Racial jokes about cultural origins were shared without rancour in a land where being Jewish and Israeli ranked higher than any previous nationality.

There were three discreet synagogues in simple buildings catering for the mainstream Jewish denominations and culturally diverse population. Beyond that a secular Ramat Yishai engendered enterprise, sometimes dubious but vigorous with imagination, flair, confidence and a largely unexpressed hope. I am so glad that we were there to be part of such a unique experience, for however short a period. Time, after all, is relative.

In Ramat Yishai we could find a blacksmith, plumber, electrician, mechanical and civil engineer, policeman, sea captain, doctor, nurses, scrap merchant, builders, grocer, fish-woman, toymaker, secretary, clerk, teacher and no doubt a dozen more professions and occupations, not forgetting the Mayor and the Rabbi. Many of us kept hens, goats, horses, harvested fruits from our land and we all cooked for our families. Readymade meals did not exist. And what a variety of international dishes you could enjoy from Sephardic baked Mediterranean fish with garlic, chilli pepper and tomatoes to stuffed baked aubergine, a vegetable you can cook in a hundred different ways; from cous-cous to Georgian stuffed chicken; from Suliman's pilaf with mutton and pine nuts to barbecued beef with hot Yemenite relish and so on and on, all served with wonderful dips and salads and followed by delicious sweets and pastries, often made from or filled with the abundant fruits of the land.

On one occasion, I added a little English colour by providing roast lamb and mint sauce for guests, having asked a friend to bring a leg of lamb from England as it was difficult to find really tender cuts of non-koshered sheep, which in Christian Nazareth was usually sold, as butchered, as a whole or half animal of uncertain age. The only problem with the importation was the fact that the joint contained a skewer which set off the security check at the airport and when discovered occasioned a remark from the security officer to the effect that he didn't know people were starving in Israel. My friend was also importing in her luggage Cheddar cheese and Typhoo tea, which I sorely missed despite the cornucopia of national produce and international cooking.

This village might have been a copy of the settlements founded by the immigrants who had gone West in America in a previous century and indeed it had a certain wildness and idiosyncracy about it which was not to be found in the suburban life of the nearest town, Tivon, or surrounding agricultural communities. It bred a degree of toughness and individuality that may be found amongst pioneering peoples who have not been required to conform for too long to an established cultural routine and settled way of life.

It was then early days in the transforming ethos born of the sudden wealth Israel was to gain from the financial protection of the United States of America. Israel was the one strategic Western democracy in the Middle East with established links to an American Jewry. As the geographical and political fulcrum of the area, not only was the country to become the mightiest military power in the Middle East, its technology in armaments and fighter planes unmatched alongside its permanently trained armed forces, but the economy generally after the Six Day War benefited from a buoyancy unknown to earlier waves of immigration before and after Independence in 1948. From 1968, the money flowed in and the Jewish State changed.

Change sparked by wealth rather than need has an insidious side to its nature, for while offering an easier way of life none would reject, it simultaneously engenders negative qualities which go largely unnoticed. When the going is good, too often need becomes greed, fear becomes arrogance, care becomes nonchalance and privilege becomes 'rights'. After all people are just people, not philosophers or gods, and common to all elements of the natural world we human beings simply react and respond to our environment and, as the Christian morning prayer says, 'there is no health in us'. I often wondered what that meant!

So we met in Ramat Yishai in the early nineteen-seventies the final fling, perhaps, in gritty post independence Israel; the fun of doing your own thing your own way, of not having to care what the neighbours thought because they didn't give a hang about what you thought; of doing and daring and laughing and caring and shouting and singing and sometimes being wicked and getting away with it. Imagine nevertheless a certain cohesion, camaraderie, a sense of belonging, a lightness and brightness, despite personal traumas or tragedies of the daily round, and that was life in Ramat Yishai at a point in time, 1973, celebrating the State of Israel's first quarter century.

Rosie's Induction

"No," said the Port of Haifa Customs' officer, "that is the wrong number. I asked for the chassis number. That is not a chassis number."

We were trying to register dear Rosie, our faithful conveyance from the Cotswolds to the Customs Shed outside Haifa. We had been given a few weeks grace to do this after our arrival in early May. As a new immigrant and the UK registered owner of an imported vehicle, I had no import tax to pay based on the value of the vehicle. This was a large concession to encourage immigration since all Israeli citizens were required to pay a hefty tax on every vehicle for sale in the country. Customs were fierce in their efforts to thwart any citizens, trying by whatever nefarious means, to privately import cars bought abroad to avoid this overwhelming tax. The tax made buying even a second-hand car in Israel prohibitive.

My husband insisted, "The chassis number VT1 is correct, I assure you. It is in the vehicle documentation here, as well on the car body." He pointed to the chassis number in the registration book.

"No, I do not accept it," replied the official, ignoring the British documentation. "Here are the lists for every make of car. Look at them. No such numbering exists. Go and get the correct number from the body of the car." He turned his attention to the next immigrant.

As I was quickly learning, most Israeli officials when faced with a seemingly intractable problem with members of the general public will say 'no', or the equally snappy Hebrew equivalent '*lo*', and indeed never ask what? where? when? or how? just in case they might find they were missing some vital evidence ... or did they know they were divinely right, I wondered? Also I noticed the words 'please' and 'thank-you' had entirely disappeared or been deliberately erased from the bureaucratic lexicon.

We waited. Another official who had gone to look at Rosie standing dusty but majestic in the yard jerked his head at the officer behind the counter and said, "It's a very old car, a Rolls Royce. I can't find the chassis number."

The first officer looked at us in disbelief and finally came out unexpectedly with a 'Why?' Presumably he was searching for the trick.

"Why are you importing an old car when you can import a new one, tax free? Why? I want to know," he barked. He looked at us with both scorn and distrust.

My husband raised his shoulders and flung open both arms, palms uppermost, in a gesture of sad defeat or admission that he was, of course, a first class fool, but he said nothing more. Secretly I felt he was sorely disappointed that the mere presence of his beautiful 1933 Rolls Royce had not evoked gasps of admiration and a free passage out of the customs shed without further ado, even if his compatriots felt disinclined to bow in a natural gesture of homage when gazing upon her.

This was my second experience of confrontational, bureaucratic intervention within two weeks of arriving in the Land of Milk and Honey proudly bearing papers which announced that I was *ola hadasha*. This was not, as some might imagine, a Spanish greeting but Hebrew for a new immigrant of the female variety. Yes, Hebrew operates like French with masculine and feminine genders for every noun but fortunately avoids the third gender, the Latin and German neuter, which has always seemed as strange to me in its nominal application as giving a window or book a male or female identity. It has to be a man who devised that, based, one assumes, on some primitive hierarchical male principle long since forgotten.

Those thoughts aside, just at that moment facing the Israeli Customs I realized that bad luck, like gender, comes in threes and there was no reason to believe mine would be different. It did not occur to me then to think of multiples of threes! Now *Ola* comes from the Hebrew word *Aliyah* meaning simply progressing upwards ... on a scale of human goodness maybe. So to be on 'aliyah' to Israel meant a definite improvement on your path in life towards higher things, perhaps eventually to a glorious state of grace in heaven, who knows? But where precisely and practically 'aliyah' stood on the modern political Israeli agenda and what it carried with it, apart from tax concessions, I had yet to find out. Being a newcomer to the country with my returning Israeli husband and two children born in England, and not even of the faith ... they were still pretty desperate for new immigrants in 1973 ... I felt I had a long way to go and a lot to learn.

The officer ignored my husband and told his subordinate to weigh the vehicle. At this Arni smelled a rat.

"Why do you weigh my car?" His voice was perceptibly rising with anxiety. With a supercilious lift of the eyebrows the first officer said flatly, "You pay a tax on the weight of every imported car, Aliyah or no. YES?"

Ah, a positive exclamation at last! On hearing this unexpected news, the *genuine* owner and only driver of the car rushed out into the yard shouting "Wait, I have to remove articles which are not part of the vehicle ... petrol and water cans, tools, etc. etc." Arni was heating up.

My husband began feverishly dismantling as much of the car as he legitimately could, without doing it damage, before driving one of the heaviest saloon cars ever lovingly built onto the weighing block. Personally I hoped Rosie would exceed the uppermost weight limit specified for the block and break it right down the middle. I also began to think quite evil thoughts, especially towards the first officer ... maybe we could steer Rosie straight at the counter and watch his gills turn yellow. The car would be barely scratched. Apart from all that it was hot as hell, for it was the last week in May and we were experiencing the tail end of a *khamsin*. This is the scorching, sandy North African wind circulating from the Libyan Sahara and Egypt over fifty days and playing itself out in Israel at 40° C, particularly on this day in Haifa's Customs Office for imported cars. The *khamsin* was boiling my brains as I watched my husband desperately attempting to reduce Rosie's weight without the aid of an instant Atkinson's diet for automobiles. I hoped my two little boys in the care of *Sabta* Klara, their Israeli grandma, were indoors within the cool of our stone house in Ramat Yishai, some twelve miles south on the road to Nazareth.

The limit was reached, Rosie having been emptied of all removables, along with the very little left in our account. We paid our pound of flesh and after re-mantling the dear lady drove silently home. I was too hot to even begin expressing my dismay, if not disbelief, at the manner in which we had been handled by those servants of the State…until I remembered the Port of Haifa. Arni by this time was worried only that after two hours standing in the sun as it crept towards its noon zenith, Rosie might expire on the road home, the contents of her fuel tank evaporated in the heat or her fuel pump refusing to work.

A Rolls Royce of course must never be seen to die on the road, certainly not allowed in Merry England or anywhere abroad normally, but Israel is not a 'normal' country by general standards and on the highway to Nazareth maybe a little miracle was needed. It happened and we arrived in Ramat Yishai with dear Rosie still purring in her gentle way as we drove her into her new housing, an old cowshed, where she could cool down and recover. Well done, gal, you've passed your first test, I thought, wondering how many more I would have to face in a lifetime in the Holy Land. Adam, came running from the patio, Matti busily shuffling towards us on his bottom, a frantic grandmamma in tow as we walked through our cool, quarter acre of orchard to the back porch of Larish House.

Place & *Realpolitik*

Politics in Ramat Yishai reflected the place and the people. In this small community, as previously suggested, there was probably a greater diversity of background nationalities and cultures than in any other single community anywhere in the State of Israel. Of course the big cities, like Tel Aviv and Haifa, had mixed populations but even those towns had their areas of settlement where like lived with like. Only on a national level could Ramat Yishai be seen to be a true microcosm of a nation which had attracted people from all corners of the world, pulled to that area by the common thread of a shared race history.

Amongst all those different backgrounds representing peoples of America, Europe, Russia, North Africa, the Near and Middle East came one further exotic group from China. These were people whose parents or grandparents had become refugees during the Russian Revolution and had run away via Siberia to China, to make a new life in the capital Peking, or Bejing as it's now known. The Chinese are famed for their merchant class no less than the Jews, so that much they had in common. But even at such a distance the promise of the Promised Land after thirty years' exile from Russia had inspired some of them to leave that home and take their chance again in the new State of Israel. Perhaps the politics of China, about to give way to Communism under Mao following the end of the Japanese occupation and Mao's final defeat of the Nationalist Party in 1949, encouraged such a move to a new and democratic homeland. True to form, some of these independent-minded people had gravitated to the eclectic social mix that was the village of Ramat Yishai in the hope maybe of building a new identity without fear or favour, with no pressure from either politics or religion.

Here, in this 'end of the road village' in the post 2nd world war years, you could get a small shack or little starter house with one room serving as kitchen and living room, one bedroom, a toilet and shower. This had to accommodate a family but the saving grace was the plot of land around the house from a quarter to half an acre. Here you could keep chickens, goats, a cow and grow most of the fruit and vegetables you needed. Additionally you were surrounded by the agricultural land of the valley which gave settlers an opportunity to find work as labourers on farming communities in the area. Such work could be varied and include not only seasonal agriculture but maintenance, mechanical engineering, building, plumbing and so on. A good artisan was always in demand.

Most of the settlers, on arriving as new immigrants to British occupied Palestine between the two world wars or later Israel, were first housed and placed by the Jewish Agency. They may have found themselves virtually in the desert in the South or in the northern hills of the Galilee. The choice was not theirs. Some remained in these places but others found time to search the land for better or different opportunities and places to live. Ramat Yishai was not under the aegis of the Jewish Agency and those who found themselves buying or renting in the village did so mainly out of choice. Employment may have beckoned or the climate seemed more attractive. Perhaps they did not want to live in a city and could not join a *kibbutz* or *moshav* farming community. Perhaps they liked the idea of having a bit of land around them to do with as they pleased. Such people effectively took over every property that had been originally built there and looked to develop more property on national or private land within the area which constituted the boundaries of the village.

Most of the small houses already described, the *shikunim*, had been built within the centre of Ramat Yishai on national land leased for such buildings, while on the perimeters and dotted around the village there was some private land and this made the place even more attractive to those wanting to build their own house and of course for developers to muscle in on the act. The private land had mostly belonged to people who had bought it in the twenties and thirties but not necessarily come to live there at the time. It was a period when funding had been made available by Jews in the diaspora, especially from Europe and North America, specifically for land acquisition in Palestine. Large plots were bought by immigrant agencies and then sub-divided and sold on to Jewry from all around Europe.

The plots were not cheap but they offered the dream of settling some day in the Promised Land. Indeed there were those of a later generation who had come to the village with direct family connections with the original sales and others who had bought from the first-time buyers.

Precisely because Ramat Yishai was such a free-for-all place with no centralised cultural boundaries and very little effective political or other restriction, people did what they wanted to do in an eccentrically free-wheeling way. So individuals who wanted to express an independent way of life, religious or secular, found the village very attractive. There were people who had left *kibbutzes*, for example, Arni among them. One such couple who had bought a house on the other side of the village were American academics who had found the communal way of life of *kibbutz* individually restrictive, not giving sufficient space for the kind of personal enterprise and independent growth they needed or were used to. They wanted both the responsibilities and pleasures of having their own home away from the city, with a bit of land around it to make a garden, grow vegetables and provide a space for the children and animals to run wild in or combination of all three. There being very few such places in Israel which fitted this bill, the attraction of Ramat Yishai was clear to our

American friends. It was indeed the only such truly independent village in Northern Israel.

The pattern of politics in Ramat Yishai did not follow in principle either the stubborn power bases or the vagaries of the national political scene. When we came to the village there were two main parties. The largest was the Socialist party, *Mapai*, the second the right-wing *Herut*, until then a small opposition party nationally. Local elections immediately followed the national elections. Ramat Yishai voted idiosyncratically for the party person they really liked and felt could achieve the most for the village whether or not this coincided with the political party people had voted for in the national elections. Naturally enough, after a four year term in the local council it was inevitable that the voters would find plenty to criticise and less to praise so that the general inclination was to vote the other party contender in next time around to see if they could do better, which of course they never did, though they might do as well. This ensured that neither of the two main party representatives became complacent and like night following day a returning member was assured of a rest from mayoral office for at least four years.

Mapai was the official Labour Party in Israel from back in the nineteen thirties and had held the reins of power for term after tempestuous term following Independence in 1948. Herut, an opposition right-wing party, was originally founded by the Irgun or Begin's Boys under Menachem Begin in 1948 but had an insignificant though highly vocal representation nationally, maybe ten to fifteen seats in Parliament out of one hundred and twenty. Herut later formed a coalition under Begin to take power for the first time as the Likud party just before we left the country in 1977. Idealistically these two parties were 'polls apart' but practically speaking in our small community both had to deal with local issues in a manner which produced the goods and found favour with the more or less fickle voting inhabitants. That is not to say that political feelings did not run high in Ramat Yishai as elsewhere but simply that the practical application, the *realpolitik*, finally held sway. The balancing independent element in our council politics was represented not so much by a religious party member as by a religious man looking after the interests of a particular community, the Yemenis.

Party funding outside regional government credits never came the way of our village because it was not aligned predominantly to one party over a long enough period of time. The constant changes every four years put it off the political map as far as the major national parties were concerned. Ramat Yishai would have been considered a political maverick in the early seventies, unlike many other communities, especially the *kibbutzim*, which had been founded on political ideology so that those voters remained an accountable figure in any general election. Equally the small population of around 200 families, maybe 600 people, ensured the insignificance of Ramat Yishai on the greater political scene. So no major funding was offered from the largest party, *Mapai*, and the council had to run a meagre budget from local taxes that was basically self-accountable, not unlike a parish council in England.

The political nature of the councils of most local small towns and agricultural communities naturally coloured their working practices and the general ethos of those places and Labour politics had been the leading voice for many years. In most cases there was sufficient work for people within their own communities. Ramat Yishai was different. By the seventies only a small proportion of the population, especially the men, had work or ran businesses in the village itself. Ramat Yishai was not a prosperous place at that time but most of its inhabitants managed to make some kind of reasonable living in Haifa, Afula, Nazareth or in nearby agricultural co-operatives.

The prosperity that followed the Six Day War with the huge input of American money had not yet kicked in during the early seventies, or at least not into Ramat Yishai, though it was on its way by the time we had left towards 1978. People had still to work hard to make a basic living and taxes, as usual, were high. The money, too, went first to those who already had it and took time to filter down to the rest of us with the development of the economy through science and technology, building and industry.

Despite this, very few people in Ramat Yishai would say they were poor. We didn't feel poor but I suppose that by some Israeli standards we were. Indeed my mother-in-law, familiar with the manicured gardens, efficient economy and regular way of life of her *kibbutz* in those years, used the word 'hole' to describe our village. Not a very complimentary description and very far from the way the inhabitants regarded their community's successful, independent way of life. Klara had always hoped her son Arni would become a municipal engineer and have a nice flat in Tel Aviv for her to visit on a day off where she might window-shop to her heart's content, her favourite past-time. And here we were 'in the sticks' with a couple of basic stores and a chicken factory off the main road announcing the entrance to the village. How very difficult it is for children to meet the aspirations and dreams of their parents and likewise for parents to fulfil the complex emotional not to mention financial demands of their children.

The Mayors of Toytown

With so many men from the village working hard to earn a living in other towns or communities, it was necessary and seemed sensible that the job of being Mayor of Ramat Yishai for the four-year elected term should pass to the women. A man could hardly give up the requisite time from his normal job or indeed give up his job and expect to find it again four years later if he found himself voted out of the mayoral post at the next election. So the political office of Mayor in the seventies went to two suitable ladies of the two main parties, one of whom had been regularly elected in the past.

The long established Socialist Mayor, professionally a nurse in charge of our clinic, was Yudit and the difference between the two lady contenders was as between fresh and salt-sea water. Yudit was a real pioneer, a brave young woman from Yugoslavia who had come to Israel in her teens, some forty years earlier, and she knew what it was to live in an outpost of another nation's empire. She was married to Alexander Shoshani, the retired *horseback guard*, and had experienced dangerous times and situations. Nothing could frighten Yudit. With her light grey hair and deep smoker's voice she had the sharpest, brightest and most twinkling blue eyes I had ever come across and an engaging chuckle which shook her ample frame. The combination of kindness, caring and no nonsense ensured Yudit was formidable, respected and deeply loved. With the fulsome figure of her later years went an equally fulsome vocabulary which she used with acerbity, brevity and sardonic wit. Everyone enjoyed her imaginative and worldly-wise expressions as long as they were not critically on the end of them. When my mother-in-law was once relating in an affectedly coy but triumphant manner how she had given up the *goy*, non-jew, she was so much in love with in her youth, Yudit had retorted drily, "Well, be thankful Klara that your son had more courage."

Yudit and Alexander had lived for many years in the village and she was very familiar with all the youngsters born and brought up in Ramat Yishai where she had been both nurse and midwife. If she saw such youth hanging around, up to no good, she would say, "I brought you into the world with my own two hands, so you behave yourself for without me you might not have made it ... eh, and the country been spared an idle layabout." Large in body and spirit Yudit knew what was right and what was wrong and most people took that on the chin, including her husband and his dogs. Among her great virtues was a deep-seated tolerance, never to be mistaken for weakness, and a woman's wisdom that could more or less ignore her devoted husband's weaker points: Alexander had a great liking for a drink, especially good vodka, and enjoyed the occasional stop-over in Haifa, meeting his drinking companions and flirting with the 'young ladies of the night'. Yudit would be suitably busy when he returned, quietly commenting to herself on the frail-ties of men-folk maybe, with a humorous shrug of her ample shoulders. She was a good and practical Mayor for the left-wing *Mapai*, firmly in control of the council even though she could often sit at a meeting and say barely one word. But her presence was always felt, her views known and on most occasions every-body behaved well around her.

The newcomer to the mayoral post was Zelda and she stood for the right-wing *Herut* party, although she admitted early in our acquaintance that she didn't know the difference between *Herut* and *Mapai* but her husband, Arie, was definitely *Herut*. Ignoring any party to which Arie was attached, he believed in getting things done his own way, for Arie was a big and burly guy who used his two hands and the roar of a lion to achieve his aims. He was a sunny Leo to his bones by not only name but nature. It came not as a surprise to us to learn that owing to his challenging way of expressing his views and doing what he thought was right, Arie had found himself at some time or another on a collision course with the law. As a result of such conflict, any chance of a career in local politics had been squashed.

Arie was thus unable to put himself forward for the mayoral election in Ramat Yishai. He saw no reason, however, why his wife Zelda could not be his spokesperson and run for Mayor in his place. In this way he no doubt hoped he would at least be able to load all the shots for Zelda to fire. This was a practical compromise solution for as long as his wife toed the marital and political line and he had no reason to imagine there would be any variation in those states. That being the case, Arie was neither required to believe in nor respect his wife's personal views or ability to do the job. She was, after all, simply his 'alter ego'.

Actually the quiet Zelda, who seemed to live at home in the shadow of the husband she obviously loved, was also a very successful and popular nurse. She was an attractive brunette with a trim figure and soft voice. Indeed it was under her running of our village clinic that a natural, democratic medical practice was taking place in Ramat Yishai. This was in attending to both the Jews from the village and the Bedouin from nearby settlements in the single surgery from a single waiting room where everyone sat waiting their turn to be seen. Occasional queue jumping took place, to which I can readily testify, since the Bedouin ladies would arrive at the earliest possible moment as a substantial group accompanied by numbers of children. They had more time, or a different notion of it one might assume, to wait around and in any case seemed to enjoy the opportunity for chatting and laughter which could reach quite a loud pitch. The Bedouin men, on the other hand, sitting separately from the women, were usually silent, no doubt concentrating as males will on their ailments and how to make the most of them when they got their turn to speak to the nurse.

As Israeli citizens, both Jews and Arabs were entitled to equal attention under the national health scheme and throughout the hospital network all were seen without differentiation. But we were told this was the first clinic operating in a strictly Jewish settlement in Israel on a 'mixed client' basis ~ a feather in the cap of our little community. It may equally have been the last to do so for many reasons apart from those of national security, sad as that may seem. This might appear strange in view of the fact that Arab Israeli citizens have the vote and representation in Israel's Parliament, the Knesset ~ equality in some areas but not across the board. Cultural differences must inevitably affect politics and certainly Israeli Arabs have many more children than the Jews, swelling their numbers and therefore citizenship ratio at a considerable rate within this young Jewish State.

Zelda, as suggested, was an entirely different character from Yudit. I believe she came to Israel as a married woman with her husband and two young children from Rumania around 1967. Her Hebrew was by now excellent. The fact that her husband was such a rowdy creature gave her an air of strength. But she was quite a modest woman and when Arie decided she should stand for election she was at first totally bewildered. He simply informed her that the *Herut* party had chosen her to represent them in Ramat Yishai and he would personally ensure she was elected! Arie, our friendly, roaring lion, enjoyed going to town every now and then to meet his mates and indulge in a solid drinking binge after which he would often be as free with his fists as his tongue. He believed he would have no difficulty persuading the majority of voters in Ramat Yishai to elect his wife.

A couple of weeks before the election Arie let it be known that he would be throwing a party in his home with an open invitation to all comers including the vocal members of his own political party. The time came and the hardier males were pleased to match their drinking prowess with that of their host. A number of ladies, who found the big, blonde and macho Arie attractive, were equally pleased to have an opportunity to flirt with him. As you may imagine, it seemed unwise to rub Arie up the wrong way so that even relative strangers living along his street felt obliged to attend the party. There was always a huge variety of interesting food at parties in the village which in this case was matched only by the quantity of beer and spirits flowing from kegs and bottles.

The party came and went and the voting took place, following which Zelda found she had been duly elected by democratic majority vote for the *Herut* party... and the usual need to change the Mayor for a further term. So Zelda gave up her nursing job temporarily and Yudit, the erstwhile Mayor had to be pulled out of her semi-retirement from nursing to take Zelda's place in running the clinic at the entrance to our village. In all fairness Yudit had hardly stopped nursing while she was Mayor as she was always on hand to back up her colleague Zelda whenever necessary.

The local *Herut* party membership in the village was jubilant for they were always deeply aggrieved at the sweeping victory of *Mapai* across the country and even in Ramat Yishai with Yudit at the helm, stating that the elections were rigged but that now at last the true voice of the people, like that of the turtle, was heard in the land.

We were very fortunate in having Yudit living next door to us for that way we not only heard all the latest scandals circulating through the corridors of power but rarely had to visit the surgery when a child was feeling unwell. We had been asked in such a case to simply pop in and see her any time of the day or night. She always kept a cupboard full of pills and potions at home and a few useful pieces of equipment, such as an enema and stethoscope. It was interesting to be living in a village where the leading figures dealing with the community's well-being, both political and medical, were from the distaff side.

The council employed a full-time Secretary, Mr. Cohen, and there was a lady to do the typing for two hours daily and an accountant for two hours daily, the latter a somewhat exaggerated requirement. Once a fortnight would surely have sufficed for regulating the affairs of Ramat Yishai but the accountant popped in as and when, keeping a wary eye on the daily 'ins and outs' and giving the office a proper air of importance.

The Secretary who had come to the village a few months before us in 1973 was Betzalel Cohen. He was more or less on his uppers after being discreetly asked to resign, so we understood, from three previous and somewhat larger councils. In most cases he had apparently been unable to provide financial clarity concerning money received and receipts given in the pursuit of his office. To be fair to the man, he was cleared of any misdemeanours in those matters for lack of substantial evidence. He subsequently found himself applying for the advertised post of Secretary to the Council in the one horse village which was Ramat Yishai and being the only candidate he received the job. In addition, and in spite of the fact that his rank in the Israeli Reserves was corporal while other villagers held higher ranks, Betzalel was appointed to be Chief of the local guard or militia which had already been established but lacked an overlord. Betzalel immediately appointed a couple of officers from the Reserves as his deputies and ran the militia with great vigour and success. This body was composed of seven or eight men in total and mixed pickles they were indeed. Our exuberant neighbour Eliezer Maman would have liked to join the militia but could not because he was a policeman. Due to the respect this brought him Eli was able to offer 'advice' now and then to Betzalel regarding aspects of the law, probably more to do with road traffic than terrorist traffic, but who knows? ' In the land of the blind......'

The council office was one of the old *shikunim* built for immigrants with three rooms in total. There was one larger room, one smaller room with kitchenette and a shower/toilet. In the main room was the Mayor's table, a table for the Secretary and a third table for the typist and accountant. There being little space, one table would be removed before a meeting leaving the Mayor and Secretary sharing a table, the typist and accountant at the other. This made room for a few chairs for the other council members

68

and a member of the public or two. From this sound base near the entrance to the village the Mayor and Council operated the general and political business for the population of around six hundred souls that was the community of Ramat Yishai.

Laffi & the Place of Birds

It was early July 1973 and the long hot summer was beginning to get into my bones, to ease out the tensions and give me the feeling that somewhere, maybe centuries ago, my antecedents had lived along Mediterranean shores where summer light and warmth were part of the pattern of daily life.

Adam, aged just over three, had a day off from the nursery school and rose early because he had seen the Bedouin boy with his goats the day before set up his tent for the summer on the dry hillside in front of our house. A bright, imaginative but somewhat introvertive child, Adam had been attracted by the young goatherd and decided to join him and roam across the local uncultivated land with the goats. At 6 am he set off with a little stick and waited until the goats came up the hill and started to be driven along our road. At this point I watched him walking among the goats, mimicking the goatherd's language and gestures as the lad kept the animals out of our front gardens before finding another spot on the hillside a little further along where they might descend to graze again. Then Adam returned home, as I had suggested he should. What freedom there is in trust and a careless sense of security.

Our goatherd was a member of a family of Bedouins who annually passed down from the North into the Western Galilee, skirting Haifa to arrive in the Jezreel Valley below us. Perhaps they had contact with the other Bedouin who had been offered land in which to settle in another valley near us north-west of Nazareth. One of their number, a young lad called Laffi aged around sixteen, was apprenticed to a local carpenter in our village where Arni had met him and offered him some gardening work in his spare time. He turned up at our house with little idea of gardening but with a glad eye on anything female even vaguely presentable in shorts, which happened to be most of the young women of the village. No women from his village would ever be seen so scantily clad, as I later learned to my embarrassment. No wonder the lad had roving eyes for such tempting and thinly disguised meat. So Laffi had to be put in his place when thoughts of familiarity crossed his mind when I offered him a cold drink on the patio of our house. But to be fair, here was a clash of cultures and a virile young man ready to make the most of it. What do you do in such a situation? Admonish and explain or cover up? A little of both seemed sensible. He got the point.

Laffi came several times to do a bit of weeding and in the course of conversation said that we, as a family, had been invited to visit his parents in a valley near Tsipori. About three miles away. We asked him to thank his family for their invitation and agreed to visit on the following weekend. So we duly set off with the children for the Bedouin village in our old Rolls Royce, fully aware that we could only go so far by car, the rest would be on foot.

We parked the car at the end of a dirt track above the valley where we found Laffi waiting for us and followed him down a footpath through the scattered dwellings that made up several Bedouin villages. It was a magical valley full of old oak trees, obviously ignored by the Turks who had felled most of Palestine's oak for railway sleepers. There were little irregular fields where straw had been cut and stacked and steep wooded slopes which cut off the area from other habitation. It was peaceful and quiet except for birdsong, reminding us that the nearby, ancient *Tsipori*, the Hebrew name for Sephoris, meant place of the birds. In the past *Tsipori* had been a seat of Hebrew learning and a prosperous Galilean city for the first four centuries C.E. Now there are only the archaeological treasures left in a wild area; beautiful mosaic floors of a palatial house and part of a well-drained early, wide paved road.

At this time our Bedouin friends were attempting to forgo their wanderings to build a settled community in the peaceful valley. Israel had encouraged this in the current unsettled political climate. Presumably the opportunity to create a more secure future for their children, in a fast changing world, made sense to these nomads whose freedom of movement was increasingly threatened. If they needed to settle somewhere then Israel offered an economically sound country whose Arab neighbours had proved not only weaker militarily but economically and politically far less stable, except Jordan perhaps who did not want these people. It was nevertheless a sea change for these wanderers against the backdrop of a nomadic tribal life that reached back thousands of years in the area. But maybe nomads everywhere were suffering from restricting national boundaries in a shrinking world, having to face new survival choices.

The footpath wound between rough, part-built villages for about a mile on a very hot day, with me wearing the then fashionable knee-length mini-dress, the only style I owned and not suitable for visiting the Bedouin since my legs were bare. On arriving at the family dwelling we were greeted with the utmost hospitality. Arnon spoke a little Arabic and Hebrew was also spoken by the younger men, some of whom worked for Israelis.

As soon as we arrived we offered our hosts a small gift and were offered in turn pita bread baked in five minutes on an outdoor iron grid over the hot embers of a twig fire. Accompanying this hot bread were small balls of semi-curdled goats' cheese or *labene* preserved in olive oil; sharp, creamy and quite delicious. We were then given a little bowl of a milky goat meat stew, containing yoghurt and saffron. The eighteen month old Matti downed this stew with great relish but his elder brother held back, being fussy about unfamiliar food. We were simply standing around the grill eating and nobody ate with us but the women and children stood with us chatting and laughing and nodding delightedly when we expressed our approval of the lovely food.

The house ahead of us was simply constructed of concrete

blocks on square columns with concrete floors and open spaces for windows and a door. We were invited into the building which was quite large in area by our standards and essentially one big living room with a floor above and flat roof under construction. The elder son who had supervised the building was talking to Arni the engineer about some structural problems while his mother swept the floor, laid down some raffia mats and fetched mattresses and pillows. Everywhere was scrupulously clean. The women sat on the mattresses, including myself, while the men sat on small stools opposite us as everyone drank fresh mint tea. I made every attempt to sit as decorously as possible with my legs tucked under me or to one side but when it became clear that I was embarrassed by the sidelong looks at my naked limbs, a young son, without a word spoken, handed me a cloth to put over my knees. The women were mostly sitting cross-legged on the flat mattresses, their limbs enveloped in voluminous skirts.

We stayed for about three hours, which was fine for Arni who was able to communicate but a strain for me trying to describe my life or understand theirs with hand or facial movements, smiles and laughter until I finally ran out of meaningful gestures. It was my first attempt at mime without being versed in the art and very trying on my imagination. But I sensed no fuss or anxiety amongst my female audience who were smiling and relaxed and perfectly natural, as were the giggling younger children with their shy looks at us. I was surely trying too hard.

Adam had stayed out of doors, running wild among the chickens and goats. The family had a well-stocked and tended vegetable garden and had planted various fruit trees. Presumably a well had been dug or some water storage organised as there seemed to be no shortage of water. The valley was irrigated naturally by a *wadi* or watercourse running through it which was surface dry except in the rainy season. It appeared that these people were basically self-supporting, as they always had been.

The view out of the large window space from the main room looked over the valley which was slowly suffused by the soft and golden evening light as the sun sank in the sky. There were no vehicles for they were all parked up the hill a mile away, so no traffic noise, no street lamps, nothing but the natural sounds of birds, animals and human beings quietly living a life which was basically in tune with nature around them. It was like any rural scene of a pre-industrialised era; something going back centuries which just then had a genuine charm for me in the beauty and tranquillity it offered.

After polite farewells and offering thanks with our hands pressed together towards our hosts we left. Laffi and his brothers took it in turns to carry Matti up the steep valley path while Adam refused help, valiantly making his own way on his small legs and often ahead of us despite a natural tiredness. It was a lovely end to a happy and interesting day amongst materially unsophisticated but intelligent and proud people whose smiling hospitality in a wonderful valley ringing with birdsong would never be forgotten.

Only later it occurred to me that it would be unfamiliar and unlikely that we could return similar hospitality by inviting Laffi's large family to our home in Ramat Yishai. Indeed these people, we were told, would surely refuse, having no wish to meet you on your own ground. And yet they had crossed that bridge in the opposite direction. They had offered us the privilege of sharing their home, their food, their conversation and their very warm welcome; giving hospitality to strangers, in every sense, remained at the heart of their culture.

Snake in the Net

I am not quite sure how we first met a singular woman called Adrienne. No doubt she had heard that an English girl had recently arrived in Ramat Yishai and was eager to speak the language with which she was most familiar after her mother tongue, German.

Adrienne had her own story to tell of the long route taken to Israel after leaving her middle-class parents in Vienna and escaping in 1938 to an Uncle who ran a linen factory in Belfast. She was then eighteen years of age and took this timely step largely, she said, in protest against and horror at watching a cultured, acquiescent Jewish bourgeoisie bow their heads before Nazi anti-semitism in the Austrian capital, with disastrous results. She was an only child and her parents perished in the Holocaust. Adrienne was even then politically oriented and an idealist. Her uncle sent her to England to find work, initially in a household somewhere outside Cambridge.

She knew some Yiddish but her Hebrew was fairly limited for she had lived in East Anglia for nearly thirty years before making a decision to emigrate to Israel following the 1967 Six Day War. She had steered clear of possible marriage with a friend of the family, a young Cambridge educated Jew with whom she would have had a great deal in common, in favour of attaching herself after the Second World War to the local Cambridgeshire Communist Party where she met an an East Anglian fellow traveller, whom she decided to marry. With little prospect of a steady income she and he set up a small market gardening business in the Fen country, where she appeared as foreign to the locals as they appeared to her. It came to her hearing that the Fen folk thought she was so foreign, from such distant parts, that she had probably never had a bath before arriving in England. Despite the not so distant war with Germany and Austria it was evident that few of her near neighbours knew or cared to know where Vienna was on the world map or what an illustrious and civilized part it had played over the past two hundred years in European culture. Of course this was some time before television really entered our homes and global psyche and certainly before package tours, for better or worse, for richer or poorer.

Adrienne had a daughter and a son with the fellow traveller before he went on his way, leaving his wife to shift barrows of manure, tend vegetable plots and bring up the children as best she might. She got a divorce and married for the second time a Welshman who was also not Jewish. He was a rather mild man who had agreed to go to Israel with Adrienne and their two children, another daughter and son. Her eldest son, then nineteen, refused to emigrate with her and was lost to the family. Her older daughter became a Mormon, married a Mormon and went to live in the Lake District. When we made her acquaintance on a visit to her mother she had four children and one on the way, but that's another story.

At the time we met Adrienne in 1973 her Welshman was working in a factory in Nazareth and she was trying to eke out their living by making and selling soft toys. As I remember it, her second husband vanished from the scene some time later, leaving Adrienne alone again with two teenage children and a very meagre pension. This was a lady full of fire, intellectual vigour and with a flaming, Zionist idealism that I felt had been somewhat lost on her mild 'man from the valleys'. But somewhere between this idealism and an extreme pragmatism that marked her ability to create wonderful things with her hands, to tend injured birds and animals like a female St. Francis and to grow fruit on stone, lay her *achille's heel*. Adrienne's valour, energy and enthusiasm were one hundred and one percent quixotic. The windmills stood fast as she tilted at them in every direction; against petty bureaucracy, local government corruption, intolerance, uncouthness, unkindness to animals and any left-wing, liberal Israeli politics.

It has to be said here that my friend's toleration of the then hostile Arab nations on Israel's borders and even bona fide Israeli Arab citizens could not be rated very high. This was not a cultural matter but a raw, militant case of fighting for survival, as she then saw it. A vigilant steering committee might note here that Adrienne had swerved considerably from left to right and that the red flag with its hammer and sickle and the *Internationale* had been replaced by the blue and white national banner with its Star of David and popular anthem from the Six Day War *Jersusalem the Golden*, not to be handed back.

Adrienne needed to talk and to some extent I became her *Sancho Panza*, though I was less a foil to the lady than a fencing partner and hapless dispenser of common sense or facilitator wherever or whenever a problem arose, which could be twice a day. All this had, of course, to be juggled with a husband and children, washing and cooking, looking after the hens and so on. But Adrienne spoke English, was interesting and I had a soft spot for her.

It was inevitable that Arni became equally involved, especially in the sort of situations that warranted climbing ladders for example or required masculine strength.

Thus it was that a distressed Adrienne appeared on our veranda one day with anxiety written all over her face and with a plea for help. Arni was not yet home from his work but she insisted that he come to her place as soon as he possibly could to free a trapped snake in her shed.

Now snakes in Israel are not generally looked upon with much favour and it was commonly said that the only good snake was a dead snake. Indeed the viper, with its handsome, diamond-shaped markings was particularly unpleasant for its bite was extremely poisonous. In our area of the Northern Galilee they were more rare than a similar looking money snake or the completely harmless to humans and very common black whip snake, which might be anything from three to six feet long and maybe a foot in circumference at its thickest.

Adrienne had managed to buy a house with some land in Ramat Yishai at an average price, only to find out after moving in that her home and garden were constructed over the remains of some Roman buildings; the ground full of stones and uneven surfaces prone to sudden collapse. She had certainly paid over the odds to those in the know. This meant that her little *shikun* was more likely to suffer subsidence than those on firmer ground, which it did, and that growing fruit and vegetables on such thin and antique masonry-bedevilled land was virtually impossible. There was little or no top soil. All this had escaped the notice of our erstwhile horticulturist in her eagerness to buy a home in this quiet village. Despite this doleful situation, Adrienne toiled to improve the land, carting loads of soil from wherever she could legitimately take it and was growing strawberries, with difficulty, in a patch at the bottom of the garden covered in green netting to keep away the bulbul, a rather voracious and large finch-like, fruit-eating bird.

It was not the bulbul that attacked the fruit but a black whip snake, attracted to the greenery and young berries and it had managed to get itself entangled in the netting. Adrienne had tried to free it by snipping at the net with scissors but this had made the snake thrash about even more and become worse entangled, the fine nylon getting forced under its scales. Before she came to us for help she had managed to carry the large creature in its tangled netting into the garden shed and shut the door to avoid predators reaching it. The average villager would have simply knocked the snake on the head to kill it and then disposed of it. But Adrienne was far from being your average villager. She was now on a mercy mission. Arni was to free the snake with her help in attempting to calm it to prevent it getting further entangled in the process.

So it was that Arni turned up that evening at the shed and was presented with a pair of kitchen scissors. His first thought too was to put the animal out of its misery but Adrienne's eyes rested fiercely and imploringly upon him. He was to snip and she was to hold. Well, the creature was strong and it was all either of them could do to hold it down while the netting surgery proceeded. Two hours went by before my husband returned home completely exhausted and neither pleased nor caring that one whip snake had been safely released into the village environs to survive another day or die another death sooner or later. It was, though, a mark of his generosity and tolerance that he had helped Adrienne without question or remonstrance. It would not be his last errand of mercy on her behalf.

On another occasion Adrienne, who had a soft but eager way of speaking and a warm hearty laugh when something tickled her fancy, again appeared at our house looking worried. I could see that another tale of woe was about to be communicated. She asked me to look through her abundant and wayward, frizzy brown hair at her scalp. Did I notice anything? Indeed I did notice what appeared to be a whole inflamed area where she had apparently been scratching at a terrible irritant. I thought it could be an allergy. There were similar marks on her neck and shoulders. I naturally asked whether she had taken this problem to the doctor. She had indeed done so and he had seemed puzzled at first and then asked if by any chance she kept chickens. She did not. This left him bemused. Was she sure there were no chickens in the vicinity?

As far as the doctor was concerned, Adrienne was the victim of chicken mites. But what seemed strange was the fact that the mites were on her head. I suppose you might occasionally pick up a chicken and hold it in your arms, but you would surely not put it on your head. He gave her some cream and asked her to be sure to keep away from any local poultry pens. This made no sense whatever to our friend. Since the problem did not go away, the doctor called to see her. It was while standing in her kitchen, drinking a cup of coffee, that he heard a clatter in the roof above their heads.

"There's something trapped up there," the doctor ventured, "could it be rats?"

"Oh, no," Adrienne gaily replied, "it's only the pigeons roosting in my roof. I love the sound of them cooing and coming and going."

The doctor looked up and noticed the considerable number of hair-line cracks in the kitchen ceiling. "Problem solved," he said, "get rid of those pigeons. It is they who have the mite which is simply dropping through the cracks and straight onto your head, thousands of them, I would imagine. I advise you to get rid of the birds today. They are, in any case, prone to numbers of unpleasant diseases." He moved swiftly into the living room and departed as soon as possible, presumably to take a thorough shampoo and shower on reaching home.

Adrienne was devastated for she had to make a choice between being house-mother to a large number of mite-ridden pigeons or asking Arni to obtain the suitable material to fumigate the roof area, difficult of access, and when the birds had flown to block up all holes to prevent further entry.

When no other solution suggested itself, especially as this was a health risk to the children, she left the house and let the man get on with the job, weeping as she watched her startled pigeons, cooing frantically as they exited in a cloud of smoke from various holes, to fly away from her house forever. Arni thoroughly sprayed the area and came home to take a long shower in steaming water and lots of soap suds. As I write this today I find myself scratching my head, my arms and feeling itchy all over, such is the psychosomatic power of mind and imagination long after the action, time and place has ceased to exist.

I did refuse my friend one other animal loving excess, as sympathetic as I was with her cause. Few if any villagers, excepting ourselves, considered the common cat a household pet, with a right to live with the family in the home and even occupy the best chair. I remember a startled visitor screaming at me, "there's a cat in the room." Mine was called Hammy because she had cost me *hamishim* or fifty lira on her first visit to the vet, a large sum for me to find at the time. Adrienne naturally had a domesticated cat.

The majority of cats in the village were wild and went through life having one litter after another which the females could barely feed as they were near starvation themselves. They had competitively to hunt for scraps and mice and those that came near the house, often pregnant or with half-dead kittens, always looked very thin and in desperate need of food and especially water during the long dry season. We tried to adopt one little family of a particularly pretty animal, but malnutrition and disease won against all of our efforts and that was distressing. Now Adrienne suddenly had the bright idea that she could practice cat euthanasia throughout the village and was prepared to humanely put down as many as possible of the newborn kittens for whom the mothers had little or no milk. She asked me if I would help her in this animal assassination by painless anaesthetization at dusk, when we could trace the nests by the pitiful sound of mewing. I refused to be involved in this harebrain scheme, on the grounds that I had no time and more importantly I felt nature had to take care of itself and that this kindly meant intervention could not possibly be effective over the short or long term.

This did not deter my friend from taking the next step. She went to the chemist to buy a bottle of chloroform and was even naive enough to explain the true reason for which it was needed. The chemist thinking he had misheard, due to Adrienne's thick Anglo-Viennese accent, asked her to repeat what she wanted and why she wanted it. Looking then over a pair of gold-rimmed glasses at her, with tight lips and a studied frown, the answer came firmly back, "No, you cannot buy chloroform without a prescription and indeed we do not sell bottles of chloroform to be administered on wads of cotton wool to the noses of either cats or humans."

Since this was not followed up by a visit of the local police, we presumed the chemist simply considered Adrienne to be slightly out of her tree but not a genuine threat to any living creature, great or small. Of course the word went around, as had other words, and Adrienne with her deep concern for all the creatures of the earth was considered by some to be a witch. She was sadly treated by some elderly neighbours to threats against her pet dog and cat and to the stony glances and superstition which age-old ignorance of a genuine 'outsider' can breed. Even our more sophisticated friends regarded Adrienne as a case for only mildly tolerant treatment, being her own worst enemy and someone born to lose yet who survives despite and still ~ a sacrificial lamb indeed in wolf's clothing or even of a witch?

Adrienne continued to haunt our lives with her passion, pessimism and painstaking but misguided efforts to 'right wrongs', avert daily disasters and to somehow be at the centre of things going topsy-turvy. A dear, crazy woman who never really forgave me for leaving Ramat Yishai when the time came and whose kindly, distracted image remains fixed in my mind.

A Personal Exodus ... Inlaws Outlined

My parents-in-law were virtually founder members of a kibbutz established near the coast between Tel Aviv and Haifa in 1935. My mother-in-law came from a Polish family, from a village much like that of 'Fiddler on the Roof'. It was on the borderlands in the south so often fought over by the Poles and Russians. She was called Klara Klieger and the wry joke about her relatively fair skin and green eyes made reference to the number of Russian invasions across the Polish border.

My father-in-law, Israel or Yis Roth, who was also fair skinned with blue eyes, was an educated man from a prosperous merchant family living on the Danube in Győr, Hungary. His family owned a granary and shipped the grain from the country's vast wheat production up or down the Danube as far as the Black Sea and beyond as business required.

The name Goren, a Hebrew translation of 'granary', was adopted by my father-in-law after independence in 1948 in order to shed the adopted European name of Rot or Roth, meaning red, which was a popular accommodation with a common word for a name that sounded harmless enough in the country in which his family had become assimilated and had lived for many generations. Little did the Jews realize that red, green, blue and so on ~ Roth, Grün and Blau ~ often with berg or stein as a suffix, would soon identify them as swiftly with their Jewish origins as any modern Hebrew name might. As the Yiddish comic said "OK, so what was your family name before it was Green?" I suppose the final reply to that might be "So, I come from the House of David"!.. which you have to admit sounds far grander than any colour or landmark.

Klara was born in the middle of the Great War in 1916 as the ferment in Russia was building up to wholesale Revolution in 1917. These were turbulent times in Eastern Europe as in the West; times of war, famine and the historical collapse forever of the power of aristocracy and the landed elite. As a young woman of seventeen in the early 1930s, Klara had left her peasant family village, joined a Jewish Youth Group and was working on the land in various farm camps learning agricultural skills that she hoped might be useful in the country in which she dreamed of living, Palestine.

The young Klara worked on the farm camps for two years. As Nazism and anti-Jewish propaganda was stepped up and Hitler's Germany sought to extend its territorial grip eastwards to Russia, Klara's Youth Group started to organize a regular exodus of young people to Palestine on a quota basis. Priority was given to married couples on a single registration so many boys and girls obtained false marriage papers from local rabbis to give themselves a better chance of getting on the emigration lists. Klara was one of those who teamed up with a lad and the pair of them set sail for Palestine as a supposed married couple in 1936. She left behind her parents and siblings, one sister managing to get a passage to the United States along with a cousin.

Klara's parents, who had never left their village, and most other members of her family subsequently perished in the Holocaust. When Klara arrived in Palestine she was sent to a Jewish settlement at Kfar Saba where she was able to study horticulture, commercial flower growing in particular. Of medium build with light brown hair and lively, flirtatious green eyes, Klara was an attractive woman who learned fast and worked hard.

Israel Roth studied law in Hungary but also dreamed of a land called Palestine, its heart the ancient city of Jerusalem so dear to so many. He was born in 1911 and since everyone needs bread, the business of distributing grain flowed on with his childhood alongside the Danube. Despite the upheavals of the Great War his life was cushioned by the commercial success of the family business. When on his student holidays to Palestine in 1933, following a Grand Tour which included Italy from which he had sailed, Yis set his mind to returning in the near future to this biblical homeland and building a new life on a kibbutz away from the insidious march of Europe's anti-semitism.

Two years later, aged twenty-four, Yis had abandoned his law studies and became one of hundreds of Jews packed on an illegal immigrant vessel, the *Vallos*, which set sail from Constanza, the chief port of Rumania on the Black Sea, towards the coast of British-ruled Palestine in the late Spring of 1935. Despite a traveling distance of no more than a few days the passengers on this crowded boat were at sea for two months in the growing heat of summer as the vessel prowled the Mediterranean waiting for a window of opportunity to safely land its illegal human cargo.

The British navy and police boats regularly patrolled the shores between the Lebanese border in the north and the Egyptian border in the south. Patterns of patrol were monitored and finally, after a suffocating eight weeks at sea with rations and water dwindling, the boat discharged its load one dark July night. Men and women with children and babes in arms waded waist deep in water up the beach of Kfar Vitkin near Caesarea, below the northern port of Haifa, while the patrol boats were in the south. Jewish settlers were there to quietly receive this weary and wet but triumphant, straggling host of humanity and smuggle them away to various kibbutzes and other communities. Today at Kfar Vitkin you can find a plaque commemorating this landing and the boat and crew who got their cargo safely ashore.

Yis found himself in the new Kibbutz Maabarot, on arid marshland two miles from the landing strip of beach at Kfar Vitkin, and stayed there for the rest of an eventful life in the shaping history of that kibbutz and a Jewish homeland. His elder brother had also spent time in Palestine in the early 1930s in theological studies at the University of Jerusalem and returned to Hungary. There he later became a rabbi and felt duty-bound to stay with his Jewish community despite the onslaught of Nazism. He too perished in the Holocaust although another brother remained in Hungary and escaped detection to finally emigrate to Israel with his family in 1956.

Soon after his arrival, Yis, a quiet and studious fellow, tall, slim and aesthetic looking but with a puckish sense of humour, was given a few rudimentary lessons in being a guard. You could not meet a more gentle and pacific man than Yis but he had to learn to use a rifle and play his part in 'guarding' the Jewish settlements. And so he was sent to guard the Jewish settlement of Kfar Saba where he met a pretty Polish girl called Klara Klieger. Klara finished her studies and went to live and work on Kibbutz Maabarot alongside her partner Yis in 1937. They had three sons, Arnon, Yigal and Itzhak and when Israel was declared a State in 1948 and registration of the population began in earnest, Yis and Klara decided to marry and give themselves the Hebrew name of Goren. Their eldest child, Arnon, my husband, then ten years old, was asked if he would like to attend the marriage ceremony or stay in the kibbutz and have a special treat, an ice cream. He naturally opted for the ice-cream and can therefore truthfully say that he was not around at the time his parents married.

Kibbutz

Kibbutz is a familiar concept in the Jewish diaspora but not perhaps to everybody. I suppose the notion of it grew out of the increasing desire of late 19th century Zionists to find a way of surviving in a new land which might incorporate their political ideals of being Jewish in a Jewish homeland without the encumbrance of religion. Religion, after all, had been responsible they felt for preventing them having a national rather than primarily religious identity. This was not an entirely convincing argument maybe but one which bolstered an idea for releasing Jews from anti-semitism and continuing pogroms wherever they lived in Europe and indeed across the world.

There were even steps taken to acquire land to set up a national home in Uganda, so Palestine and the Promised Land was not the only target for this aspiration. But despite negotiations with the then governing bodies of that central African country the attempt failed.

No doubt there was also a hankering in the minds of generations of ghettoised Jews to own land and cultivate it and be physically self-supporting and, idealistically, in the old land of Israel from where their descendents had originated, the pull of the Book being still irresistible to many.

Certainly my father and mother-in-law had some of those thoughts at heart when they settled in Kibbutz Maabarot along the coast between Haifa and Tel Aviv in the nineteen-thirties. The land, largely a malaria infested swamp, had been purchased from a distant Arab landowner who lived in Syria. Maabarot affiliated itself with a left wing, non-religious party, which suited Yis and Klara.

The kibbutz community was based on pure communism: a shared way of life in which all partners were equal with an elected and regularly re-elected Secretariat to manage all the finances and the living rules by democratic consent. Every member could have their say at weekly meetings. This was the administrative and ethical system adopted by common agreement. These communes were naturally small and made up of like-minded people from similar backgrounds. They were able to pool existing professions and skills and acquire further education to meet their needs from within the wider kibbutz organisation.

The majority of founder kibbutz members were of course young people whose physical strength and energy could be harnessed to maximum effect. Children born were looked after in children's houses, twelve to a nurse and teacher, and they lived and slept there, spending only three hours a day from 4pm to 7pm in the small one-bedroom shacks of their parents. Under that system more adults were available to work all day. There was a communal kitchen, dining room, laundry and so on. Everybody took it in turn by fixed rota to be involved in those day to day tasks of communal cooking, washing and cleaning. There was a pooling of labour, knowledge and ideas.

At Maabarot, the swamps were drained but it took more than twenty years to turn the kibbutz into a thriving agricultural community and at some individual cost to health. My father-in-law, amongst many others, suffered from malaria for many years. As the membership slowly grew with different waves of immigration to its final figure of around three hundred, the agriculture ~ milk and its products, fruit and fish farming ~ was augmented with small industries such as dog food, baby food and pharmacological products. It tickled my explosive Monty Python imagination that the Hebrew word for suppositories manufactured in Maabarot was 'nerot'- candles!

The kibbutz soon developed a fine reputation for music and after the Second World War became home for a period to the family of an idealistic French 'cellist, taken by the idea of pure communism, the famous Paul Tortellier. Maabarot was also nicknamed 'the garden kibbutz' due to the efforts of its members to make it a place of beauty, each little shack surrounded by a personally planted garden and with communal areas also planted out with care and imagination to give pleasure in shade, colour and architectural design.

So when I first walked into this little Eden in 1973 I was duly impressed, for by then the shacks had become proper dwellings and the communal areas spacious and attractive. There were simple sports facilities for the youth and a wonderful full-sized swimming pool with well-watered grassy banks and a baby pool for the children. Houses and other buildings and corners of gardens and the landscaping were set off by the art work, ceramics and sculpture of the members.

But I was not born with my back to the wall, a need to find a homeland or with a traditional sense of persecution. Communal living to me would, I knew, have been very difficult after the initial feeling of euphoria at such a successful social way of life had worn off.

The entrance of the kibbutz from the main road had a tall, tree-lined security fence stretching away from it to its perimeters and large metal gates with a sentry-box, if you like, by which you passed and were checked visually every time you came in and went out. You enter but do not travel through a kibbutz as you would an English village. It gave me sometimes the odd sensation of being caged, a mild claustrophobia. More unkindly, one might equate it to an exotic goldfish bowl. Whatever ripples, light or intense, disturbing the majority would be properly stilled by consensus action. That meant that any highly individualistic members rocking the boat might obviously need constraining or be given the opportunity to leave.

Arni threw himself out of the 'goldfish bowl' in his early twenties to get a university education, working on road building to pay for it. In the post Independence years the kibbutz could only support two out of three of its sons at university and the Secretariat, with membership approval, voted that Arni should be the one to be turned down, despite academic achievement, because some members judged him to be an 'unruly' character from early childhood. In fact he was a bit of a dreamer and not exactly self-disciplined. When woken one day from a beautiful dream by a sarcastic and loudly declaiming teacher in front of his 'siblings' and house group when he should have been working at his maths, he was startled and shamed. The same teacher upset him so much on another occasion when they were outdoors that he picked up a stone and tossed it in her direction. Unfortunately it hit her, but with very little force and no real damage to more than her dignity. So perhaps it was hardly surprising that he later 'lost the toss' to further his education at a university but it was a bitter pill for him to swallow. No matter, he left his kibbutz in his early twenties, succeeding under his own steam in the real world.

Across the years, while some other kibbutzes economically foundered, Maabarot adapted and has prospered until today, not only from hard work but also the cohesion of shared beliefs. It is nevertheless difficult to hand those pioneering beliefs down, more or less intact, to more than two or three succeeding generations who will have profited from the communal ideology. The affluent children of members in today's world no longer fully recognise that ideology as the fundamental corner stone of the continuing life of a kibbutz or any commune. Many of these youngsters leave the kibbutz to take their chance on a bigger world stage. Many travel and return home confused, disappointed and discontent. Life ain't easy anywhere.

The younger generations have not had it economically hard. They have been spoiled and one is reminded of the old northern saying "clogs to clogs in three generations." But the way of life, dependent as it once was on its communal ideology, precisely now challenges its members. Numbers of kibbutzes are still enjoying the fruits of their and their forbears' shared labour and skills, with a very high standard of living and leisure time in which to think about where they go from here to maintain and increase it ~ privatisation, perhaps, the ultimate antithesis? Only history will show what happens to probably the most successful experiment in communism ever undertaken, in some cases for over a hundred years, and to the descendents of those pioneering forbears of its practice.

For me personally, I have the enduring memory of an incident one day when I was sitting on the grass around the swimming pool having a thoroughly lazy time and enjoying it. I was joined by a kibbutz member, a woman of much my own age and neighbour of my mother-in-law, who attacked me in the friendliest way by firmly asking why Arni, myself and family did not become members of the kibbutz. I said "We are very happy the way we are, thank you Haiuta." It had been an almost imperative suggestion with a hint of criticism behind it.

"We would like you to join us," she continued, smiling enthusiastically and then looking down at my feet commented decisively, "Meggie, you need to cut your toenails!" I rest my case, m'lud.

Getting Accustomed

The children and I were four months into a new culture in a new country when the entire family went down with the 'flu early in that first hot September. Arni was worst hit but fortunately had a permanent job for the time being and could only sweat it out in bed. Whatever the doctor decreed seemed to have little effect on the course of the virulent virus. He suffered quietly, shrouded in sheets. Meanwhile, having just recovered from my bout, I mused on our progress to date.

We were missing some of the English vegetables like beans, peas and spinach but our garden was full of fruit so we were bursting with vitamins ... which nevertheless seemed pretty ineffectual against a crop of children's diseases and the common cold. We were also looking forward at the end of the month to eating some of our first eggs from our first ten layers, delivered by father-in-law as chicks in the Spring from the children's farm on the kibbutz. The birds had a nice coop above ground with a 'stairway' and a grassy run-around safely wired off to keep them in and predators out.

Adam was already picking up the language quite quickly in the nursery and had no trouble switching to mother's tongue when he got home. Just as well since Matti was still busy trying to sort out basic English and shouting or laughing when words failed him. I had learned enough to go shopping and pass the time of day with folk but really felt the need to improve my Hebrew at a smarter pace. We had just purchased an old, apple green Saab for everyday use at an exorbitant price and as soon as I got used to its layout I felt I should make the effort to attend *Ulpan*, the State organised system for new immigrants needing to learn Hebrew. Evening classes were to start in October, twice a week for two hours each session.

Everybody in the village enjoyed practising their English on me even if it simply began and terminated in 'Hi! and Bye!' Some, indeed, spoke it very well so that I was rarely allowed to flounder about in Hebrew without someone rushing to my rescue and completely undermining both effort and confidence. I was looking forward to formally coming to grips with this difficult language for a Westerner visually bred on the Roman alphabet. My only attempt at learning the new script had foundered when realising that the dots representing vowel sounds were left out in 'grown-up' writing i.e. everything available to read from instructions on tins and packets to newspapers and all higher forms of literature.

I duly set off on October 2nd for my first class in Modern Hebrew. I was one of several English speaking immigrants but the rest were from the United States. Following all the introductions the class started with an attempt to find out how much we basically understood, the teacher asking each of us to briefly describe in Hebrew our countries of origin. Apart from the Americans, the next largest contingent of students hailed from the U.S.S.R. All were Jewish except myself ~ so that much the rest of the class had in common.

You may imagine my displeasure when a two way conversation began to take place, at first in Hebrew, between the Russians and the Americans concerning life in their respective countries. I was eager to learn basic alphabet and grammar and not get involved in the socio-economic advantages of living either in the United States or Soviet Union. It soon became clear that a little competition was about to take place on the lines of 'my place is better than your place' and since Hebrew soon failed those engaged in the developing argument, English took over. The rest of the class yawned, tired after a day's work and our teacher, though tetchy, seemed unable to control what immediately followed.

One Russian student said that she had come to Israel not because she was poor and downtrodden and living under a Communist regime. Far from it. She had come out of choice to the land of her forefathers. She went on in good English and considerable spirit to suggest that the Capitalist Americans trod down the poor to make the rich richer (or words to that effect) and had nothing to offer 'Miss Ukraine'!

"So you gave up a fantastic house, all mod con, a new car and choice of anything to eat and plenty of it, did you?...I don't think so," said the woman from Wisconsin.

"I left a nice flat behind me and could eat and drink as much as I liked," Miss Ukraine replied.

"Why do you lie?" shouted Miss Wisconsin. "We know better … there's no country in the world like the United States. It has the most and the best of everything...*and* we are *free*."

"I'm not lying and what do you know about it? What do you know about my place? I bet you don't even know where it is on the map," shouted Miss Ukraine.

At this point I jumped into the argument from Middle England.

"Ladies, do you mind, *bevakasha!* We're in Israel here and now. An hour has gone already. I want to learn Hebrew. If you don't … feel free to carry on in English outside the class and leave the rest of us in peace to get on with it."

The teacher had her hands on her hips and now rasped "*Sheket*", shut-up, and something else loudly in Hebrew which I didn't understand, swearing maybe. All eyes turned upon her and the class shut up.

Emotions were running so high by then that it seemed unlikely that anyone understood a word of that first lesson … which was to be our last. Within a few short days, political differences expressed between competing super-powers in a classroom of new immigrants, *olim hadashim*, would be swallowed up in the most effective force for uniting a common people ~ war!

Grapefruit & Guns

On Saturday 6th October, 1973, Arni and I had taken a little stroll along the dirt track which led past our house and the end of the village to descend through grapefruit orchards belonging to the nearby *moshav*, Sde Yaakov. It was the evening of Yom Kippur and as usual on that one Day of Atonement in the year, Arni had fasted from sunset of the day before. Sitting on the tilled ground around a grapefruit tree, we picked up a couple of fruit that had fallen and began to peel them and enjoy their bittersweet juices as the setting sun shafted low through the dusty leaves of the neat rows of fruit trees and cast its shadows over the dry, red-brown soil. Rain had not yet come to the country after the long hot summer.

As we meandered back to our home in a village which in six short months had become a haven of friends and magic circle of good fellowship we were chatting away as usual on any subject that entered our minds. The peace and calm of that lovely October evening at the head of the beautiful Jezreel Valley was so much for which we could be grateful, despite the fact that Arni had that week lost his second job since arriving back in Israel. His recent boss had been an unsettled character, an engineer with a number of strange neuroses, including a belief that staff were daily stealing the office pens and pencils, which he checked out every night. Arni had found this man difficult to professionally navigate. They had quarreled and Arni had unceremoniously left, leaving us temporarily without an income or the formal notice and certificates attached to officially leaving employment. My husband never let the grass grow under his feet and I knew within a few days he would have found another job. My mind was at rest.

Walking up the track to the first house belonging to our neighbour, someone came towards us at a brisk pace. "War has broken out, Israel is under attack," was the blunt and incredulous message we received.

"What are you talking about?" we replied.

It was then explained to us that first the Egyptians and then the Syrians fast on their heels in a concerted effort had attacked Israel from both South and North on a day when even men of the regular armies in both areas would have been ritually observing the most religious day in the Jewish calendar. The nation as a whole was resting from strife and its citizens asking their God for forgiveness for sins committed to their fellowman over the year that had passed. Yom Kippur is, of course, the most solemn occasion of the Jewish year, time to think and pray and ask in the privacy of one's thoughts to be cleansed of sins, whether of ignorance or deliberate injury to others, with the determination to improve one's behaviour in the coming year. It was also a good time for men to mull over last year's business and next year's hopes.

Since our arrival in May of that year, Arni had been so busy sorting out a living that he had forgotten to contact the artillery unit to which he belonged as a Reserve officer and in which he had served during the 1967 Six Day War shortly before leaving for the U.K. He had been away from his country for more than five and a half years and from the regular training given to all men and women of service age every year. This considerable force constituted Israel's Reserve Army; highly trained young men and women aged between eighteen and forty-five years of age who would be ready to respond immediately to a call to arms. Such a Reserve army was necessary in a very small country of just over three million citizens who were surrounded on three sides by hostile nations of far greater numbers.

Arni hurried into the house and had difficulty contacting his unit on the phone. Obviously a great deal of confusion reigned and telephone lines were buzzing non-stop but within half an hour he was given a location, which he did not pass on to me, and with a swift kiss and shouting over his shoulder that he would be in contact as soon as possible, he disappeared with the car in a cloud of dust to rejoin his old unit. I do not remember him even picking up his toothbrush. The children were in bed and asleep when he left that night.

I was aware that under normal circumstances the Reserve units were not usually on the front lines but following up behind the Regulars and the Servicemen, or so I had been told. In this war the rules were varied to cope with the suddenness of the attack and its unforeseen consequences. Such a well-oiled military machine, however, did not take too long to get its act together. In the circumstances there were considerably more immediate casualties in the wake of the gap of awareness and receipt of Intelligence in this sudden strike compared with the Six Day War, when the unexpected had been the card the Israelis had played in attacking and decimating the Egyptian air force on its own airfields very early in the morning so soon after the Arab nations had commenced that war.

Yom Kippur was a *coup* indeed for Israel's hostile Arab neighbours and in particular for Egypt, wanting to restore its lost and burning pride left smouldering since 1967.

Before hearing from my husband I received a frantic letter from my parents who considered that as I was not an Israeli, I had no need to feel involved and should consider my safety and that of my children first and foremost and return to England. They had, perhaps, temporarily forgotten what it is like to be in a country at war when you feel you are defending your legitimate right to live in peace and security, not to mention the commitment of marriage. My younger brother had been born in 1939 on the outbreak of war and my parents already had two other children by then, my elder brother born in 1936 and myself in 1937. Despite having been idealistic members of the Peace Pledge Union during the 'thirties', they had got on with reality when the Second World War broke out and did not emigrate to safer climes but remained in London to play their part in the war effort on the home front, my father then working in a reserved occupation at the Home Office and as an ARP warden in the centre of London during the worst of the Blitz.

I assured my parents that the children's safety would naturally take precedence in my mind but that my place was also to be in Israel for my husband, supporting him both morally and physically as best I could. The villagers of Ramat Yishai were being hugely supportive of each other and to myself on realizing that Arni had just lost his job and not received leaving certificates enabling the government to pay him directly while on active service. There would be some delay before that finance could be organized.

I was given carte blanche to buy all necessary provisions on tick from the local stores in the village for they knew us and were sure that any temporary debts would be sorted out sooner or later. In fact they insisted that I should not feel at any disadvantage, for which I was extremely grateful, especially to the lovely Ben Lulu family who ran the main store and whose women clucked after me like a harem of broody hens. They loved my two little fair-haired boys, so sharply contrasted with their own dark, curly-haired Moroccan children and jokingly called my youngest and fairest, the palest blonde baby Matti, *kushi catan* or *little black boy*.

Arni had finished his training in officer course before the Six Day War and finally became a captain in the Reserves at the end of that war. I knew that all the officers of any part of the Army would be put to the test in this present military situation and naturally was desperate to know where he was and to what extent he might be in danger. News of casualties or the missing was passed immediately to the next of kin.

Following grapevine information on October 7th that Arni's unit had moved north from Acco on the coast north of Haifa, and hearing nothing for the first few days, I assumed they were making their way towards either the Lebanon or the Syrian held Golan Heights. It was from this latter area we were being fired upon by

Syrian 'frog rockets' which had a range of 70 kilometers. In the first two days of firing these were aimed primarily at the northern airfield of Ramat David, which lay about three miles from our village below us in the Jezreel Valley and just about at the end of the rocket's range.

It was obvious that the Syrians had hoped to put as many Israeli planes out of combat with these rockets fired from hideouts some short distance from the edge of the Golan Heights, the border from which the Syrians looked down on the Galilee and its numerous Israeli agricultural communities. But within two to three days of the Israeli forces getting into action, the Syrian rocket emplacements had been struck by the airforce and only two or three of those rockets came anywhere near their target. The first had exploded on the edge of a town on the other side of the airfield, Migdal HaEmeq, 'Tower of the Valley' with some damage to property but not to life. A second rocket landed on our nearby airfield but only managed to destroy a bicycle shed, making its crater where runways were unaffected, or so we were told. No single aircraft was hit.

At the time of that explosion we were sheltering in the basement of a neighbour's house along the road which had been furnished with makeshift bedding, as the village shelter for our street was a few hundred yards further away in the centre and not so 'convivial'. The siren had sung its eerie warning song and I had decamped in an orderly fashion to the house of Etush, where the children were settled in cots and the adults blanketed and chatting on its dry, earth-based floor under the re-inforced concrete stilts on which the house stood.

The rocket made its wayward mark on the nearby landscape with a tremendous bang which shook the very foundations and sent up a cloud of dust to settle all over us. The noise was so horrendous and sang so in our ears that for a moment or two our hearing was slightly impaired. The dust settled, there was a little coughing and then the all-clear sounded. We clapped and fervently hoped and prayed that no-one nearer the explosion had been hurt. That happened in the first two days of this three weeks' war which was to keep our men and women away from their families over the following six months, despite the formal ending of the war in the last days of October 1973. For the most part, the servicemen and women were allowed home over that period for alternate weekends.

I received the first official army postcard from Arnon six days after the war began and was delighted and happy to see his writing on the simple, plain card. It was dated the 10th of October and had been posted from an army bag in Haifa which meant that he was fighting on the northern front. Despite the ambush of Israeli posts on the Golan Heights, resulting in numbers of deaths and the scattering at night of the remaining men who escaped into the safety of the valley, many arriving barefoot from the scrubby one thousand metre slopes of the Heights, Syria was virtually out of the war by the sixth day. Five of their airfields had been wrecked by the Israeli airforce taking off right above our house with a great roar of engines and so close that you could see the pilots in the cockpits. By the twelfth of October the Syrians had lost twenty-six planes and numerous tanks had been shelled and put out of action by the artillery, in which Arni had a hand.

At the end of the first week of the war I had taken the children, at the request of the grandparents, to Kibbutz Maabarot a few miles from Hadera on the coast, halfway between Tel Aviv and Haifa, where we were considered to be safer than in our village near the airfield. This sudden exodus to mother-in-law's required timetable had not allowed me to organize myself properly so that soon after arriving and dumping our bits and pieces I was obliged to return the fifty kilometres home to organize the feeding of our chickens and after being requested by Klara to bring to a kibbutz that had everything in plenty some extra articles for the children which she thought necessary. After a long wait I managed to get a bus to Haifa and then a lift to Ramat Yishai.

My return journey with a foldaway high chair tucked under one arm and clutching bags of extra clothing with the other arm was difficult. From Haifa I managed to get transport to Hadera from where I started to walk the three miles along the highway towards Maabarot. An army car carrying high ranking officers took pity on me and stopped to give me a lift the rest of the way. I was asked what on earth I was doing trudging with my bag and baggage like a refugee along the road streaming with army vehicles and no public transport in sight. "There is no need for an exodus, lady" they told me, "the war is being won."

Following my arrival in Ramat Yishai I had noticed how quiet the place had become except for the planes roaring north in waves over the village. People were calm and unexcited and already assured that indeed the war would not be long in the winning, despite numerous difficulties on both fronts. Women were of course anxious about their menfolk and everybody was very sad that such a senseless war had been launched in an attempt to get Israel once more off the map of the Middle East.

In spite of this, morale was very high indeed and it was known that volunteers were again pouring into the country and finding little they could do. There was an abundance of nurses but not enough surgeons and other medical specialists. The blood banks were full. Arnon's brother Yigal had received superficial shrapnel wounds to the leg but was soon on the mend and rearing to get back to his unit. I wrote to my parents...

"I want you to come out here so that you will be able to appreciate and understand the 'climate' of Israel, which is culturally not so different from your own. I think you must see for yourself and then you may realize that your daughter and grandchildren are not living in an alien, backward *desert* place."

Of course it was important to feel that you would be on the winning side but despite having been attacked, my personal feelings about the war then were those I have now. In view of our so-called civilized thinking and any progression towards international co-operation, it seems incredible that the only way we can still settle our difficult problems of co-habiting within and across borders is by killing each other with the nastiest weapons we can invent.

As I see it, in a world contracted by time and technology, geographically and culturally, we still fail to fully acknowledge and deal with the problems of inequality, those fearful gaps between rich and poor as far as nations go. In a world crowded with human beings of natural ambition, both personal and national, the fear of losing the economic advantage and plain greed inevitably leads to power struggles with those attempting to share or reverse those advantages. Too often we see internal struggles in States spearheaded by individuals who are power-crazed, greedy and despotic to the point of civil war ~ and the have-nots continue to suffer. Among the affluent nations, worried democratic governments work both to maintain the status quo and their political popularity. Shady deals are done in arms for trade or influence. Out of the inequalities, problems arise that are ably fuelled by cultural and religious differences. *Survival catastrophes*, I call them.

In Israel the unsettled business of ownership of land and borders was behind the present war in which so many beautiful young lives were being lost. For them I shed my tears and for this I was brought closer to my husband's country under attack, but I cried for all the young men whose lives were being wasted in war on whatever side they might be fighting and for its cruelty which takes place under State sanction.

After a brief stay of three unsettled days in the kibbutz when extraordinarily I bumped into my friend Tovah, last seen in beautiful Florence, visiting her cousin Masha because she couldn't get a plane out of the country, I returned with the children to our village and to a continuation of our lives in our own home with our own good friends, waiting with my two little boys for Arni's safe return.

My mother-in-law, on whose insistence I had trekked to Maabarot, had suddenly decided that I could no longer stay on the kibbutz and told me so without giving even a hint of an explanation. This time, fortunately, a visiting family member Yuri, a professor of metallurgy at the Technion in Haifa, took charge of the situation. He had been shocked at Klara's decision which did not appear to have anything to do with the kibbutz Secretariat and after an angry exchange with my quiet father-in-law in Hungarian he got me, the kids and the luggage bundled into his car and whisked back to Ramat Yishai.

Tovah was able to visit me before she left for England and we chewed over the good times we'd spent together and discussed the political implications of the present bleak situation. Mother-in-law's behaviour also did not escape attempted explanation but remained a mystery; she had no need to cook for us because we ate in the communal dining hall and washing was done by the communal laundry. There were empty flats for accommodation. There is much to marvel at in mothers-in-law in general which remains unfathomable to the simple or serious minded and I certainly never got to the bottom of mine. There was, however, a later occasion when the twins were born when Klara had no doubt as to how my mind worked but generally we smiled and avoided confrontation. Her cakes were very good!

Postcards from the Front Lines
(as Written!)

First card received on 12th October 1973:

10 Oct.

Dear Meg and Kids

I'm OK. We're just having sort of resting and others doing the job now for us. Everything look quiet until we roar in with our mess. Keep moral up (you're the poor one). Love, love to all.

11 Oct.

Darling Meg and Kids,

The first rain flashed through our tent during the last night and I was simply "floating" in my sleeping bag. Didn't know whether to laugh or cry, soaking and cursing the lot managed to find a dry corner and after borrowing somebody else's blankets continued my disturbed night. Anyway is not cold now and we spend the day drying ourselves. Saw the first snow on 6000 ft high mountain, beautiful, soft and "creamy". Got new coat a bit too big; but if I carry on eating as now, will probably fit. Wonder if it is raining down there. Miss you so much. My thoughts constantly around this boy from Kibbutz Maabarot [classmate of Arni's killed] seems that the devil is around nearer and nearer. I love you so much, kisses to the kids.

13 Oct.

Dear Meg,

Having now few minutes to write. This business going on slowly [by Israeli standards] and one hopes it won't last but it drags on and on. We suffered quite heavy losses in the first few days mainly on Sunday. By the way, I joined the lot on Sunday night in the same unit, same place and surprisingly same crew of the 6 day war. Evidently feel like at "home". Unfortunately and unlike the "6 days" there is a slow motion which saves lots of lives so we accept it. With a bit of luck we might get it over in a week. Having a substitute [in rank] I'll probably be first at home. Love to you all. xxxxxxxx.

14 Oct. 6am

Darling,

Am OK, a bit chilly in night but not bad at all. Improvising our own food and it's very good. Want to see you soon. Love to all xxxxxxxxx

To Arni, 15 Oct.

Darling N,

Hope you got my first card! Am back in Ramat Yishay. Your mum is not too well ~ has a skin complaint due to nerves and I was told we could not stay in Maabarot . Got your card yesterday and happy to hear you are fine. What would you like me to send you by parcel? Soap, blades etc? Saw Yigal [Arni's brother] yesterday at Maabarot. He can't wait to get back to it and left this morning. Itzic [the youngest brother on the Egyptian front] is still OK. The kids are alright and nursery school has started again. …It looks like a longer job this time but morale is high here and the neighbours have been splendid. Spent first night in a week in my own bed last night and missed you. Lots of love and all our thoughts are with you darling. Yours waiting. Mag.

Darling N,

Hope to hear from you again today. All village is in shelters at night except our street, but we have a basement under Lustig's house set up with beds... it would be a great help if I had the car. Is it at your base with key inside and if so can I take it? Hens laying 2 or 3 eggs a day. No mail from England yet, perhaps it's just as well! BBC news is rotten so I have to get a translation of our news from Ruthie. It would be lovely if you could come home for a few hours. ... Keep well and tell me how you feel. Lots of love as always. Mag.

15 Oct. Somewhere. 8am

Darling,

Things getting quiet here and if the U.N. will take some decision I'll fly home immediately. God knows what your family think? I wonder how you're getting on, probably upset. I was thinking last night and don't know if I had the moral right to take you from the paradise over there (England) to this <u>bloody</u> chaos. Am glad you've got Ruthie and Eli [our neighbours] am sure they will help. Ring again your family in U.K. and assured them we're all O.K. Think that anyway I would have volunteered so it is better that you're here. The morale is indeed high, ample of food and if (the hell with "if") Love love love .

17 Oct. 7am

Darling Meg, Adam & Matti,

Lovely morning. Life here gives the chance to see the sun rise from full dark. Mount Hermon appearing strong violet with darkish lines. Sky is dark blue which turns slowly lighter as the red sun rolls over to full view. Their Migs are usually here to say 'good morning' at this time so we start earlier. Met last night Chief of neighbouring unit who was with me last time and we discussed industrial design (he is a production engineer) while shells (ours) were going out at full steam ahead. Absurd I think but terribly real. Hope some business will come of it. Our own Chief is not so brilliant and this doesn't help, but things roll more or less O.K. There is a boy from Maabarot (Itzic's class) who is really a promising leader and he helps a lot. We've become very good friends, he has a lovely sense of humour which is required here. Sorry for all this rubbish. Love, love to you all. xxxxxxxx

7.35am

Darling Meg and Kids,

Just heard the [Bach] Double Violin in the radio and became intolerable to the boys. Poor lot, not their fault that so many [… illegible] are around that …! Just received your card thanks. Hope you're getting mine. I've got everything that one is required. Parcels are pouring in from hundreds of organisations and private. We are simply flooded with the lot except <u>peace.</u> The transistor is now on "Spring" of the Four Seasons. My god, what a distance, what a gap, are we going to do the same every few years? Oh Hell! We "collected" the pilot (Iraqi) of a Mig who answered that we play the politicians. He was lucky and in a few months will go back to his family. Love to you all xxxx xxxx._

To Arni, 17 Oct.

My Darling N,

Got your card and am worried. You seem to be right in it, and I'm longing for you to be safe. Of course all wives feel the same ~ and mothers. Israel is fighting so hard and it is so depressing. But morale is high generally or at least people have lots of stamina even though their hearts are heavy. When can we expect an end to this senseless killing? Your mum is a bit of a nervous wreck and your father still floating in his own philosophical world, but at least I've had sensible and solid friendship from Yuri [a cousin's husband]. Sweet old Adella [neighbour] sends her love and offered me money, which I refused of course. Your friend Palo is arranging some money for me as I'm down to my last 50 lira ~ so don't worry, all is well! Eli has offered to get me eggs and veg etc. and is also a great morale booster. Will send you a jumper for the cold nights, meanwhile you have all my love to keep you warm and that's lots and lots. Be well, darling. Yours always. Mag. xxxxx

To Arni, 18 Oct.

Darling N,

Palo has just brought this quick delivery card so that you can get news quicker. Thought a lot about you last night and was a bit worried now I know where you are (approx.). Phoning parents on Sunday. If they are not happy it can't be helped. I hope they'll boost not lower my morale. Yigal [brother] has a car and is going to look for you today to bring back good news. Your mum sent cakes and I will send a sweater tomorrow and tell me if you want anything else. Everybody sends their love and a kiss from Adella. Matti is blooming but Adam asked for you today and wants you home. Tried to start Rosie [our vintage Rolls Royce] but forgot to switch petrol on ~ then it went dead. Will try again later today. Lots and lots of love Darling. Mag, Adam and Matti xxx

To Arni, 19 Oct. 9. 30am

Darling N,

Have sent parcel of clothes including "woolly hat" though I hope you won't be needing them much longer. I'm very anxious but had phone call this morning from a comrade-in-arms, which was nice. Please God it will end soon as nerves are getting a bit thin ~ otherwise all is well. Most of my cards don't seem to have reached you, though I've sent them every day. Please look after yourself as we want you back home safely. Did Yigal find you?

[Arni arrived home unexpectedly midday for 2 days leave, 19 & 20 Oct. Great rejoicing.]

21 Oct. 2pm

Darling Meg and Kids,

Am O.K. In my absence we've been moved backwards so it's very quiet and almost "pleasant". We've got now some rotas of "leave" so hope to be home for the 24ᵗʰ [my birthday and our wedding anniversary]. In fact all the region is down to exchange of artillery, so we've got to fight the boredom. Too much food is being pumped on our heads and one hopes to survive this … without upsetting the tummy. Being urged to finish this letter because the guy is going. Love, love xxx

22 Oct. 5am

Darling Meg,

The radio just announced about the prospect for peace, am two foot above the ground. I suppose that the boys will stay here for a while [to be 6 months] but sure will manage to get away. When back yesterday it was understood that I'm volunteering to help give leave for the boys and I'll try to keep it this way. A bright windy morning is rising up and the sun reaching more and more while shadows running short as though were afraid. I love you so much.

23 Oct. 7.50am

Darling Meg and Kids,

The Bl– Syrians won't stop this lot, probably didn't get the message. Still hope to be home tomorrow although think this card will get you later. Pastoralic atmosphere, a few donkeys around us but afraid that without water won't survive. Meg I miss you so much. Can't express those feelings. Yours with lots of love and to the Boys.

To Arni, 30 Oct.

Darling N,

We seem to have been waiting a long time for you but one musn't complain. I keep hearing so many tragic stories that it's no matter if you are delayed. At least you will be coming home ~ hundreds never will. Itzic's friend Danny payed a surprise visit yesterday. Home from Suez (East). His brother-in-law was killed. His sister has a three month old baby. Danny stayed here with his girlfriend for two hours. He wanted to find your brother Itzic. Your friend Palo is optimistic about political situation ~ more than I am. Was going to Maabarot today but Matti came out in spots all over ~ chickenpox, so he must not go out of the house for a week. Masha's friend has one son killed, one son wounded and one son unconscious from a road accident coming home on leave. It's all very depressing. Sorry I can't be light-hearted but it all affects me very much. I'm angry. They must never be allowed to start it again. Got your cards today and there's mail including a cheque from the army I think. Chickens laying 6 eggs a day now! All my love. Mag.

Arni sent postcards regularly during the 6 months he was actively serving with occasional leave. The last two cards I have were sent on:

6 Feb. 1974

Darling Meg,

Got new arrangement so will go home every 8 days for 4 days. Will come on Sunday, but if I'm going to be a bit later than expected I'll continue to Maabarot for the memorial service [of classmate] and will come home probably on the same night or Monday morning. This is a bright, windy morning and nothing is getting warm. I mean I'll have to find something to do to keep moving. Things are quiet now and the ground is drying slowly after all those showers. All well except that you are so far. Love N.

15 Feb.

Meg,

Just remember what have left out of our telephone conversation last night 'twas that on Valentine's Day so wanted to tell "I love you". N.

Unshifting Sands...

It is inevitable that feelings should be partisan when under attack but the broader and more impatient view I had of war during those first three weeks when Israel was under fire on all fronts was strictly female. Why can't men get around a table and come to some sensible consensus regarding co-habiting adjacent territories, finding economic links for the benefit of all and allowing for cultural differences and a different pace of growth for each interested nation where obviously space allows for it? Envy and greed are, of course, the main protagonists in territorial wars and what Israel had managed to successfully build out of badlands and desert since 1948 to 1973 was now something to be desired and 'morally' fought over by the neighbours, yet again. Refugees are the sorry ones in the cross-fire of war whether they have fled their homes with justification or through plain fear. If Egypt, Jordan and the Lebanon cared so little for their Palestinian refugees, how much less they cared for a Palestinian State on their borders. What land Israel held was up for grabs.

Egypt, Lebanon, Syria and Jordan had more land than enough of their own to stimulate modern agriculture with modern technology to boost their economies. And none of these States had any intention of absorbing and settling those increasing populations of Palestinian refugees from previous wars; they were the burning tinder to light new wars and their spark had to be kept alive by keeping them huddled in awful camps with no escape and no hope

of a future. This action was politically pragmatic but morally inde-
fensible ~ and the world turned a blind eye. The Palestinian Arabs
who had remained in Israel after 1956 and 1967 had become
Israeli citizens, had a voice in Parliament and the freedom to build
their own lives within their own religious cultures. They lacked
only one freedom ~ to displace the new Jewish State and call that
territory Palestine.

Yet Israel occupied a very small stretch of land in relation to
its neighbours and even the West Bank then offered more than
enough space for Palestinians to build a viable State, stretching
as it did from the Jordanian border right into the heart of Israel
between Haifa and Tel Aviv, leaving only seven or eight miles of
Israeli territory between the West Bank border near Tulkarm or
Kalqilya and the sea. But where was a desire for consensus when
the world's largest players had already staked their interest in
this strategic centre of world power with its vacillating, burning
needle-point poised between global East and West?

So it seemed to me in those days that history had nowhere to
go that it had not been before. Nor, I was sure, would that alter
in the years to come. Circumstantial details may have changed in
the Middle East across history since the Greeks, Romans, Turks,
British and Israelis had conquered or commandeered the area
but the desire to fight over the land was as strong as ever. The
dunes may change shape with the weather and time but underneath them the bedrock sands remain historically unshifting, with
bedrock opinion hardening on all sides.

Of course by comparison with the two World Wars and their
obscene human loss, the Yom Kippur War was just a short, sharp
blip on the screen and of the three and a half million or so Israeli
population in 1973, just under two thousand seven hundred were
to lose their lives in the three weeks of the sudden attempted coup
to push Israel out of the area for good. But being such a small
nation we all knew of individual losses, someone's son or husband,
and one life lost in barbaric and bloody war is one too many.

By the 15th of October, 1973, I was writing home and explaining that Israeli troops were doing well in the North and that if control could be established in the South a cease-fire would be imminent. Since the first three days of the war, no more 'frog' rockets had been sent our way in the north and it was rumoured that the Russians had removed both rockets and personnel from Syria when victory had not been quick and decisive, in order to maintain some kind of political balance in global terms with their fellow super-power, the U.S.A. So whose war was it anyway?

My mother-in-law's skin had erupted in a very unpleasant manner when her three sons had disappeared to various fronts with their military units. The middle son, Yigal, was wounded when his armoured car was attacked by four Migs but this had resulted only in shrapnel in the leg and after three days in hospital and convalescence he had reported back for duty. This did not help mother-in-law's nerves or skin.

Her husband, Yis, that pacific and gentle philosopher, remained quiet and imperturbable. If he had feelings and thoughts, he kept them to himself and carried on loving the grandchildren and patting their heads as usual. His coolness of character reminded you of one of his own favourite poets, Kipling, who had suggested that *'if you can keep your head while all around are losing theirs...'* and so on. The only time that Yis had fired a gun, as far as I know, except in training perhaps, was in the air to remind the night-guard that he was late in relieving Yis on his shift at the gate of the kibbutz. The fact that this created havoc, having been interpreted as a call to arms to defeat terrorists trying to enter the community, had left Yis equally imperturbable. Being late and not polishing your shoes were the two matters that might really move Yis to sudden speech and action. Wider crimes within the community or society might be quietly considered but were hardly ever mentioned.

Arni managed his first trip home on the 19th October and I drove him back as far as the northern shore of the Lake of Galilee where he would be picked up by an army vehicle on the 21st. It was very early morning and the Golan Heights rose like a misty

113

Chinese watercolour, blurred browns and yellows above the dark Lake. It was very quiet and except or maybe because of the abundant presence of troops everywhere waiting for orders to move into or out of that ethereal landscape, it all seemed as unreal as a backdrop for a 'midsummer morn's dream'.

Up to the latest front line on the Golan Heights where Arni was headed, he said the earth was a rich red-brown but remained, as it had for centuries, un-watered except for the sporadic rains. The Syrian peasants who toiled at it to make the most meagre of livings also remained as primitive as their ancestors in tools and know-how. The land lay agriculturally untended and unfulfilled in the sun. But from these Heights the Syrian military had set up, at great expense and with technical knowledge, rocket emplacements for bombarding Israeli targets in Northern Israel as far as the Jezreel Valley. One kibbutz had virtually been raised to the ground with one of the first rockets set off at the beginning of the war and an Arab village in Israel had offered free labour to re-build that kibbutz at a cost of £300,000 … a telling and unique gesture of Arab citizen solidarity at that time.

Both Christian and Muslim Arabs in the *Knesset* (parliament) had vocally disassociated themselves from the invading 'brethren' as a mark of solidarity with the State. The Bedouin in our valley who had not been volunteered for service within the Israeli forces, continued to tend their goats, ignoring all but the changing weather and the grazing land. News from abroad, especially home, appeared decidedly influenced by Arab oil and only the Dutch had taken anything like a moral stance in defence of Israel. My own moral indignation with the British government at that time was naturally high and I wrote to The Times about it. My letter was not published.

When I got home after that strange journey dropping Arni off close to the war zone, I had to calm the three years old Adam, who could not understand why his Daddy had gone away again. Well, I said, he's not so far away and maybe will be back again to see him soon, in a week perhaps. What is 'soon', 'a week' to a tiny tot?

Meaningless. What was unsettling was the evident disruption in mind and body even in such a small person. So far the war had been waged for two weeks and there was another to go before a cease-fire could be signed. But surely the greatest war damage lay ahead in minds influenced now to take a hard-line stance in the future on both sides, in the young and not so young.

Bin Hur ... and the Politics of Rubbish

One of the most delightful sights in the village, especially in the winter when a strong wind might be whipping up from the valley, would be to see our rubbish collector going about his duty early on a Wednesday morning. This observation may excite a little curiosity and the story around it either complement or deplete your view of human nature, depending on your philosophy.

Pinye was our man. He was a lean, though I have no reason to believe hungry, immigrant from Rumania whose background in detail was held a private matter to him, shared only perhaps with a few of his cronies over a bottle of schnapps. That said, Pinye was not often seen socialising at village events for he was a bachelor with no children, as far as we knew. No doubt there were some like the nurse and Mayor who knew a little more about him than we did. Generally speaking Ramat Yishai folk did not pry into your past, which might involve a long story, but were anxious to know about your present life. For example, when we first took on a middle-aged Yemeni woman from the village, Yemina, to help clean the house, she greeted me with affectionate effusion and the first question, "Eh, so how much does your husband earn?" That was, and still is, quite common introductory chat. Needless to say, coming from an English background, I found the question extremely rude but fielded it by saying I had nothing to do with the finances. Yemina laughed loudly and wagging a finger at her new employer replied, "Hm, more fool you, lady." On later reflection, Jemina had a point.

But to return to our subject, Pinye seemed a mysterious character whose claim to fame in Ramat Yishai was based on the fact that for many years he had been collecting and disposing of the household waste. He also kept a black and white part Fresian, part Arabic cow on his small plot on which he grew alfalfa and clover to feed her. She was kept in milk and probably yielded no more than three or four gallons maximum daily. Pinye milked her twice a day.

Soon after we had arrived in the village I had declared my total dissatisfaction with the watery milk on sale at the local shops. Virtually all the fat is skimmed off the Israeli milk because there is a large industry in its by-products, such as cottage cheese, yoghurts, sour cream and similar foods. Fat milk had also received a government health warning and no choice was available. The milk was simply white water. Learning that we could obtain fresh milk from Pinye's cow Arni spoke to Pinye and agreed with the man that he would drop off a small churn at his gate every other morning and pick it up after the late milking. We were happy to do the pasteurisation and cooling ourselves at home. The milk was delicious and totally destroyed our ability to drink the 'proper stuff'. But Pinye, apart from owning a cow also had a horse and a cart and it was these tools which had enabled him to apply for and get the job of rubbish collector in Ramat Yishai some years earlier.

You might be immediately reminded of Steptoe and Son, except that Pinye had no son and was a far more grave and proud person than old Steptoe. There was also a fundamental difference in the design of the cart for Pinye's cart had only two very large wheels between which was slung a chariot body which could be tipped on a rod towards the ground for the bins to be received into its belly or discharged. I don't know how many bins Pinye could collect in one trip to the tip but he was up early and had finished serving the two hundred or so properties on two or three mornings a week before the sun was too high, promptly returning the waste bins to their owners the same morning as the collection.

Pinye's horse and chariot, its rider seated high, could be seen coming at a great lick along our outer road as we were the first point of pickup at the end of the village on the western escarpment. So the horse got a good gallop before the weight of the bins slowed it down on the return journey. It was seeing Pinye on a cold and windy morning, his head clad in a close fitting leather helmet with ear flaps rising and falling with the movement of the chariot and the wind as he spurred his horse on, which prompted me to call him *Bin Hur*. Bin Hur provided great excitement for the children and was admired and respected by us all.

As previously mentioned the council of our village was elected on party lines. There were four members elected from the two main parties, *Mapai* and *Herut*, an Independent party member and of course the Mayor who held the casting vote. *Mapai* and *Herut* both offered candidates for Mayor and the losing candidate stood down. The council employed a permanent Secretary. This was the general structure of council politics in Ramat Yishai and at this time the Independent member represented the Yemeni community in the village. For this particular term of office a Yemeni Rabbi had stood and been elected although he did not live in the village. The Rabbi, true to his particular faith, considered that the Yemeni Jewish culture was a head above the other divergent religious branches of Judaism which had developed out of the European diaspora, a diaspora scattered to seek fortunes across the world from Babylon to Brooklyn.

The Rabbi councillor would sit in at council meetings and utter not a word about any matters that did not directly concern his community. He would remain silently aloof, contemplating the squabbles between *Mapai* and *Herut* ~ discussion over whether the village could afford a second-hand fire-engine and so on ~ with complete detachment, perhaps even praying for his 'unorthodox' colleagues who might well admit to an entirely secular approach to life, heaven forbid, for there were still acknowledged communists in the community who had jettisoned all but party politics. If he voted at all, our Rabbi would simply raise one finger of one hand just above the knee where it had been resting but remain silent.

Arni was present one evening, as the only member of the

public, at a particularly rowdy council meeting. The business was to include the matter of the sacking of our rubbish collector and personal milkman, Pinye.

Now Pinye had done a first rate job as bin man for a number of years with his horse and cart but despite constant inflation and a request for a rise in his wages he had received no increase from the council for more than three or four years, the Secretary hoping Pinye would thus be forced to resign. Arni had already intervened in this matter on Pinye's behalf with the Secretary, Betzalel Cohen, who was a townie at heart, happened to be Pinye's neighbour, objected to the smell of his cow and generally did not care much for the man. He also believed in the 'modernisation' of Ramat Yishai for which he intended to make himself personally responsible and famous. He was ashamed for the council to be employing a horse and cart in the jet age, believing it made a laughing stock of the village.

We did not remember hearing anyone complaining about the regular collection of our rubbish or how it was done. It was done quietly and efficiently and that was that. Then suddenly Pinye was taken ill. It may have been the 'flu or some stomach bug but it was a sickness from which he would recover within a couple of weeks. He did not have a second-in-command to do his work while he was in his sickbed and this gave the council an opportunity to vote him off the job, especially after they had received a couple of complaints after the first week about the rubbish mounting up. It seems also that two young men, prior to the council meeting, had approached the Secretary with an offer of mechanising the rubbish collection with a tractor and trailer and the promise of speeding the process up ~ at twice the price.

Pinye was a simple man with only his cow and sturdy horse for company at home and apart from badly needing the job to keep the wolf from the door, we really believed he felt that being the Ramat Yishai rubbish collector gave him a certain status in the village. He was recognisable to everyone. He was indeed somebody important to the community. Although not a very talkative man, surely a great advantage in terms of getting a job done speedily, he was absolutely reliable and loyal and he had never before allowed the odd bouts of the common cold or sickness to interfere with his work. All in all Pinye was a thoroughly decent fellow nearing his sixties and looking to retire with a pension with some few years yet to go.

Since my Hebrew was basic, I asked my husband to attend the council meeting on this occasion to voice genuine local disapproval of the underhand way Pinye was about to be treated and his livelihood threatened with this attempted move behind his back, especially since he had no-one to represent him at this meeting deciding his future. Lying on his sickbed, he was not even aware of his threatened redundancy without pay.

The subject was introduced by the Secretary, Betzalel Cohen, who held forth at some length in favour of Pinye's sacking, although in his capacity as Secretary he had no right to offer opinion but only present the facts. It was soon made clear that he was primarily behind the 'mechanisation' programme and had persuaded the Mayor to put the matter on the agenda. He then opened the item up for discussion and nodded to the Mayor, Yudit our neighbour. Yudit declined to speak so it passed to her deputy to comment, who also declined to speak. This was a touchy subject. Our Yemeni Rabbi simply gave a cursory negative nod in the direction of the Secretary which could mean that he either did not wish to speak or was against the motion. Betzalel moved quickly on to the opposition party to express its viewpoint. Following that, a paper ballot was to be conducted.

True to party politics, the opposition member started leading off in grandiloquent language with a speech which appeared to be neither in favour nor against the matter under discussion, for during his exuberant outburst the edges of his argument became distinctly blurred. Nobody knew whether he had eaten something unwholesome, been stung by a bee or simply had another row with his wife but he evidently felt he had an excellent platform from which to run down the party in power. This he did in relation to Mapai's every conceivable idiocy, mistake, unprincipled action, corruption and wickedness since they had been elected to represent the people, not only in Ramat Yishai but in the local government area and indeed across the State. As the minutes passed without interruption his voice grew louder and louder and his face redder and redder. Arni and the other councillors, except the disdainful Rabbi whose eyes were closed by this time, exchanged glances with increasing irritation. A full seven minutes had gone by before Yudit looked the opposition member straight in the eye and told him he was not speaking to the point, he'd had more than a fair hearing and it was time to sit down and allow the business to be concluded properly. At this the member became utterly incensed, shouting ever more loudly that he would not be censored, he had a democratic right to speak.

Now the ideal of democracy was dear to all and this set everybody off, except the Rabbi. No doubt the neighbourhood was beginning to wonder what on earth was going on since such a decibel level issuing from the council office was not a habitual occurrence. Indeed, it looked as though matters might come to blows as the Secretary waved his arms about and the member threw his fists into the air. Finally Yudit purposefully stubbed out her cigarette and in her gravelly voice declared the meeting adjourned forthwith. Rising from her seat, she vehemently pushed aside her table to proceed towards the door, declaiming fiercely that she was used to children in the clinic, in the kindergarten and in the junior school but did not expect to find them in the council office.

To say that one could make a grand exit from such a confined space as that little room of three by four metres with a full council meeting, two tables, six chairs and a member of the public present, would be exaggerating somewhat. Furniture and folk had to move swiftly and awkwardly to allow the well endowed lady Mayor to reach the door. The Red Sea, however, parted and Yudit strode out into the warm night air that was nevertheless cooler than the atmosphere of the room she had just vacated.

No decision had been made about poor old Pinye at this meeting but it was not too long before we realised we had seen the last of our charioteer when a noisy tractor and trailer appeared to collect the rubbish bins. In place of the brisk clip-clop of Pinye's horse and his gruff but kindly words in its ears, we would be woken from our slumber with the revving of an old diesel engine, acrid smoke pouring out of its tail. Pinye did not live long enough to collect his pension.

For the Beauty of the Earth ...

It was the third week in March 1974 and Arni was home from the army for a weekend so we did a little trip around the Western Galilee, going north right up into the mountains overlooking a valley and the hills to the south. We were standing in brilliant sunshine while a fantastic rainstorm swept across the mountains opposite us. It was pure Turner landscape, grand with its formidable rocks and sky alive with changing deep and dark greys and purples enveloped in incredible turbulence. The light from our side lit up this majestic scenery which was breathtaking.

We parked the car in a small Arab village to buy some bread and cheese and soon found ourselves the guests of the proprietor of the village shop. Having served in the British Army between 1944 and 1948 the owner spoke reasonable English and was obviously proud to demonstrate this. During the pleasant hour we spent with the family we heard a long tale from one son about his new bride to be, a first cousin and a resident of Jordan. Problems had been encountered in the attempt to get the fiancée into Israel as a permanent resident. She had received a number of permits for short stays not exceeding three months. A decision was taken for the girl to get pregnant, not a normally accepted pattern of family events. Having succeeded, this still proved useless in face of Israeli immigration law. Finally it was the usual personal contact with an Israeli friend of some influence which provided the 'open sesame'. With Israeli citizenship for both the girl and her baby assured, the couple were organising their shot-gun wedding.

The young mother-to-be had been nursing in Jordan for six years, spoke English well and was quite charming. Arab Israeli problems were discussed openly and hope expressed on all sides for a permanent settlement and 'shalom'; peace for all. I wonder what became of those young hopefuls. Meanwhile, having learned that I was not Jewish, I was asked questions about Christmas in England as our hosts were Christian Arabs. They wanted to know exactly how we celebrated Christmas in a country so far removed from the authenticity of the towns and surrounding landscape of Judea and Nazareth. I explained as best I could about nativity plays in schools, Christmas trees, turkey and pudding and they smiled at our 'quaint' customs as though somewhere along the line we had completely lost the plot.

We then talked not only about the lovely local landscape but Israel's hugely varied landscape in one very small country; mountain and desert, the Galilee, Dead Sea and the amazing Jordan Valley. We had earlier been on a trip in the countryside below Mount Hermon on the Lebanese border at the head of the Hula Valley which we had followed down to the Sea of Galilee, which had greatly impressed me. This was my first Spring in the country when Israel is at its scenic best.

It had been a beautiful day with the Hula Valley landscape wonderfully green and smothered in many places in wild flowers, amongst which there randomly stood the architectural beauty of wild almond trees crowned with their delicate, palest pink blossoms. In some places old olive trees stood sculpted in the meadows, gnarled but silver-green and bright in their new foliage trembling in a light breeze. Their remarkable brown, twisted trunks and flashing silver leaves rose out of carpets of mauve flowers so dense that no green could be seen between them. There were beds of scarlet anemones amongst the wild broom and pale cyclamen with pink rock roses in profusion. You could not fail to notice the tall wild iris, deep blue with bright yellow centres alongside huge bee orchids. It was a wild, colour festival for the eyes granted to the onlooker because insecticides had neither been used nor blown that way. Israel hosts 2400 species of wild flowers against Britain's 1500 species. This was a wonderful place for any student or lover of natural history.

Mount Hermon stood snow-capped beyond and above us, benign enough at that time only six months after battles had taken place on its slopes bordering Lebanon. One wanted to forget then that the mountain had been captured and lost and in an abortive attempt to regain it many young Israelis had been killed, including one lad from our village. The Hula Valley, prosperously farmed by the Israelis, was loomed over by the mountains of Lebanon on one side and the Syrian Golan Heights on its other flank. Looking down from our vantage point near the high northern town of Zefat I realised how vulnerable those farming communities below us must feel.

We descended, as did the rushing waters from their source on Mount Hermon, until we reached the valley floor and walked alongside the only turbulent river in Israel fed by many springs along its course to become the famously quoted, dreamed of and sung about *River Jordan*, a river which could be crossed in most places by a few stout strides. In my mind I had always imagined the Jordan to be as wide and grand as the Mississippi, as no doubt had many others. But this was it, in a land encompassing the mountains and green landscape of the Lake of Galilee at the Northern end and the great rift of the Jordan Valley going down to four hundred metres below sea level at the Dead Sea. Beyond that was the desert of the south and all within a six hundred mile range north to south. This was the dramatic topography of a small but dramatic country sharing that same landscape on various fronts with its four neighbours: Lebanon, Syria, Jordan and Egypt.

Our four-year-old Adam had picked up a twelve-foot long piece of papyrus stalk which he dragged behind him across rough terrain and rocky pools for nearly an hour before we got back to the car. Having explained what it was and how the ancient Egyptians had used this plant he seemed quite fascinated, asking more questions to satisfy a curiosity we had obviously whetted. He held tenaciously to the light stalk, wanting perhaps to drag a little history along with him, to take it home or think maybe for a few seconds about the meaning of time. Adam was upset that we had to cut his stalk in two to get it into the car. Strange it was, on reflection, that the subject our first son later chose to study at university was Ancient History.

Kushi Galore'

We first met Kushi at a party in nearby Tivon. He stood out in a crowd, being tall, well-built, darkly handsome but quiet. I quickly discovered that the only other 'foreigner', apart from myself, at this jolly, *al fresco* get-together was Kushi's wife, the pale skinned, red-headed woman they called Ruti. She was in fact a Bernadette from an Irish immigrant family to Britain, most of whom had done very well in the construction industry since the Second World War. Ruti had been brought up a good Irish Catholic in north-west London. How she met and married her Israeli husband, Shimon, is a tale for her to tell one day. But just then it was a joy to have not only an English speaking person to converse with but, as things turned out, a delightful, zany and funny London Irish girl with whom I became heavily involved for the rest of her stay in Israel and subsequently for the rest of our lives.

At that time Ruti was struggling to bring up their two young sons, Uri and Eyal on a *moshav* in the Jezreel Valley and keep her marriage afloat to a wayward loner who, like the legendary cat, preferred to 'walk on the wild side'. Indeed, Shimon was widely known in Israel for a particular exploit around the Six Day War in making it through enemy territory to the Rose Red City of Petra in Jordan and back to Israel without discovery or getting shot as a spy by either side. It was reported that during the war he had excelled as a desert tracker. I was given the impression that there were few scents, sounds, footmarks or other indications that someone had gone before, that Kushi couldn't trace over the rocks and sand of the Judean, Negev and Sinai deserts when to normal senses there was nothing at all to be observed. Although sallow of skin with dark brown eyes Shimon was not as dark as some Jews from Yemen or Ethiopia and yet Kushi, a slang term for 'black' in Hebrew, was the affectionate title given to him by friends and the rest of the nation. There was no doubt, however, that suitably dressed, Kushi would be indistinguishable from many Bedouin who still wandered the deserts and border lands.

Kushi indeed made it by foot, or whatever means available to him, to Petra and back without harm to a hair on his dark head, and whether he 'crushed any snakes' along the way is left to the guessing. Shimon, as I prefer to call him, had met Ruth in London sometime after this escapade and following a whirlwind courtship they were married and shortly afterwards war broke out and first Shimon and then Ruti decamped to Israel where the boys were born. Looking at her on the evening we met, automatically brought to my mind a real life picture of that biblical heroine withstanding the best and worst of a new life 'amidst the alien corn'.

Ruti also reminded me of the *Girl with the Green Eyes*, if not her authoress, Edna O'Brien. There was, and still is, about my friend a strange mixture of the innocent and dreamer of romantic dreams oddly combined with a fierce ability to mobilise a deeply pragmatic side to her character. This latter strength she used without fear or favour, firstly to protect her family and secondly herself when setting off to engage upon numerous adventures, her marriage to Shimon but one.

The choices Ruti made in navigating through life would be out of the question, if not unimaginable, to more prosaic souls, with the outcomes of her instinctive actions and reactions often unmeasured and certainly unforeseen. But Ruti always worked very hard to establish and secure a safe base for her children, paramount in her life. Despite this priority, she had more tales of the surprising and unexpected to tell than anyone I have ever met. Her armour and sword were a natural candour and child-like curiosity. Though such innocence might get her into trouble, her startled pragmatic nature would rescue her time and time again. Or was it the other way around? She was naturally fearless because she did not scent danger, real or imagined, as most of us do.

Ruti was of medium height and build and her voice lightly soft and warm but lilting no Irish accent. She was very attractive in a totally feminine, unselfconscious way. Until today, she has aged little in any respect despite a tough and independent life throughout the thirty years that have elapsed since we were first fated to meet at that party. The milky skin of her face is still soft and mostly unlined, except around those green eyes which indicate that she has laughed a great deal ~ but abundant laughter as often as not accompanies abundant tears. Ruti's heart is forever young and even now unprepared for the more obvious shortcomings in human nature which become evident and understood to most of us over fifty. Her observant and whimsical humour, however, has not lost its zest nor her laughter its lightness and spontaneity notwithstanding the troubles and traumas of her life, sometimes quirkily self-inflicted.

The circumstances of Shimon's birth are shrouded in myth as far as most people are concerned and Ruti admits that Shimon didn't know precisely where or when he had been born. He sometimes adopted her birthday, Christmas Day, for convenience. His parents, a Jewish mother from Iraq and father from the Yemen living in Palestine, had died shortly after he was born and he had been put into an orphanage in Jerusalem until he was fostered. There were many children like him in Palestine under the British mandate. Some had arrived as Jewish orphans from abroad or been sent to Palestine for their safety. Others maybe were the result of impossible unions and there were no doubt a dozen more situations that might occasion such children to be either adopted by a kibbutz or individuals wanting a family. In Shimon's case, he was fostered as a baby and brought up in a straight-laced manner by a German Jewish immigrant couple in an agricultural settlement in the Jezreel valley.

With impossible unions in mind, it might be interesting at this point to recall the sad story of a pair of young lovers from different backgrounds in our area. The girl was the daughter of a Bedouin family who had settled in a village near us. The boy came from the nearby middle-class Jewish township. Their chance meeting followed local history. The Bedouin, unlike the Palestinian *fellahin* (farmers) for whom they have little fellow feeling, have led a nomadic way of life across the centuries. These Arabs normally moved from place to place with their tents, camels, goats and chickens, eking out a living from the land which had no borders or ownership in their eyes from Syria in the north, Jordan in the East and the Sinai in the south. Those who had settled across the years did so mainly in Jordan, the present Jordanian King being from Bedouin stock. After the establishment of the State of Israel, succeeding governments had attempted to control these wandering peoples for reasons of national security. In our area, in the north, Bedouin had begun to settle firstly near Tivon and from there eastwards along the beautiful valley near *Tsipori*. This land, although within the national border, had not been settled by Jews or legislated for settlement. It was a 'grey' area.

The Bedouin in the north, who had earned good money during the 1973 Yom Kippur war acting as trackers for the Israeli army, continued to build dwellings along the valley with successive Israeli governments turning a blind eye throughout the 1970s. I have written earlier of our invitation to one of these Bedouin villages where we were hospitably received. The parents of our host, from personal preference, were still living in the traditional Bedouin tent next to the house. Although the Israeli State provided no infrastructure such as roads, running water, electricity and so on, these people it was understood would no longer be on the move. They worked as truck drivers or took up similar jobs that suited their nomadic temperament. These settled Bedouin made themselves responsible for primary school education and subsequently their children were given secondary education in the nearby Jewish schools. Those who did well were latterly sent by their families to universities abroad, often in Italy or Germany, to learn professions such as medicine, engineering, law and so on, a huge cultural change.

So that is how one young and beautiful Bedouin girl, aged seventeen, met by chance and fell in love with an Israeli boy from a good family in the adjacent Jewish town of Tivon. For her traditionalist family this was a major crime that could not be tolerated. When her father discovered the liaison he killed his daughter.

In a changed scenario from the Moses story there were no doubt occasions when babies that survived mixed parentage were secretly adopted by Jewish families. Tales such as this had attached themselves to Kushi, only to be properly repudiated in the press by the man himself.

After the Six Day War, Shimon was like a caged creature suddenly deprived of purpose. He desperately sought friendship and approval despite his rather taciturn manner and the *macho* appreciation that courted him in his homeland for his familiar exploits. He was anti-establishment, excepting the Army, and enjoyed taking risks. This involved him in some adventures of a sometimes dubious nature which on one occasion involved his being remanded in custody to await a Court appearance, the evidence heavily stacked up against him. The threat of imprisonment was anathema to Kushi and he asked Ruti to help to extricate him which she did by approaching the wife of the war-time General Moshe Dayan of the eye-patch fame, whose son knew Shimon personally. A straight case of 'who you know...' Six witnesses gave him character references and he received a suspended sentence.

Indeed, Shimon was not without admirers in the upper echelons of the Israeli governing parties. Israel is a very small country where nobody brought to the public gaze goes unnoticed. So it was considered sensible to offer him a place in a farming community, away from the city lights and any temptation to demonstrate how he could go where no other man might, retrieving goods no other man could carry single-handed. He was singularly strong and apart from his witness support in Court it was deemed that he had committed a solo crime and was not in league with Tel Aviv's gangland, which would have worsened his case. From October 6th, 1973, Shimon was gainfully employed again for six months by the Israeli Army during and after the Yom Kippur War but the same boredom and consequent trouble was to follow in the post-war period.

Farming was really not Shimon's scene, a little too domestic and dull and monotonous in its demanding daily routines. Equally, you are never very far from the city lights in such a small country. In fact Tel Aviv was not much more than an hour and a half's drive from Moshav Ram-On in the Jezreel valley where the family were living. I remember visiting Ruti on one occasion and being told not to lift the lid of the dustbin on the garden path because the bin contained a large and possibly venomous snake. Shimon liked wild animals, maybe even felt a kindred spirit with them but this did not encourage him to leave them free in their natural habitat. Indeed, after a few years out of the country, being detained for further stupid misdeeds at the pleasure of the German State judiciary, he was returned to Israel and set up a restaurant and small zoo on the desert road to Eilat, which has since attracted a wide and varied clientele from all stratas of Israeli life. But I am shooting forward in time and we were in fact in the early summer of 1974 at a party where Ruti is telling me how difficult her life had become.

Towards the end of July 1974, my Irish friend decided she would have to pack up and return to England. Her father had recently died and after a visit for the funeral she considered that her sons and herself stood a better chance of a more stable life on the old stamping ground of north-west London. The six months reserve service attached to the Yom Kippur War was over and Shimon was no longer regularly at home and seemed to be involving himself with an unsavoury crowd from Tel Aviv whom Ruti thoroughly distrusted and termed *The Mafia*. Her instinct turned out to be very much on the mark.

It was time to go quietly. She needed help, she said, to pack her goods into the few suitcases, boxes and tea chests she had got together. The only problem was that she was unwell, had no energy to do it and no idea of packing efficiently. Although by now more than two months pregnant, I took a couple of days off from my family and drove down the valley to be her packer, a job at which I had become fairly expert over numbers of years of travelling hither and thither and back again. She marvelled at the speed with which I sorted out her home contents according to size, malleability and fragility. I then eyed up the containers and began carefully to stuff them so that not a single square inch was left with air in it before being labeled with the contents. Everything was finally ready for despatch which had to be organised as swiftly as possible in case Shimon re-appeared and before Ruti, with her two boys, had disappeared to spend the last three weeks of their time in Israel in our little caravan in Ramat Yishai. This time would give an opportunity to sort out paperwork, get tickets and prepare for her second exodus, this time with two lads aged six and four in tow and no husband.

Ruti had good women friends in the moshav but there were also those who considered that Shimon and his family did not pull their agricultural weight or fit in socially. So Ruti had to be very discrete about her departure, especially as she wished to keep her whereabouts unknown to her absent husband. There were problems, as well, of contract and moneys owing to her or to the Moshav which needed to be sorted out but not, she preferred, under present circumstances. It is difficult enough to take a decision to leave a marriage when you have invested all the love that you could into it and this had left her drained and weary and certainly in no mood to fight with officious members of the community with little love for her, despite the few strong protagonists.

So Ruti shut the door quietly on Moshav Ram-On and came away to Ramat Yishai where the next three weeks proved momentous enough. Of course it took Shimon no time at all to find out where his family was encamped and he naturally paid us a visit or two.

Arnon and Maggie tie the knot in Harrow, 1970

Rosie and her charge in the Alps near Italian border, 1973

Massada by the Dead Sea

Young Arni after Reserve Service, 1959

Arni (centre) on Golan Heights, Yom Kippur War, 1973

Arni's parents, Yis and Klara Goren

*Maggie's parents, Herbert and
Molly Evans, with twins in the
garden, 1975*

*Pinye's cow in front of our house and
our view of Mt Carmel*

Mothers and twins in our garden, 1975

The house we built but never lived in

Our Garden of Eden

The Judas Tree, March 1977

The young family at Kibbutz Maabarot

Wild flowers in the Western Galilee, 1974
Spring on Mt Carmel, Maggie and the boys, 1976

The River Jordan, Tel Dan, N. Israel, where Adam found his papyrus.
It doesn't get much wider than this!

140

Bedouin boy with his goats outside our house

Friend Jo, who came to help with the twins, at Belvoie above Jordan Valley, May 1975

Bedouin lady cracking our olives

*Our fertile Jezreel Valley and
Mt Tabor*

*Adam and Matti dressed
for Purim Festival outside
house, 1976*

Sunset at Ein Gedi, looking over Dead Sea to Moab Mountains in Jordan

✦

Turkey in the Melons

I suppose we had all expected Shimon to discover where Ruti had gone with his two sons but had not expected either the manner or spirit in which he was to turn up at Larish House one Friday afternoon, shortly after her arrival. A half truck pulled up on the verge of the road beyond the low stone wall surrounding the wild area of our front garden shaded by its tall pine trees. We were all at home on the eve of Shabbat, our four boys playing around the caravan.

Shimon greeted us and pointed to the back of his truck which was piled high with water melons. Now everybody loves water melons but especially the kids who began hopping about like Spring lambs. They are for you, he indicated to Arni, after greeting Ruti and the children with an ironical grin, but quietly enough. We went inside for a chat and there was a basic exchange between husband and wife as though nothing untoward had taken place. Ruti explained that she had already bought the plane tickets and she and the boys would be leaving Israel within a week or so. Shimon merely shrugged his large shoulders and since he obviously had not come to argue on this point or cause a problem we left them alone to talk about the financial implications and responsibilities of the marriage split, the children's future and whatever else they had to say to one another. The children soon disappeared to play in the garden.

Shimon then asked Arni to help him unload the contents of

the truck, a gift for us all, a peace offering to let us know that he had no intention of behaving in any kind of threatening manner. Indeed, as mentioned before, he needed to be liked and maybe feared that Ruti had given us a less than complimentary picture of him as father and husband. I think he was intent on balancing the scales. But we had no reasons to dislike Shimon for he had always been pleasant enough to us and despite our practical involvement in providing a temporary sanctuary for Ruti, we felt the personal problems between husband and wife were for them to sort out, especially as peaceful co-operation appeared to be the agenda for that day. We were quiet and cordial with Shimon.

We had no idea how we could possibly eat so many melons but did not want to offend our unexpected guest so they were unloaded and piled in the front garden. It was only then that he removed from a sack in the truck a live turkey and it wasn't Christmas or even Chanukah. It was a little amusing to think that Shimon had passed the chicken factory at the entrance to the village where turkey meat, though dead, was abundant, cheap and ready to cook. However, along with the melons, this was also part of the peace-offering. No doubt it had been farmed on his moshav. Shimon tied a thick piece of string around its neck to prevent it wandering off and it stood by our front steps, making the usual turkey noises, a large stone placed on the other end of the string to stop the bird wandering off.

Arni looked at me and I looked at Shimon and we both asked him what we should do with the turkey. "Just kill it," he said in his deep voice "you can slit its throat." At this point he produced a large sharp knife. Arni paled visibly and protested loudly, pointing out that he would be unable to do that, it was not something he was accustomed to doing, it would upset the children …. He was fast running out of excuses and manliness and suggested that Shimon could surely do the job for us at the back of the house away from the children. Though we naturally did not speak of it, Shimon did have a reputation for daring and courage in wartime military forays, searching out infiltrators or spies crossing borders at night into the wild desert terrain. It would only take a second or two to deal with the turkey with his sharp knife and very little strength was required for the job. Arni was about to lead him around the house and leave him to it, not wishing to even watch that performance. Shimon then surprised us. No, he said, it didn't appeal to him either. He looked a little embarrassed to admit this but we liked him the better for it.

So here were two soldiers of the Israeli army, one from the artillery and one from a special unit used to close encounters and dangerous operations, and neither could kill the turkey. Shimon came up with the answer. Surely the slaughter house in Ramat Yishai would still be open, it was not yet dusk? They should take the turkey there to be despatched.

Shimon could not be bothered to put the bird back into the sack and gesturing for Arni to go with him proceeded to walk with the turkey on the string across our back garden onto the track which led to the village centre. I gathered later that a surprised slaughterman was not pleased to see either *Kushi*, Arni or the turkey and took a little persuading to do the job, saying that he was not authorised to deal with the bird on his premises in the required kosher manner. It was against the rules and could bring him trouble and so on, and so on …he stopped, sighed in the ensuing silence and went on …. however, on this one occasion only and as it was for *Kushi*…he'd do it. Being a man of few words Shimon simply shrugged again, the bird was killed, singed ready for plucking, brought home and shut in the wash house. I was left wondering who on earth was supposed to pluck the damned thing. Well, that lot later fell to Arni and the eventual cooking to me. It was enough to put me off turkey for life.

Following the turkey trot, we sat with Shimon and Ruti drinking coffee on the patio, the late afternoon sun rosily filtering through the light green leaves of the pomegranate tree leaning against the patio pillar by the garden steps. The children were busily biting into and sucking large slices of water melon like moon-shaped mouth organs, their mouths and vests by now stained crimson. There was a sure irony in the conversation which then developed.

Shimon liked our stone house in its fruitful garden and we explained how we had been promised by the woman owner when we first rented the property that we could buy it within a year but now she had changed her mind. We told him that this miserly woman wanted only to make as much money as possible from the renting and that she and her family had never had any intention whatsoever of parting with the property, before, during or after our tenancy. The matter had been discussed on numerous occasions already and each time the question of purchase was put off. Recently the owner, Mrs Larish, had wanted to raise the rent but we told her that we would be neither paying more rent nor leaving. We still felt she should honour her original promise.

At this point Shimon immediately offered his help. He would gladly 'persuade' Mrs Larish to stick to her promise. He asked us for the landlady's address, saying that he would call on her and have a little chat to settle a sale in our favour. We immediately envisaged the elderly woman suffering a heart attack or worse, depending on what powers of persuasion Shimon had in mind and begged him not to take the matter further on our behalves. We suggested that we would prefer to build a house in the village instead, which is what we shortly afterwards did. He was difficult to persuade, so great was his eagerness to do us some kind of friendly favour. Although he now knew the landlady's name and the fact that she lived in Nazareth Illit, the Jewish settlement above the old town, we hoped he would respect our wishes. Once again he simply smiled and shrugged. Kushi was intelligently observant, he tuned in to atmosphere and was not a totally insensitive man, but I would not have rated him high for humour. He had too much personal baggage to carry to find life more than superficially amusing. Despite some uncertainty and concern for a short period, no doubt totally unwarranted, we soon realised and were thankful that he did not visit our landlady for a friendly or even less than friendly chat.

After this rather unexpected conversation, following the delicacies of the turkey incident, Shimon raised his tall body out of his chair, smiled charmingly and thanked us for looking after Ruti and the boys and we in turn thanked him again for his generous gifts. He left as quietly as he'd come. We soon recovered from that extraordinary visit of an extraordinary man, though we never forgot it. In due course Ruti was taken to the airport with her sons to start a new life in the suburbs of London. That must have seemed very strange to those young boys after their wild life of freedom in a farming community, off the beaten track, in a land of heat and plenty where virtually anything could happen at the drop of a hat, and so often did.

Encounter of a Closer Kind

When we realised that the 'Larish' house in Ramat Yishai would never be ours with neither the owner nor her children prepared to sell, despite promises to the contrary, Arni and I started thinking about an alternative way of life. Arni had come from an agricultural kibbutz and he felt his heart was in the land even if his head had been trained for engineering.

I was taken to a place very near Nazareth in the hills of Galilee and shown the most superb and peaceful view it offered across wooded hills and valleys towards the sea. It was the land attached to the somewhat rundown moshav of Tsipori and I started dreaming. When I was around eleven years of age, at a post war Ideal Home Exhibition, I had been approached by someone with a microphone, probably the BBC, and asked "Well, young lady, what do you think of the Show and what would you like to be when you grow up?" A friend of my parents had been exhibiting some cloches he had patented for growing salad vegetables on a small plot and it was the gardening exhibits which had interested me. Beyond that I told the interviewer that I wanted to be an "agri... agri...cultrist". I really had difficulty getting the word out and why I didn't simply say farmer is beyond me, for that's what I meant. I was in love with the earth and the countryside at that time, and still am.

Arni and I started to make enquiries about becoming members of the Tsipori farming community or moshav, which at that time was basically a fraternity of Rumanian families from years before. Since we were so insistent, after a lot of suspicion on the part of the moshav Secretariat, they eventually decided that it might not be a bad idea to have a live-in engineer and just hoped I would be up to the job. There was something strange to me about the whole 'carry on' but I put those thoughts aside. We were shown a little shikun, which had definitely seen better days, and it was called Bet Shemesh or House of the Sun; unfortunately or fortunately, depending on your take on it, the word Rising had been left out of its name. We were told that it really needed cleaning up a bit because over the past year it had been used to house turkeys. I was not impressed with the moshav members we first met. They seemed somewhat uncouth but later we made the acquaintance of a very nice elderly gentleman member with a house in a superb place on a hill with a magnificent view. He told us there was a plot going next to him and we should apply for it and build our own house there. Bet Shemesh was just a stop-gap.

He said that the Jewish Agency currently had a lien on the community, which had been growing beef cattle, as it had got into debt and they were running the business of building it up with new immigrants.

Naturally, I did no more than rush home and take out pad and pencil and start drawing the plans for our new home on that particular plot. It was all very exciting. Then Arni reminded me that we were being tested and had been asked to clean up the turkey house the following weekend, ready for our use within a few months. That brought me down to earth rather fast. There was an awful lot of muck in there, never mind feathers.

Matters progressed. We had to offer our handwriting to a graphologist and were then called for interview. As it happened we were not the only ones there waiting outside the 'office' of the moshav in the summer heat to be grilled by the Jewish Agency bureaucrats. Unknown to any of us at that time there was, isn't there always, a hidden political agenda so the recruiting was not quite as straightforward as it should have been, although Arni as an ex-kibbutnik had been tipped the wink that there would no problem as far as we were concerned.

Suddenly we heard a lot of shouting and crying and a young girl in her teens dashed out of the office and in a very distressed manner told us that her father had a weak heart and that he was so upset that she feared it might bring on a heart attack and please could we do something about it. At this stage the whole family came staggering out of the office and the father, a man in his fifties, certainly was a very bright red and shouting in a strange language while the mother and other kids were crying. We tried our very best to appease them.

It appeared that the family were from Georgia on the Black Sea and among an exodus of 30,000 Georgian Jews fleeing to Israel from that Russian State from 1970 following awful anti-Semitic persecution there; the latest rounds starting with a new outbreak in 1965. Jewish history, going back two millennia in that area, had been very chequered at different periods but this was the first and most massive immigration in modern times. There was an urgent need to settle these people somewhere in the land of Israel.

As I said, the politics of the situation was unknown to us but the rough treatment meted out before our eyes was only too obvious. The family had been turned down in a totally uncivilised manner after they had been more or less led to believe they could settle in a new home in a new country to start a new life. The parents had virtually no Hebrew but the youngsters had a little. They were simple working folk who had left everything behind them when they ran away from Georgia.

My virtuous morality got the better of me. I was so incensed that I did no more than write to the Head Office of the Jewish Agency in Jerusalem, telling them how appalled I was that Jews could treat fellow Jews like that at this time, or any time, in Israel's new history. Of course I laced it over two pages with more critical appraisal which was polite but sharp. An innocent indeed!

A short while later I received a letter from the office of Raanan Weitz, head of the Jewish Agency and one of those men who had helped build Israel up from 1948, playing a leading role in the research and development of rural areas. He would have been around sixty at that time. The letter asked me with Arni to meet him at the Zim House offices of the Agency in Haifa on a particular afternoon. I was pleased, thinking some kind of redress was in hand for those poor Georgians. Maybe we will be given tea, I suggested. Once more, how innocent could I be?

Having dressed as smartly as I could we arrived at Zim House and eventually found our way to the offices on the third floor. We knocked timidly and a door was opened and we were asked to wait. A woman came out and we went through one office into a very small ante-chamber with an L-shaped row of desks, behind which sat a tall and well-built man in the centre with two people either side and one studious looking man with glasses on the short end of the L. I was fairly close to him and only about two feet away from the desk where the boss now stood. Arni had been motioned to a chair in the corner of the room on my right and I was given a small chair in front of boss man. He was still standing, leaning on the table, and addressed me with a slight smile and a disconcerting introduction. He told me he was Raanan Weitz and had read my letter. He asked me some questions about my background and having ascertained from my replies that I was just a little housewife and obviously not a journalist from The Times maybe or any other paper, his smile became a little more tight-lipped. "It is many years," he said slowly in impeccable English "since I have read English of the high literary standard of your letter," he paused and added ominously "but you know what I did with it? I tore it up and threw into the wastepaper bin". The mouth curled and his stony eyes looked at me with silent anger. As you can imagine I was deeply shocked by this planned attack while he carried on saying what he had to say. It became obvious to me that they had been shocked by my letter in which Nazi Germany had been somewhere mentioned and the treatment of Jews by Jews. That was the crux of the matter. And here I was sitting in front of 'the Godfather' and receiving a blazing and passionate discourse against myself. At one point his henchman to my left, the young man with the glasses, leapt up from his seat and attempted to grab me around the neck. "Shev" or Sit, barked the Godfather at him in a totally commanding tone and the man immediately sat down. I think I may have started trembling a bit but was not going to be bowed. Weitz told me he had been an officer in the British Army in the Second World War and at no time throughout his entire career had he been laden down with the kind of conscience I seemed to be carrying around with me, with or without a genuine excuse, or words to that effect. I took in a breath, looked him in the eye and said I felt pity for him as life without a conscience is hardly worth living, or words to that effect. He stood tall, controlled his anger and peremptorily dismissed us, telling us to wait in the corridor outside.

Phew! Arni, who only had to state from which kibbutz he had heralded, was speechless and I felt weak at the knees but suggested we just get up and go. My native husband told me we could not do that. Meanwhile it seemed all hell was breaking loose in the office nearby, a lot of shouting until the Godfather over-ruled and a lower level of discussion took place. It felt as if half an hour went by before we were called in again and told that a decision had been made to give us a place in Moshav Almagor. A letter would be sent and now you can get out said the renowned Professor Raanan Weitz. When we got out into the sunshine and rather fresher air of the port of Haifa, not known for its freshness, I was still trembling. On the way home, and Arni drove, he explained that the moshav we had been offered was one of the most prestigious, if not the number one in the country, where many of Israel's crack pilots were given places. People would give their eye teeth to go there. It was in a beautiful site just above the Northern end of the Sea of Galilee beneath the Golan heights and close to Capurnaum. This time my lip metaphorically curled.

When we got home, where my Irish friend Ruti had been looking after the children, I sank into a chair and having been asked if I'd like a cup of tea, explained that a double brandy would be more welcome. Within a week we received the Moshav offer and spoke to the father of a client on Israel's first ever Moshav

Nahalal, next door to us. He was or had been a Chief of the Moshav Movement. A friendly and useful discussion followed but I had made up my mind. They could stuff their offer. It was Tsipori for me or nowhere and after that outrageous débacle I actually preferred nowhere. And so we decided to remain in Ramat Yishai and build our own house. I wrote a curt but polite reply refusing the Moshav's offer, which may have been the only one they ever received. I naturally never heard from either the Jewish Agency or Raanan Weitz again.

Sometimes you kick a stone with bare feet and find a scorpion underneath it. On this occasion a scorpion had kicked the stone and found another scorpion lurking there. Were there any winners? Not really. Professor Weitz had wasted his time on a journey to Haifa when he realised I was not a journalistic or other threat ... and I had simply lost a beloved dream. But we surely both recovered and got on with life, as you do, and fortunately Arni and I had only spent one horrible weekend trying to clear the caked-on turkey poo in the House of the Sun. I often wonder whether Weitz ever remembered that encounter of a closer kind. It was not a pretty story but to be fair I was not aware of all the complications of mass immigration into a tiny new country in transition and years later I could well understand how my words, especially as a non-Jew, had bitten into and hurt even those hardened officials of the Jewish Agency. But perhaps it was a salutary lesson too, for all concerned, who knows? I realised then that the old adage 'the pen is mightier than the sword' does indeed hold sway. And yet I do so wish in general that the world would stop using swords and, if not pick up the pen, at least talk ... all sides tolerantly with some humility. But of course that is wishful thinking when the personal or national stakes are so high.

The Case of the Crippled Fire Engine

In 1974 the little roads in Ramat Yishai were full of pot holes. The water tower needed maintenance but the Secretary to the local council believed that the village lacked only one thing … a fire engine. To find a fire engine had been Betzalel Cohen's primary ambition since coming into office. He searched the papers and made enquiries until one day he found just what he was looking for in a small town which had bought the engine from a larger town near Tel Aviv and they had got it from Kibbutz Bet Alpha, whose business was the manufacture of fire engines. In fact this shiny red monster had been constructed from a light lorry produced by the American company Fargo for use during the Second World War. These brown lorries had been used in the service of the NAAFI and eventually some had turned up in Israel.

Kibbutz Alpha built fire engines from these trucks by putting a tank on them, giving them a petrol engine, pump, hoses and valves and painting them a bright, glossy red. Betzalel was duly impressed when his eyes first alighted on the third-hand fire engine for sale. It was, after all, specifically built for use in small, rural communities. His joy was so great that he bought in *on spec* without even having a professional check the mechanics and he bought it with the council money on a repayment system to be spread over ten years. Was that some kind of a guarantee? It was delivered to Ramat Yishai and a place was proudly found for it right next to the council offices.

Now one day, at about eleven o'clock in the morning, council handymen under instructions from the Secretary were burning the thistles on the waste ground around the two small buildings housing the village nurseries for children from eighteen months to two years old and from two years to five years old. The children finished nursery at one o'clock. It was a very hot day with a dusty wind blowing from the desert in the south. Nursery school was in full progress and as I rode past on my bike to the nearby post office, the children playing outside, including my Matti, were quickly herded into the nursery and the doors and windows firmly fastened as the wind continued to blow billows of smoke around the nursery buildings. I could hear the children coughing and crying.

The new antique fire-engine was standing nearby in case the fire got out of hand ~ an occasion no doubt organised by the Secretary for its first trial by fire. A man was getting it 'primed' as it were and the vehicle appeared to have about as much pressure in its old hose as might be expected from the intermittent peeing of an elderly gentleman. There was also not enough hose on the reel to cover the whole area of burning brush so the engine stood first at the back of the nurseries and then the driver laboriously reeled up the hose before driving it to the front of the buildings to start unreeling again, at least prepared for some kind of action.

I quickly parked my bike outside the Post Office where several mums were gathered chattering loudly about the children and the smoke but doing nothing else about it. Grabbing the phone on the counter, to the surprise of the postmistress, I asked for the Secretary's number and getting him directly shouted at him to get over to the plot *'maher, maher'* (fast) to make the men beat out the fires as quickly as possible, adding in curt and direct language what I thought of his management and timing for testing his new acquisition .. *meshigine!* Dark looks came from the postmistress who, being *yekke* (square), told me the public had no right to use the post office phone.

The other mothers stood ogling me as though I'd just landed from Mars. Ignoring them, I ran across to the baby nursery and

155

commanded as firmly as I could, "everybody outside please". The nursery teacher, Rachel, a lovely but rather shy and gentle girl, obviously wondered what she should do without authoritarian permission but agreed to evacuate the small building with my help. With each of us carrying the youngest in our arms, we marched the other toddlers holding hands in pairs to the Post Office on the higher ground well away from the wind direction and smoke where they were kissed and cuddled and their little faces washed in cool water.

The lumbering engine stood dismally to one side of the road with hoses dangling having proved itself pretty much of a white elephant under duress. It turned out that the fire crew recruited from the village had been 'dry trained' and not entirely sure how to proceed with water. The appointed fireman was still doing his best to maintain an emergency service with the limp hoses when his engine died. After a number of spluttering attempts it started up again and was able to reverse away from the creeping fires, having no chance of hosing itself down if the fire got out of control.

By the time Bezalel's car came screeching around the bend I was already running towards the second nursery to go through the same operation, the Secretary hot on my heels echoing the command that the children should leave the building. We totally ignored each other. Not so much smoke had penetrated the closed windows of the bigger nursery and, to be fair, Bezalel got the burning fully under control within fifteen minutes with other men joining in the beating, leaving only an acrid smell in the hot air.

The fires virtually out, it was decided that the children should not go back to the smoky nurseries but could proceed to the primary school for the rest of the morning. They were assembled again into neat crocodiles and with the help of a number of mothers toddled off to the smoke-free zone of the primary school to cause a happy distraction until it was time go home.

Later that day a shiny red fire engine, sadly impotent, was inspected back on its parking lot. Its tank was found beneath the red paint to have rusted in several places, exhibiting numbers of little and larger holes so that under any pressure it leaked like a sieve. Additionally, images of a broken-down fire engine itself catching alight and exploding in a fireball remained etched in the imaginations of all who later jokingly told the sorry tale of Betzalel's pride and joy.

We do not know everything that was said at the next council meeting about this embarrassing matter but the subject was avoided in the street in front of the Secretary, who could be very tetchy and outspoken and was not renowned for a sense of humour. We later heard that Betzalel told council members they had been swindled and he would therefore be paying no further instalments to the other council from whom he had bought the fire engine and who in turn, having never had to use it, stopped paying their ongoing instalments to the previous owners on the same grounds and so on … .

And so the village fire engine gradually lost its brilliance as the pine trees under which it was parked dripped their pine needles and dropped their cones over its body. As time passed it slowly sank into a sad decline … a reminder perhaps that *all that glistens is neither red nor gold* … just a cheap deal.

The Night of the Long Rope

The night of the long rope followed Yom Kippur of 1974, the holiest day of the year for the devout. Muscal, our next door neighbour, was indeed devout, being one of the few inhabitants of our street who regularly went to the synagogue every Sabbath. Being of Eastern European descent he went to the Ashekenazi synagogue about two hundred yards along our road.

As Muscal was coming home at dusk, Yom Kippur slipping away for another year along with the eloquent prayers and promises, and while old stars were beginning to sprinkle the heavens with a little brightness, our neighbour happened to notice a long piece of rope lying on the road. He picked it up, as he later reported it to us, took it home and tied it around the balcony of his wooden verandah. After all rope is always a handy commodity to a small-holder.

The next day someone known to Muscal from a nearby settlement came to visit him. The two men had something in common, a love of fine horses. This was also shared with Muscal's neighbour on his other side, our friend Eliezer who was a natural with the animal and might easily have been a 'horse whisperer' had he not been a policeman. They both had enough land and outbuildings to stable a beast or two and certainly Eli did just that. Muscal had a good eye for a good horse but I felt his interest was primarily financial, as it was in most things.

After exchanging the usual pleasantries at the front of the house, Muscal's visitor started talking about his horses, which was natural enough. He told Muscal he had a particular filly amongst a few in his stabling which had real class and unusual markings.

"The blaze," he said "is like two white lilies and the rump a deeper shade of red than its flanks. It is a high stepping, beautiful creature and so spirited that it often tries to get out of its paddock," he concluded.

The visitor then asked Muscal if he had ever seen that horse when he was visiting their place, or at any other time for that matter, to which Muscal replied in the negative.

"Aie, aie," said the visitor, sighing a little and continued "and are you growing calves this year, my friend?" and with this naturally took a few paces towards the side of the house from where Muscal's plot stretched out behind the building.

As he did so the visitor's eyes fell on an elegant chestnut mare with a blaze like two lilies tethered to the verandah at the back of the house. Muscal, following his uninvited guest, expressed enormous surprise saying that he had never seen this horse before and on examining the situation found that the horse was in fact tethered to the long rope which he had picked up and tied in a good knot to his balcony the night before. He assured his visitor that he had simply found a long piece of rope on the road as he was coming home in the dark from praying in the synagogue and tossed it over the verandah rail.

"I would have known if there was a horse on the rope," he said solemnly and murmured as an afterthought, "so, I have saved your horse from straying, what a lucky chance."

It need only be added that despite repetition of the rope story which filled out with more and more detail concerning the humbling address of the Rabbi at the previous day's service, the stars in the sky that night, the heat of the day and ever more confused mumblings, the visitor was seen not to be listening but leading his lovely young mare on the rope back along our road and off to his own village.

Well, whether the horse had come loose and strayed from its own domain on Yom Kippur while the family were observing their religion or whether Muscal had found himself wandering through the other village in a state of reverie and repentance after his prayers of atonement and promises to God, no-one ever found out. Muscal stuck to his story but what he could never explain to anybody who asked him at the time, or any other time for that matter, was why he had bothered to tie the rope with such a healthy knot to the verandah instead of simply leaving it on the ground.

"Aie, aie, not everything has a simple answer," he would reply. How very true.

Simply Synagogues

When we first came to Ramat Yishai we were made aware that the synagogue was a converted dwelling place some halfway along our road. I say the synagogue, as though only that one existed in the village, because my husband was of central European parentage and it was assumed that if the family had any religious inclinations at all they would be expressed through the offices of the mainstream Ashkenazi synagogue. The Ashkenazim, with Palestinian roots to their customs and rites, represented early migrations of Jews settled into France and Germany in the Middle Ages, many of whom later moved eastwards to Poland, Czechoslovakia, Hungary and on to Russia. In an unwritten pecking order the main synagogue is that of the Ashkenazim, as the Church of England is the official church of the United Kingdom.

Getting closer to the sun, however, the next in the hierarchical pecking order are the Sephardic Jews from the 12th and 13th centuries, using rites and customs from ancient Babylon, who first settled in Spain and Portugal and then spread to North Africa, the Balkans and elsewhere in the Middle East, a large number now living in Israel. But other religious customs and rites had also developed amongst the Jewry in other cultural areas where Jews became firmly established. These included Persia and southwest Arabia, particularly Yemen, its ancient equivalent being Sheba with its famous Queen, later taken over by Abyssinia. Today's Ethiopia, previously part of Abyssinia has its African Jews who share the same Yemeni oriental rites and are currently increasingly migrating to settle in Israel. The Yemenis have for long years been a considerable cultural component of Israel's population.

What happened to the Christians, followers of a good Jew from the Galilee, who split West from East, Rome from Byzantium, happened before to the Jews. Exiled or displaced Jews who migrated to new areas often widely separated by natural geographic boundaries, were naturally encouraged to changes in cultural behaviour in the assimilation game; the necessity to merge with larger indigenous populations of differing customs, religious beliefs and languages. Out of such historical adaptation emerged those schisms in Judaism, in interpretation and power. So what's new, except that the world is smaller and the same process faster and ongoing. But that process of assimilation, constantly changing and complexly diverse, is never complete, which is what makes for our rainbow coloured world today, if you choose to see it that way.

The rainbow according to Ramat Yishai arched over all those differing Jewish cultures and were duly accounted for in a good Jewish compromise. After establishing in conversation that there was more than one synagogue representing our small village population, Arni was shown another building which looked just like any other house but which had above its door the *Magen David* or Star of David. This housed the Persian community. Then we discovered yet another synagogue in a modest house belonging to the Yemenis. A bolder building in the village was the more obvious synagogue for the Sephardic Jews, looked after by the largest Moroccan family, the Ben Lulus.

Now the Persian community has a similar form of prayers to the Ashkenazim but they had no regular Rabbi in Ramat Yishai. That synagogue would of course always be open for special holy days throughout the year, like Yom Kippur, when a Persian cantor would lead the prayers. At other times the Persians in the village might attend the Ashkenazi synagogue if theirs was shut. Ashkenazi Jews who were uncomfortable with some of their Ashkenazi neighbours might drift to the Persian synagogue whenever it was open.

Likewise it sometimes happened that individuals or whole families from the Sephardic Jews, the Moroccans particularly in our village, would change their place of worship if there had been arguments or acrimonious dealings amongst their own kind, which happened frequently enough. But these Sephardim would only use the Persian synagogue and would not enter the Ashkenazi place of prayer, as a matter of principle. Thus the Persian synagogue could be said to represent the most ecumenical and accommodating practice of religion in the village and would obligingly adapt its prayer forms and its rites for whichever happened to be the predominant congregation at any one time; Persians small in number, Sephardic Moroccans large in number or wandering Ashkenazim. From the wisdom of their philosophical past, perhaps, the Persians had discovered that the connecting links of language and culture within the Torah could form a bridge to span the worst divides.

Only the Yemenis had a regular rabbi or other officer who would lead the prayers in their synagogue with no less than ten men present every evening. It was the most well attended synagogue in Ramat Yishai with a good congregation every Friday night and on the Sabbath. It was small wonder that the Yemeni community felt more religiously righteous and true to their faith than all the other disparate Jewry put together making up our religious 'rainbow' population.

It is a fact commonly observed around the world that religious houses sometimes house less than religious or saintly people. Regular attendance can be put down to superstition, to the fact that habit dies hard, or simply that good or bad deals might be undertaken within reverential confines with a hope thereby to inspire trust and confidence!

An example of less than saintly behaviour occurred at one harvest festival service of *Sukot* in our village, involving the discreditable and extraordinary behaviour of some members of both the Council and synagogues.

There were two pieces of no-man's land sloping down the escarpment side to the valley in front of our house. These areas had been farmed independently and continuously for many years by Muscal, our Romani-Hungarian neighbour and by Pinye, our rubbish collector at the time. One day both men received a letter from the council Secretary, who desperately wanted to turn our village into a thriving town and stamp out its small-scale farming which threatened that kind of development. He had received, it was broadly understood, legal information suggesting he might advise our farmers that the council could and would be appropriating the two plots of land in question to turn them into communal parkland, though no-one knew from where any funding would be coming for such a community enterprise. There had been no prior discussions, no terms, just a brief letter out of the blue from Mr. Cohen to the two smallholders.

Muscal and Pinye were both livid with the Secretary's perfunctory and ill-mannered communication threatening their livelihoods and they chose the only sensible place to meet for a dust-up. That was to be the synagogue on the feast day of Sukot where they knew they would find our Council Secretary. Muscal went in shouting with all fists flying but the usually quiet, controlled Pinye approached a surprised Secretary in a different manner. He so demeaned his mother in public with the longest string of obscene epithets without pause that you could imagine that all hell broke loose in God's house. The protagonists indeed became so worked up that all three appeared on the brink of apoplexy. Suddenly the Rabbi intervened above the din and sent the three men out of the building to calm down and ask for God's forgiveness for their language and behaviour before thinking of entering the synagogue again.

We learned later that the Secretary had decided to sue Pinye for slander, which saddened some but amused others who were aware of a longer history between the two men who lived acrimoniously next door to one another. Due to this very public fracas the Council considered it necessary to look more closely into the question of the appropriation of the land and finally for any suing by the Secretary to be delayed in view of the 'slanderer' having no money. The Secretary later found a more subtle way, as we know, to achieve Pinye's downfall.

Another commotion took place on the Sabbath following a Yom Kippur, when the same neighbour Muscal, who religiously and financially supported the synagogue for the saving of his soul, took upon himself the honour of taking up the scrolls with the books of the Torah. One of the elders, who knew Muscal well, objected to this self-appointed role on principle, personal not religious one must assume. Once again Muscal started loudly declaiming and waving his fists in the air and then towards the elderman. Pandemonium once more broke out until both sides reached an impasse and Muscal finally sat down muttering to himself, giving way to the elder at the behest of the rest of a noisy congregation.

The final incident I recall, though no doubt many more took place, was also on that holy day of Yom Kippur. I went along to the synagogue to look for my son Adam who was visiting it for the first time and had been there for over an hour. On approaching the entrance I heard what sounded more like argument in a market place than devotion. It appeared that a reader had been hired because he was the cheapest to be found in the area and the man was mumbling at an ever increasing speed and obviously trying to get through the words as quickly as possible and make his getaway. Needless to say with a nation where you can find eleven opinions among ten men and where a *maenean* of ten could shout that they had been attacked and outnumbered three to one by a band of three, everyone began voicing his opinion of the reader instead of quietly praying ~ or minding their own business. The reader took no notice whatsoever of this interruption as voices rose ever higher and he left soon afterwards to contribute his services elsewhere. Adam, at the tender age of five, probably understood very little of what was going on and since I knew little more, I beckoned for him to join me outside and we went home without alluding to the scene.

It occurred to me then that the Church of England had a long way to go to compete with such overt demonstrations of democracy and market manners at its services but maybe Baptists and Gospel Evangelists were somewhere in the running.

Eli ... & ...

Our dear friend Eli Maman was a character whose inventiveness and creativity may never have been fully exploited or appreciated by the police with whom he was employed during our acquaintance with him as a close neighbour. Eli worked at that time in the traffic department and rode a large, white motorcycle for many of his duties but this could be boring and repetitive for such a man as he. He was an expert with horses and other animals, his home a menagerie for many creatures hidebound, furred or feathered. His wife Ruthie, a Canadian immigrant who was the long-suffering backbone of the family, a loyal and true mate, mother of their two boys and two girls, was a superb cook. Both husband and wife were hospitable with a capital 'H' and their house was open to all comers. Ruthie might have enjoyed a little more privacy, room for her own thoughts and feelings, space for herself but this was not really an option while being married to a man like Eli. Many were the wonderful barbecues in their garden at which the liquor flowed and our expansive host with his booming voice and laugh made sure everybody was enjoying themselves to the full. But this generosity and other economic problems no doubt put a strain on the family income which was not always under expert control of the breadwinner. Ruthie, after raising her children, finally took some additional training and returned to teaching and taught at the junior and high school in the village. Life was not easy for them.

I suppose one of Eli's biggest problems was self discipline, or lack of it, and a great desire to please people and be liked, whether or not he could afford this sometimes expensive luxury. And it was quite often his inventive imagination which caused him more problems than a few. His rank was consequently often yo-yoing between promotion and demotion, which naturally affected his income and upset his wife along the way. But Eli believed in the timeless mercy and fruitfulness of the Almighty, perhaps only qualified by the age-old Hispanic expression *mañana*, for today is surely only waiting for tomorrow ... which, of course, never comes.

As a traffic patroller of the main highways we might assume Eli was often engaged in the misdemeanours of others and involved in highway accidents of all sorts. One night Arni was sitting up late when he heard a tapping on the front window. He supposed this was someone we knew who perhaps did not want to disturb the whole household. It was indeed Eli, who explained to Arni that an articulated lorry on the main Haifa highway not too far away had slipped a couple of coils of re-inforcing steel onto the road. As I understood it, and this may be an exaggeration, the driver heard his load shift but knew as he was pulling up that he had no lifting gear with which to get it back on the lorry. Fortunately, or so we may believe, he was on an inside lane and not an immediate danger to other traffic. Eli had been passing in his patrol car and stopped to investigate the matter. The driver let Eli understand that he was anxious to get the rest of the delivery under way. If questioned about the missing coils he told Eli that he would simply shrug and say he was only the driver and had not loaded the vehicle. For this reason he was glad Eli had come along and he hoped he would take over the responsibility for dealing with the coils, or disposing of them, without further involvement from himself. That, at any rate, was the story Arni received. Eli had waved the driver off, coned the area and headed back to Ramat Yishai knowing that we were then in the process of building our own house and that one of the more expensive materials we had to use was steel re-inforcement.

The idea of fetching a load of 'police protected goods' that had fallen from a lorry rather appealed to my 'subversive' husband but even if they could find another two men to help and a suitable vehicle, it was unfeasible without some proper lifting gear. The rolls probably each weighed at least a ton. It then occurred to Arni that even if they succeeded in removing the goods to Ramat Yishai there might be other consequences, questions asked and so on which he did not feel he would genuinely be able to fence. He was, after all, a respected engineer with a family to support. So after an hour's interesting discussion on hydraulics and heavy weights, Eli and Arni decided to abandon the project. What happened after that remains in the realms of conjecture. Somehow Arni felt it was a generous and disappointed officer he had left to contact his superiors with the news of the traffic accident and its precise whereabouts. The subject was never mentioned between them again.

Another incident which pinpointed the ready skills of our policeman which had not escaped the notice of the force, happened when the Home Office Minister was paying a visit to the municipality of Haifa. This was a formal visit in a large black American Cadillac, chauffeur driven from Tel Aviv to Haifa. The Minister of State was to first join the Mayor of Haifa at the imposing Municipal Offices so that they could be photographed by the press as they publicly shook hands, signalling some recent agreement enabling money to flow from the Treasury to Haifa Municipality, no doubt for proper reasons to do with immigration or other Home Office business. Both the Mayor and Minister belonged to the same party, *Mapai*, thus easing the flow of cash presumably from one coffer to another through correct bureaucratic channels. Yes, Minister!

Unfortunately, after the car had drawn up at the steps of the Municipal building both the chauffeur and the Minister left the car at precisely the same moment, slamming their doors as they did so. The chauffeur quite rightly had moved quickly to get out and open the car door on the other side for the Minister. That independent government official, without due sense of protocol, had in an ungracious manner let himself out of the Cadillac without formal aid. Thus the keys had been left in the ignition and with both the doors closing a security mechanism had come into operation which locked all of them simultaneously. The Minister went into the Municipal offices with the Mayor and journalists while the chauffeur was left on the steps of the building with egg on his face and a burning need to remove it before the Minister re-appeared within half an hour to take a ceremonial trip around the town of Haifa in the limousine, escorted by twenty-four police outriders of which Eli was one.

The Chief of Police in Haifa was on the spot and asked someone to summon Eli to his presence. Eli was motioned to turn his shiny white motorbike around and drive back to where the Cadillac was immobilised. Here the Police Chief stood and his ultimate employer said to him, "Eli, open this bloody car." Having delivered this command the Chief immediately turned his back to him.

Eli muttered, "Yes, sir," as he drew from a pocket a number of hairpins. Our man looked at the Cadillac lock and skilfully bent one hairpin as required. This he entered into the lock and a few seconds later the car door was open and ignition keys withdrawn and handed to a relieved chauffeur. The Chief of Police, still with his back to Eli and having ignored the entire procedure, waited judiciously until the hairpins had been restored to the pocket and Eli had driven back to his position. This happened seconds before the good Minister descended the steps to a car door held open this time by a chauffeur for the Minister and Mayor to be deferentially seated. The parties proceeded on their way with Eli and colleagues at the head of the cavalcade.

It might be interesting to make a point here about Israeli protocol. It is well known that formal dress for MPs, Ministers, members of the Judiciary and all government officers had been abandoned before Israel ever became a nation. In a bid for political equality and freedom rather than concern with climate, the formal tie had been cut out of any sartorial rules from the earliest days of immigration, when bodies were formed that would later become the democratic bedrock of a new State of Israel. An open-necked, white shirt is all that is required above a pair of trousers of indiscriminate grey, blue or black. The shirt sleeves may be short, rolled up or left down and unbuttoned for most government or other business. Jackets and suits hardly exist unless a man needs to diplomatically defy the rule, as with a Prime Minister and his henchmen having to appear on an international stage or TV.

Such sartorial 'cool' had needed no law to frame it, receiving for once in this politically argumentative nation one hundred percent approval. This surely contrasts strangely with the dressing etiquette of many ex-colonial countries, where officials have continued trying desperately to look as well groomed in forty degrees of heat as the ex-colonial masters whom they have deposed. In the case of those earlier British colonies it would seem that not only do officials like *'mad dogs and Englishmen'* go out in the midday sun but do so inappropriately dressed up to match an indelible sartorial precedent which the born-again Israelis, in their pioneering spirit and democratic wisdom, chose first to flout and then to ignore.

But I return to our friend Eli who on coming home from his police patrol duty somewhat earlier than usual one night found himself investigating the strange case of ...

... The Midnight Tomato Picker

As previously mentioned, Mrs Larish was our landlady who owned and had lived in the house we were renting two plots away from our very good friends Ruthie and Eli and their four children. This redoubtable woman, in her late sixties, was generally regarded as a bit of a witch, liked neither by her neighbours and not greatly by her children, as far as we could gather. When love and human kindness were being dished out, Mrs Larish was no doubt hiding from the possibility of being asked to contribute rather than to receive something. So she missed out, as did all those who came into contact with her. Of course, she may well have been a beautiful young woman at some time and life dealt her some bitter blows but of those circumstances we are unaware so we could only judge as we found.

The family Larish had arrived in Ramat Yishai from a kibbutz some time in the nineteen forties or fifties and purchased one of the few private stone houses from its original owner with its half acre plot looking west across the valley and on which fruit trees had been planted. The Maman family had bought their stone house many years later but were living there before Mrs Larish moved out of the village.

Eli Maman loved gardening and planted his plot with fruit and vegetables and had good crops which helped to support his growing family. Our policeman very often worked on night shifts and came home fairly early in the morning and went straight to bed. On this occasion the shifts were changed unexpectedly and Eli was sent home halfway through his shift, arriving around midnight. As he approached his house he became aware that somebody, a shadowy figure, was in his garden doing what he had no idea. Everyone in the house was fast asleep so he took his hand pistol from his belt, went out into the garden and quietly approached the intruder whose back was bent over a row of his tomatoes, picking them at a great rate. The person appeared to be dressed in a long white robe and his first thought was that it might be an Arab. This seemed highly unlikely since none of the Bedouin nor *fellahin*, the farmers, would need or want or take the risk of stealing from a private garden in a Jewish settlement. Eli knew no fear but rather felt excitedly challenged by this situation.

"Stop what you're doing, stay where you are and raise your hands or I'm going to shoot you," he growled loudly with convincing strength of purpose.

The person stood up immediately and as quickly raised their hands whilst dropping the basket they had been holding, with the result that some kilos of tomatoes spilled onto the plot. The thief turned around quickly and Eli recognised in the moonlight that he had his pistol pointed at his neighbour from two doors away, Mrs Larish in her nightgown.

Eli then asked his familiar intruder, "what are you doing in my garden?" to which the swift reply came

"I am not in your garden."

"So where do you think you are?" Eli asked gruffly.

"I'm in my garden," Mrs Larish responded, "and this is my house," she added quickly as an afterthought pointing at the Maman property.

Unsure whether the lady was blatantly lying to cover being caught in her embarrassing misdemeanour or simply sleep walking, he stuck his pistol into his belt, took her gently by the arm and propelled her back to her own house without a further word from either of them.

Meeting Mrs Larish later that day on the road, he asked her

with a wicked twinkle in his eyes if she remembered having visited his garden after midnight. The lady emphatically denied with outraged indignation that she had been anywhere near the place, saying she was always in bed by ten o'clock and why would she do that and how dared he suggest such a thing.

That Eli had not been sleepwalking himself had become evident when he'd returned to pick up the fallen fruit before finally going to bed, still chuckling at the outrageous *chutzpah* of a neighbour, neither poor nor honest, who had not one single tomato plant in her own garden. Until today, Eli could not say for certain whether Mrs Larish was sleep walking or not but had a pretty shrewd idea where the truth lay.

The Mad Militia

Soon after the Yom Kippur War, the second major defeat for the contiguous Arab states in six years, it became clear that feeling was running high amongst many Palestinian Arabs. They were not happy with the additional land that Israel had taken on the Golan Heights but especially with the continuing military occupation of West Bank Palestinian territory and the increased Jewish movement into that area. So it was inevitable that this should lead to a spate of terrorist incursions into Israel proper in 1974 by guerrilla groups or individuals, with the killing of numbers of Israeli citizens in border towns or even deeper into the State. The worst of these in May 1974 was the massacre of twenty-one schoolchildren at Maalot on the Lebanese border. The Israeli government followed this with an equally horrific reprisal bombing raid on a border refugee camp where the innocent also suffered. Two wrongs…as they say!…though no doubt not everyone would view it that way.

Because of the increased terrorist activity in the country it was agreed in government that small towns and villages should mobilise security guards from within their own communities, a sort of Home Guard or local militia. The militia was formed from men who were in the Reserves, having all received military training. In our village the organizing Chief of *Dad's Army* was the Council Secretary, Betzalel Cohen, then a Reserve sergeant. They were a band of seven men from various units including major Goren from the artillery and other ranks from other divisons. They were not supplied with uniforms but were each given an *ouzi* sub-machine gun which, in Arni's case, was kept under our bed at home.

Following its formation the militia met regularly in the council's office where they were instructed on procedure in the case of an alert. They were also taken to the headquarters of the civil defence in Nazareth where they were given a long lecture on the use of their arms in a local civilian setting; what they should or should not do with their guns in particular circumstances and how to act if terrorists took over a house with the occupants inside and so on. It was all rather gruesome but no doubt necessary and having recently served in the war they were none of them lacking in a general understanding of these matters, though close encounters with the enemy had not been everyone's experience.

Beyond forming a local militia, Parliament had previously passed a law that every able-bodied man between eighteen and forty-five could be called upon to guard his community at any time and had to be prepared to give one day a month in that pursuit. This guarding of a village or area of a town normally involved nightly patrols arranged by rota.

In our village a list of patrolmen was in operation and two of them would take it in turn each night to patrol the village either on foot or by car. The men on the rota were warned to expect a simulated attack to take place at some time in the immediate future during which the Ramat Yishai militia would be alerted to respond in accordance with their training.

In the case of any alert, simulated or real, the siren would be sounded and the men of the militia had then to meet as quickly as possible at the council office. On this first occasion of the Secretary's mock terrorist incursion, he was anxious for everything to go as smoothly as possible with an efficient performance from his militia. He therefore phoned his seven-man band that evening and gave them a good ten minutes warning prior to setting off the siren, asking them to converge at the double at the meeting point with their arms primed ready for the 'surprise' attack.

The siren went off some time after ten o'clock that evening and the militia ran, biked or motored with haste to the council office to receive instructions. They were told that a certain house at the centre of the village had been entered by insurgents. The force quickly and silently reached the place and surrounded it in a military fashion to contain both terrorists and whatever simulated action might take place. Beyond initial containment, and unless unforeseen developments demanded an immediate response, it was understood that further counter terrorist action would be within the official domain of the military police, who are immediately summoned in the event of a terrorist incursion. Well that was the procedure by the rules. On this occasion the rest of the community had no idea whether the siren had heralded a real attack or not. People had been told to stay in their houses if the warning siren went off and that if shooting began to take place, they should hit the floor or at least keep their heads well down, holding small children in their arms.

Just when the militia were ready and waiting for some second stage of this practice to take place, something happened that was not in the plan. A few hundred yards from the house they were surrounding and towards our end of the village a sub-machine gun was repeatedly fired. Taken so completely by surprise the Secretary and 'commander in chief' looked at his men in shock. He had no *walkie-talkie* and since mobile phones had not yet been invented and there was no way of getting on the phone immediately to the military police, some action had to be decided upon. But just as the militia were about to sally forth towards the area from which the firing was coming, guns at the ready, the whole village was blacked out. Every light was extinguished, every electrical appliance went dead. At this point Betzalel got in a real panic, turned to Arni as the highest ranking officer among them, having been promoted to major in the Reserves after the war, and told him to take over. Arni reminded Betzalel that he was the 'commander in chief' and had to make the decisions but was told by the Secretary that it was his job as commander to get back to the base and get hold of the military or border police without further delay. He rushed off in the dark to the council office and the little platoon waited for more firing which did not take place.

The border police arrived quite quickly but not before Eli Maman, headlights blazing on his old jeep, came careering up the road towards the militia. Being a policeman, our neighbour Eli was excluded from serving in the militia, which had upset him as he liked to be involved in most male exploits in the village whether boar hunting or man hunting. Eli had naturally received wind of the simulated attack taking place that evening and knowing that most of the militia had been prepared for this, he had decided that a real element of surprise should be part of the practice. So Eli and his good friend, the large, jocular and hairy Chaim, known as 'gorilla', a man of great loyalty but little wisdom, had got into Eli's rattling old World War Two jeep and set off from our road along the perimeter of the village with their own submachine gun. Eli shot into the air a couple of times and it was this that was supposed to put the militia on their mettle and create the real alert. Unfortunately with the second volley it happened that Eli was passing under the main power line across Ramat Yishai and managed to shoot through it, cutting off all the electricity supply to the entire village. At that point he ceased further shooting for obvious reasons of safety to man, beast and commodities.

Although many versions of this story were later told and no doubt cover was given to our good policeman who was very popular, the episode could not go unnoticed and could certainly not have helped Eli along his police career from corporal to higher ranks. As he soon found out, red alerts may be paved with good intentions but seldom with promotions. Whether or not Eli had informed his own family of what he was doing, which was unlikely knowing him, he nevertheless left his neighbours, including me and the children, doing as they had been ordered. On hearing the gun fire, we hit the deck in the dark where we remained for quite a while until shouting had grown to the proportions of argument and, recognising the voices, I began to realise it was all part of a practice rehearsal, dangerous as that might have been. I had thought that the black-out was a bit over the top before I learned how it had occurred. Fortunately our two boys were too young to be afraid and in their innocence decided it had all been rather exciting.

When Arni got home an hour or two later, the children were back in bed. Candles had been lit awaiting a return of power and we popped the cork of a bottle of wine grateful for our delivery from reality and sat laughing at the antics of our neighbour and his crack shot that could pass through an electric cable, surely an impossible feat had he aimed to achieve it with a single volley. Whether Eli was laughing quite as loudly at that time in the presence of the military police, to whom he had been summoned, remains doubtful but the tale served up in good company in the future sparked considerable hilarity.

Considering the grimmer background to this amusing incident involving all the frailties as well as strengths of ordinary village folk, it was universally understood then, as it must be in all theatres of war, that life has to go on. The cat has to be put out and the washing brought in. Shortly after the abortive efforts of 'the mad militia' in Ramat Yishai, another eight men, women and children going about their daytime business were gunned down in a town on the Lebanese border. Such situations bringing tragedy and death for the few cannot be dwelled upon by the many to a point of mental and physical paralysis ~ even for those close to the victims. We have no choice but to keep going.

Like pebbles on a beach, smashed time and again by giant waves, we shift and slide, continuing to chatter or sing as the tide draws us out to a different line. Even stones may laugh, for all we know.

Landscape of Many Colours

We were running up to Christmas 1974, fourteen months after the Yom Kippur war had officially ended but in its wake with Arni waiting to finally complete his extended Reserve service on the 27th December.

Around the same time *Chanukah* (dedication) with its celebration of the festival of lights was taking place to commemorate the re-dedication of the Temple by Judas Maccabeus in 165 BCE. There were to be parties for the children at their *'ganim'*, nurseries, with traditional *suvganiot* or doughnuts, candles lit every night for eight days and presents for all. A second-hand, two-wheeler bike had been repaired and painted for Adam by an old boy in the village and a wooden train was waiting for Matti with other presents from England to be opened on Christmas Day.

Arni could not be with us on the 25th but he had wangled a good week at home from Friday 13th to Friday 21st December. On the Sunday we suddenly decided after lunch to jump in the car, in my case heave myself in as I was over seven months pregnant by then, to enjoy a few hours at Jodfat in the lovely hills above Kefar Cana. Cana was the small, Christian and Moslem Arab village not far north-east of Nazareth famed for the 'water-into-wine' story of the wedding at Cana in the New Testament. It was a beautiful sunny afternoon and since the rains the area was greening up again, looking fresh and lively. Where we finally stood with our boys in those lovely hills was of special interest historically. Our knowledgeable Israeli driver and guide outlined the story for us.

Arni explained that we were standing on the very hill on which the final battle had taken place between Josephus Flavius, General in command of the Jews and later simply called 'Josephus', and the Romans under Vespasian during the Jewish Revolt of 66 C.E. Following an all-out siege which could only result in victory to the Romans, Flavius and his men decided to commit suicide rather than be captured. But just in the nick of time, as it were, and luckily for both Flavius and chroniclers of history to come, the young Jewish General received a 'message from God' telling him to surrender and offer his services to Vespasian with the flattering advice, from heaven-knows-where, that the man would become Caesar within nine months. The life of Flavius was spared, with hopefully that of his men, and indeed within the nine months his prophecy came true. Vespasian was made Caesar and Josephus thenceforth became the official 'Roman' historian of the times.

You may look upon that story with as much cynicism or credulity, blame or praise, as you wish. Certainly it smacks more of an existentialist expediency, if you prefer, than hard-line ideology but if one is to judge history by the results it was a fine move. Josephus became the greatest historian of his day leaving a legacy of what reads as surprisingly dispassionate and objective reporting of the continuing struggles in the area between the Roman Empire builders and the indigenous Jews.

It was as a Roman subject that Josephus looked on from within the Roman camp to recount for posterity that heroic last stand and communal suicide of the revolutionary Jews living on the fortified desert mount of *Masada*. One wonders what his true thoughts and personal feelings were when the Romans had finally got their battering rams hoisted into place after a very long siege and were able to enter that redoubt high above the Dead Sea, dwelling place of dissident Jews fighting for freedom from Rome. The battering rams on their scaffolding built high on the sheer side of the Mount crashed into the fortification with no response. Nothing stirred within the walls of that quiet place under a quiet sky where they found only the bodies of all the men, women and children lying dead by their own hand in silent testimony to a final victory. Was it possible that some Roman hearts and minds were stung by those self-inflicted deaths after so much energy wasted for so long upon achieving them? Such ultimate sacrifice is awesome.

Where we now stood in a high, wild place not far from the bustling city of Haifa, we could see the Mediterranean peeping through the hills, the Valley of Beit Netofa running towards the Western Galilee and the Jordan Valley and Golan Heights beyond. It was a view point of magnificent historical and landscape proportions. We left it in an amazing sunset which had the Carmel hills ablaze and those hills nearest to us steeped in pinks and purples, browns and violets, while the sky above the sea was streaked with salmon and pale green. For nearly an hour colours shifted and collided across that sky, deepening the tones reflected on the landscape until suddenly the crimson ball of sun disappeared dramatically below the horizon into the sea. We drove back through a Nazareth nestling in its hills and silhouetted against a dark violet night sky alive with the shimmering yellow dots of its lights; sights, sounds and stories in a lifetime not to be forgotten.

The Yemeni Coffee House

Ramat Yishai was attractive not only for its idiosyncratic ways and colourful population but also for its mild climate in the north of Israel.

There were three large Yemeni families who had arrived there from part of a huge *aliyah* from the Yemen in the early fifties, shortly after Independence. They lived together and largely kept themselves to themselves and were responsible for building the Yemeni synagogue in the village, having no difficulty then or later in ensuring a *mineaen*, ten good men and true, for every service. In fact the Hebrew word *mineaen* derives from the ancient Semitic language of the Jews of the Yemen.

Among other goodies which some of these immigrants had brought from their country and hoarded like treasure were coffee beans, regarded as a mainstay of Yemeni life. Somehow these had survived or others been brought over and members of the family decided to try their luck with cultivation. They planted the seeds in pots and nourished and nursed them in the general hope that they would grow and develop to a stage where they might be planted out. This had failed on one or two occasions already and the matter had rested there until the idea struck that the plants might survive if protected throughout the winter period.

More seeds were potted up and the plants responded as usual to the initial care they received and as before began to flourish in their pots, growing as tall as one and a half meters. The decision

183

then had to be made as to what they should do about protecting these plants in the northern Israeli climate, hot in summer but chilly in the winter, down to as low as 12° C, which obviously did not suit an outdoor coffee plant of the Yemeni variety. Coffee is grown in many parts of the world, each genus adapted to a particular climate and altitude, each producing its individual flavour. To be fair, the Arabic and Turkish coffees available in Israel were very good but perhaps there is nothing quite like the reminiscent smell and taste of a coffee you were reared upon.

The families set about erecting a rough timber rectangle of tall posts with a few cross beams joining them over which plastic sheeting had been secured. The whole area covered about six by six meters and was around four meters high. Holes were being dug within this cage and the growing coffee plants placed in them when the family was visited by a member of the regional council planning department. The officer advised them that they appeared to be contravening planning regulations by erecting a dwelling without planning permission and that this should be immediately rectified with plans drawn up and presented to the council.

At this stage the village engineer was called for a consultation. Arni duly went along to the site and the whole story of the coffee production was put before him and he offered to explain all this in detail to the planning officer. After a brief call to the officer, a meeting was arranged on site where Arni showed the man the 'coffee house', which might have had something in common with a castaway's shelter but hardly a family dwelling within a village community.

The officer, in a somewhat patronising manner, suggested that Arni, being new to the village, did not fully understand the situation or have the information to hand which he had. He asked my husband to follow him and walked to the far end of the Yemeni house, where indeed an extension had been built, originally as an outhouse for the laundry. The 'laundry' had been converted to accommodation, housing an extended family which was able to produce children annually, almost as fast as coffee beans. Sex for these orthodox Yemenis meant children, for like 'love and marriage … you can't have one without the other'. It appeared there were a couple more extensions which had been built next to the house for chickens or for goats and so on. All these extensions were now housing the ever extending family.

Arni nevertheless re-iterated that these earlier structures surely did not compromise the obvious 'greenhouse' in which thin rows of coffee trees had already been planted, somewhat tall and spindly rather than bushy as one might hope them to grow. The inspector was not impressed and simply said he had a job to do to ensure that the planning laws were adhered to and would report the matter back to his chief.

The chief, a woman architect and chairman of the regional planning committee, contacted Arni to express her support for her officer and her disapproval of any attempt to contravene the planning laws. My husband insisted, however, that as an engineer the structure under inspection on this occasion was far too flimsy to be used as a dwelling now or later and only suitable for the job for which it was designed, a 'coffee house'. After further discussion it was agreed that she would personally visit the site and asked him to be present.

In due course she turned up with another four members of the committee and the former inspector and they all walked around the 'coffee house' where the plants had been watered and were looking reasonably healthy. The lady admitted that she had never seen such a structure before but that experience had made her suspicious of the owners' intentions and she was still not convinced that it would not be converted to a dwelling later, however rough, rude and without foundations it appeared at that moment. She spoke briefy with her inspector and then drew her committee members to one side and out of earshot they discussed the matter further between them.

Finally, the lady called Arni over and said that it had been decided by her inspector that the framework under viewing could now be regarded as a 'coffee greenhouse' and as such would not require planning permission. However, as an addendum to this agreement it had been decided by all the members present that every other extension that had been previously erected required retroactive planning permission.

So the case of the Yemeni 'coffee house' was settled with Arni applying on behalf of the family for belated planning permission for all the extra rooms that had been added over the previous five years. Of course this cost the family something but at least they did not have to pull the extensions down, leaving family members without a roof over their heads. Arni was also paid for his professional services with politeness and gentle, knowing smiles.

Now whether our Yemeni friends ever considered that the planning costs they had brought upon their own heads were truly worth the unfulfilled dream of growing their own coffee remains in the realms of speculation. We have no idea whether or not those thin caged trees on that shrinking Yemeni plot in Ramat Yishai ever bore beans for grinding into good oriental coffee. But there can be no doubt that the aspiration to whatever scheme the Yemenis were dreaming up had acted on their minds and imaginations in as stimulating a way as any thick, dark Yemeni brew.

Two For the Price of One ...

I was writing home, scratching my legs like mad, sniffing and suffering from the wintry weather outside and the cold in my head. This was just a day before being rushed one month early to Afula hospital around 10.30 pm to give birth. The scratching was a last minute reminder that pregnancies produce as many strange symptoms and addictions towards the end of the nine months as in the early morning sickness of the first weeks, which happily I had avoided.

It was the 7th January, 1975 and although I was weighing no more than sixty-four kilos, ten stones, the baby felt much bigger than I'd experienced before. No matter which way I turned I was unable to bend, although bending over backwards seemed slightly easier but of little use if I wanted to pick toys off the floor. I also found it difficult getting my shoes on. We had unfortunately sacked our cleaner, Jemina, that lady of the fast tongue and slow hand, not simply because she wanted to wash the floors with the carpets in situ but because raising her hourly rate ~ according to union rules she said ~ was becoming a weekly demand and beyond both our pocket and our patience. Anyway, I always had to clean up after her.

In my letter to my parents I said that our cat, Hammy, was putting on weight in sympathy without being pregnant and I had been amused by Adam's neat explanation to our neighbour that the baby would not come out of mummy's tummy yet because it was too cold. I also mentioned that I had been reading an article suggesting that Georgians can live for ever, well almost. Just then, having difficulty in breathing due to totally congested nasal passages and the problem of a rash on my nether limbs, I was just longing for the day, a few weeks ahead, when I might get back to normal. Living for ever was not uppermost in my mind at that moment. The Georgians, however, were an interesting diversion for an expectant mum sitting down to read a magazine for five minutes.

The Georgian credo I read, according to one of their youngsters of just a hundred years of age, stated that apart from a largely vegetarian diet of yoghurt, nuts and honey, life should be free of extraneous tension. In other words, it was alright to pull or push a plough but not to pull or push around your own or other people's personalities. Temper was considered as potent as poison and prolonged emotional excesses or stress were to be avoided as far as humanly possible. Ah, so they were not talking about the gods here! Exercise, on the other hand, that wasn't forced or putting you under pressure...how? ... was very important but equally the body should be perfectly relaxed in repose. So laughter, I presumed, had to be gentle and nothing like the loud guffaws I usually let out when hugely amused. Environmental pollution was out of the question.

I had pondered on all that, wondering whether Georgian women, who did most of the work, lived as long as Georgian men ~ and how did the girls manage their pregnancies in that culture spanning east and west, ancient and modern more or less. I realised that taking the basic recipe for longevity seriously, few of us today and fewer Georgians in the future would be able to employ or enjoy it. I say 'enjoy' because living longer has to be healthy to be even vaguely desirable. But even Georgia was now 'on the map' and no longer out of reach of tourists or the effects of global dust and greenhouse gases.

So in bidding farewell in 1975 to a Georgian who had just died aged one hundred and sixty eight ~ a man born when Napoleon was fighting at Austerlitz yet who'd outlived the Second World

War by thirty years and had three wives, or widows, present in the *cortège* ~ we were probably saluting not only the last hope of a quiet life away from it all but the last 'old soldier' who'd never fought a war: a 'soldier' who was literally still in the saddle well into his hundreds and whose final bride of twenty-four he had married aged eighty and with whom he'd sired several more children. Apparently the old man believed that it was far healthier to be involved with the community than with yourself, which was obviously borne out by his multiple sexual successes ~ and possible proof that morbid introspection never won fair lady.

Here was I, and indeed here were most of us, fighting or recovering from wars, breathing dirty air, competing for a place on the ladder of life, arguing, jogging even but still reproducing and looking for happiness at any price, whether on our supermarket shelves, in our sex shops or with our super gurus. I was learning where we had gone wrong but it was too late now and I could do little but get on with it. And so it seems to happen in life whether you're a Georgian or not.

As the old story began, 'it was a dark and stormy night', the rain was lashing down and poor Arni had to get a wife in labour, late on the evening of the 8th January, into the car and drive about twelve miles to the hospital down the valley. He left me there in a birth room and rushed home to look after the children whom he had been asked to take to their grandparents when I went to have the baby because Klara did not want to come to 'the hole' that she called Ramat Yishai. I had stated that the kids should stay at home with my neighbour and continue to go to the nursery with the least change from routine, a request that was ignored to keep mum-in-law happy in being seen to do the right thing.

It was close to midnight in the Afula hospital, two nursing midwives were on duty and I had no notes with me. Never mind, time was running out and the pains were coming faster as they tried to get a temperature reading by sticking a thermometer in my mouth. Regrettably I had to spit it out since there was no other way I could breathe with my nose totally blocked. I tried between contractions to explain and asked them to stick it under my armpit. They were not amused. By this time the baby was on its way out at a quarter to midnight and only then did the nurses begin to look surprised as they prodded my abdomen. Something like panic started to cross their faces on suddenly realising there was yet another baby to deliver. They had been given no instruction that twins were on the way from me or anybody else and this seemed to throw them right off course. They began rushing about looking for an obstetrician who was not 'in the house' at midnight and then appeared to be upset with me for not informing them. I seemed unable to convince them that I had not myself been told.

Well, we all had to get on with it, no alternative. The first baby, 'a boy', they told me, had slipped out with little difficulty. If only '*he*' had been a '*she*' I thought in a flash; the second could have been either, I would not have minded. With only five minutes between the births I was too busy to be able to ask them not to tell me the sex of the second baby but to keep it as 'a little surprise'... I already had my doubts. I really needed a breather to get used to the fifty-fifty last chance, not intending to get pregnant again. "IT'S ANOTHER BOY"...they said confidently at two minutes to midnight, simply glad that both had arrived safely, expected or not. It never occurred to me at that moment of gender naming to worry about whether the twins were identical. Just as well. I was later overjoyed that at least I had given birth to two non-identical brothers, although I'm sure other mothers of twins might not have been so 'picky'. So Abigail never arrived but Ben and Dan took her place and they were lovely and still are.

Next morning, when staff had found me a proper bed after I'd spent a fretful night leaking from my nose downwards in a make-shift fold-up bed on the floor in the centre of a crowded maternity ward full of wailing Arab mums from nearby Nazareth, my first thought was naturally to hold my babies. They had been taken straight to the premature unit after their births. Realising I had a nasty cold I accepted that this initial contact might be best left for a few days until I recovered but little realised it would be weeks rather than days I would have to wait before I could hold them for the first time.

Being a month early the twins were small, just over two kilograms each. In their modern medical wisdom, the Israeli hospital doctors in 1975, who were fine and clever but somewhat arrogant in their approach to the mother, decided they knew best and that the twins would not only have to be taken to a special unit but the mother would not be allowed to touch them or be with them in that unit until they had gained sufficient weight to go home. That way the small babies would avoid the additional hazard of germs from outside. Strange thinking, when you consider how important the mother's body is to a newborn babe and how its immunity is built up with that contact, not to mention the immunity from breast feeding as soon as possible. Surely the babies could be taken to their mums in a room set aside for that purpose.

Some years later they learned from experimentation with the new-born 'joeys' just out of the kanga's pouch that their survival in their tiny, vulnerable and hairless state depended absolutely on their clinging fast to the warm and humid body skin of the mother before they began to feed. This principle, no doubt long understood and practised by less privileged mothers across the world, is now applied to mothers of premature babies in the developed world! I wondered how on earth they could imagine that a healthy mother might infect her own baby more than nurses coming in and out of the premature unit daily? The agony of only being able to look at my twins during five long weeks with my face pressed against an outside window of the unit was pretty traumatic. Not a happy memory. After the helpless feeling of several such visits, I would not go there again until the babes were ready to come home despite yearning for them.

The next hurdle I had to cross concerned my desire to breast-feed my babies and therefore the need to ask for advice on expressing the milk while I was still in hospital. I had already been given pills to dry up my milk without being asked whether I wanted to do this or not. When I made a bit of a fuss about this it was arranged that a consultant would come and explain matters to me. He arrived in due course and despite my somewhat frail emotional state due to the circumstances of the birth and lack of contact with my babies, I was firmly informed that babies would never feed from the breast after having been put on the bottle for days, if not a fortnight or more. In asking why that was, seeing that breastfeeding was the most natural and instinctual thing for any mammalian, the man shrugged his shoulders and ignoring my question in a most condescending manner, repeated his mantra of 'never never'. He smiled at my ignorance, it seemed, and ordered more 'drying' pills. I was furious, threw them in the bin and was determined when I got home later in the week to obtain a breast pump as quickly as possible.

Getting my hi-jacked older boys back from the kibbutz, dealing with an affronted mother-in-law (who'd arrived on my doorstep with flowers and cake for my homecoming) and expressing milk without clinical support was hard, especially the latter. I remembered the Georgian way of life and wondered where and how I could relax in repose or even find repose. But having stuck to my guns for the full five weeks, nature rewarded me with the biggest blessing. Following the huge joy of collecting Dan and Ben from the hospital on a bright Spring day at the end of February, I sat on the sofa in my bedroom with a twin at each breast and behold... they sucked and sucked and the milk flowed. It was one of the most wonderful moments in my life.

Life was indeed hectic and Dan and Ben very different temperamentally. Dan was determined, eager and physically alert while Ben was a cuddly lazybones who would have been happy to be nursed all day long. Dan had his feed and then got on with life. Ben hung around sucking slowly and crying if you tried to hurry him. I fed Dan for an indulgent thirteen months, while he still wanted it. We decided Ben was probably not taking enough on board to put on sufficient weight and after a couple of months I weaned him onto goats' milk in a bottle which seemed the next best thing. I felt both babies had received as good a start in life as nature had allowed and despite Israeli medical misunderstanding. More of the goat to follow!

Brother Itzhak & the Wayward Saab

Once again Arni was away on Reserve service and I had been left with Emma, the goat, as well as holding the babies. As it happened I just could not master the knack of milking Emma, though the twins appeared to have no such trouble in my regard. Well, one of them at least. Daniel was a fine little feeder and sucked briskly to his complete satisfaction, turning to other matters when he'd had his fill. Ben, as I said before, was a dilettante who surely thought I was available to sit and nurse him all day at a leisurely pace, as he frequently stopped to stare at the world around him. It was all very well for that Super-Tramp, W.H.Davis, to lean on a gate and rant on about *'What is this life if full of care, you have no time to stand and stare'* ~ but what about the mothers!? … was my thinking. So Ben was getting plenty of practice at staring but his increasingly nervous mum found it hard to let down the milk in these circumstances. Just such nervousness overtook me in regard to milking Emma, who plainly refused after the merest dribble to let down her milk despite a full bag and all my tentative pulling and squeezing. She simply held on, reproaching me for not relieving her of the weight of her bag and getting tetchy with my clumsy handling of her teats.

We had bought Emma, a lovely white Saanan, from the children's farm at Arni's kibbutz and she had been delivered with two kids to Ramat Yishai so that we would be able in due course to bottle feed the slow-coach Benji with milk closest molecularly to mother's milk, since he was not getting enough from me. So here was I with a goat to milk and a baby to feed and drying up in both quarters. My friend, Adrienne, offered to come to the rescue when Arni was away if I could pick her up from her house in the car and take her back, as time was precious to her first thing in the morning. Adrienne was a natural with any animal and had kept goats herself at some stage in her life in England, so she was a godsend to me. On this occasion the twins were blissfully sleeping in their cot, so I thought I would quickly take Heidi home following her milking Emma, without disturbing the children.

It was a hot August day and the two older boys were spending a few days holiday on the kibbutz to give me a rest. As we crossed the village at eight o-clock that morning Adrienne asked if we could just pop in very quickly to see somebody living on the track behind our garden at the end of the village. I parked the car in first gear, I thought, as the handbrake did not work properly. Now the Saab had an overdrive which I did not use but my husband frequently used. So the car was without a handbrake and neither was it apparently in gear. After momentarily getting out of the vehicle to greet Adrienne's friend, I watched in slow motion as the car began to roll silently across the road. Before I could get to it, the Saab had run down a slope into the woman's garden, missing an empty children's playpen by inches, to stop after hitting the mains water pipe at a corner of the house.

There was no damage to the house and little to the car but the pipe burst and the water spurted out, leaving the woman without water in the house. I was so hugely relieved that there had been no children in the playpen that I hardly thought about what to do next. Suddenly I was aware that my babes were at home on their own. Adrienne was sent hot foot to look after the twins while I placated the woman whose acquaintance I had only just made, assuring her on absolutely no authority whatsoever that I would get a plumber to mend the burst main immediately.

I then had to think whether or not I knew a plumber in the village. There was one. He was the cheeky brother of our friend and neighbour, Eli Maman. I managed to start the car without causing further damage, backed up the garden slope onto the road and went off in search of brother Itzhak. I had little hope of finding him, I thought, because it was by then nearly nine and most folk were at work by eight. I just wished someone would know where he was. There was, however, a further difficulty if not acute embarrassment to be faced.

Itzhak, with his wicked, dark eyes and sexy looks was married to a nice girl called Varda and she was well aware of the fact that her husband was a lady's man, forever flirting with the women and generally behaving in a less than reliable fashion as far as earning and spending was concerned. Eli and he came from a large family of Jews, Algerian on their father's side who had settled in Palestine from around the late nineteenth century. As fine craftspeople the Mamans had been invited to live and work in one of the country's oldest and most prestigious agricultural communities, Moshav Nahalal, a couple of miles from our village. All the males in the Maman family that I knew were clever artisans and very artistic but tended to live on a 'come day, go day' basis, a happy-go-lucky approach to life which did not always bring home the bacon, or beef I should say.

It just so happened that a couple of months before my little accident, Arni and Itzhak had fallen out over a payment due to my husband for architectural plans. Itzhak's business tactics had gone down badly with Arni who had unfortunately lost his temper, falling right into the wrong court. This had given Itzhak leave to act offended and to refuse to have anything more to do with Arni, for as long as it suited him to keep payment at bay, which could of course be indefinitely, despite brother Eli's embarrassment and protests with his younger brother. Now Itzhak was the man I had to seek out and from whom I had to ask a favour to get me out of an equally difficult and embarrassing situation for me.

Meanwhile I knew that the longer it took to get the pipe mended the more metered water I would have to offer to pay for apart from paying Itzhak. Eventually I found my plumber doing some work for himself and told him of my predicament with red cheeks, as he obviously knew I was aware of the 'awkward' relations between him and Arni. He unashamedly looked me up and down as I stood there in my shorts and sun top and laughed with ill-hidden glee. The situation quite obviously appealed to his sense of humour. Well, he was on a job and if he came, it would be another hour, he told me. I swallowed my pride and smilingly said, "Fine, I'll wait for you at the house, you wont let me down now, will you Itzik?"

"How much is it worth?" he joked, winking at me. He had a penchant for blondes, like his wife.

I went back to the burst pipe, wishing I could bung it up like the little Dutch boy at the dyke. I also wondered, as you do, why this had happened to me and upon whom I could legitimately place the blame for my acute humiliation and embarrassment. But again I thanked my lucky stars that no-one had been hurt, especially children, which did not bear thinking about. So I put on a brave face, told the householder that Itzhak would be along shortly and waited a full hour before he turned up with some pipe, the necessary unions and a bag of tools. "Thank goodness," I thought, "he has finally come to the aid of this lady in double distress, if only for the wicked pleasure he was getting out of it."

He set to work immediately, adding a final touch of piquancy to the situation.

"I need a plumber's mate," he said, grinning from ear to ear, "do you know what these tools are called?" He pointed to an assortment of spanners and wrenches and a mole grip for which I could only guess at the Hebrew.

"Sure," I replied with a confident smile that belied the fact..

"*Tov*. So, when I want a tool, I'll ask you for it. You will be the plumber's mate."

Just so Itzhak put me in my place. I was the architect's wife brought low but he did it with such a mixture of *chutzpah*, flirtation and malicious humour that I could do nothing but laugh and hand him the tools he could well reach for himself. I secretly wanted to crown him with them. He did a good job, though, and I offered with alacrity to go back to the house and get the money to pay him on the spot, so glad was I to see the water flowing out of the kitchen tap and not into the garden. And surely I could make my moral point with no haggling and a prompt payment. But he smoothly told me he would accept cash the next day as he knew I had to get back to the babies. Naturally I honoured my end of the deal and he had more than the cash out of this little misadventure. He made sure the story of Arni's wife bursting a water main with her incompetent driving and pleading for his help went all around the village.

That incident may well have given Itzhak some temporary moral high ground following the dubious dispute and it was not long before he and Arni were speaking again and compromising over the question of what was owed to whom, the compromise basically being all on Arni's side of course. But since both men had a sense of humour and in the game of life this was given the priority on this occasion, they were no doubt able to joke about their respective wives, as most men enjoy doing given the opportunity, or one wife in particular in this case.

Somehow Adrienne's part in this story got temporarily lost but I always had the strange feeling that I could never feel one hundred per cent safe with my friend for whom life inevitably turned up the bad penny. Of course the incident had absolutely nothing to do with poor Adrienne and everything to do with an unreliable car but you know how the 'ifs' come out on these occasions … *if Adrienne had not asked me and I had not agreed to take her to see that lady…*and so on. I pondered on all the strange mishaps that seemed to involve my friend on an almost daily basis.

Poor, good, kind and 'flying crooked' Adrienne, what will happen to you in heaven, I wondered? Wasn't it Robert Graves who said in his poem about the butterfly, the cabbage-white "… *its honest idiocy of flight, will never now, it is too late, master the art of flying straight.*" There was something light and bright and uneven about Adrienne's character and a certain emotional fragility.

Perhaps she was a butterfly in a former life. Graves went on in his poem to describe his butterfly's artlessness as a *'flying crooked gift'*.

Notwithstanding Itzhak and the wayward Saab and no matter how Adrienne's flight through life might be measured, I realised that my friend was indeed a gift to me, and certainly to poor Emma the goat, even if she was not always her own best friend.

Avigdor, Alexander & the Yemeni Funeral

One day the two veteran horsemen Avigdor and Alexander of *HaShomer*, 'The Guards', found themselves on the outskirts of the village at a funeral of one of the revered eldermen of the Yemeni community who had died simply of old age and good fortune. It was only when the family were gathering in the cemetery that some of the men felt they were short of a required *maenean*, the ten men necessary for any religious office. There were actually more than ten men present but in this instance the family decided the basic *maenean* should be augmented to twenty in honour of the deceased who had been very well respected.

Arni was working in his office that day when a Yemeni villager knocked on his door and told him about the imminent funeral of his relative Hamid. He asked if Arni would kindly join the *maenean*. It was not really a question for a man could not refuse such a request, being one of those occasions where *noblesse oblige*. My husband's irritation at being pulled away from a job that was running late was only increased when he found there were already more than ten men present but was glad to see his good friends Avigdor and Alexander among the throng of wailing Yemeni mourners. They too had been corralled in for the occasion and Arni stood behind them on the bare hillside of the village cemetery.

Avigdor and Alexander had belonged to *HaShomer* from the 1930s to the 1950s. The Guards had been set up in the very early days of the 1920s when there were few Jewish settlers in the land called Palestine, which had been under the Turks for several centuries to 1918 and then under a British Mandate from 1920 to 1947. In the days between the two world wars the members of *HaShomer* had dressed like the Arabs or at least wore the *keffiyeh*, the traditional Bedouin headdress, and had surely looked dashing on their fine Arab steeds for which they paid good money. These young men had patrolled the small Jewish settlements in the Galilee with pride and courage.

Where these two 'old guards' were now standing in the cemetery of Ramat Yishai they were looking across the wide, cultivated floor of the beautiful Jezreel Valley to the high, sloping banks of the Carmel foothills and to the cemetery belonging to the small, suburban township of Tivon. Within that cemetery was a special plot for the guardsmen of *HaShomer*, which was within their sights and was well established under a grove of huge pine trees. The guards from the old days were all buried in this shady plot in nice neat rows. Every year a memorial ceremony would take place there to pay tribute to the many courageous young and older men; some had sacrificed their lives in guarding scattered Jewish agricultural communities from marauding Bedouin who often made surprise raids on the settlements to steal livestock, occasionally killing some of the inhabitants in the ensuing fray.

The funeral service progressed and the Yemeni rabbi began reciting the prayers for the dead, the *Kadish*, which is basically the same for all Jewish denominations in any country. However this rabbi was taking his time in his own language which none of the *Ashkenazim* like my husband and our two friends could understand. The whole performance seemed at least five times longer than the service they were used to attending, once a year perhaps. They tried valiantly to follow the core of Yemeni men, nodding when they nodded and shouting Amen when they did.

Boredom was setting in when Arni heard Avigdor whispering quietly to Alexander asking him if he liked this place, to which Alexander replied, "Well it's very nice but it's a little open to the elements on hot days like this." There was not a finger of shade. Then a fiercely quiet discussion followed concerning where they both wished to be buried.

Alexander loved his home in Ramat Yishai and did not associate himself with the nearby town of Tivon at all and felt he would be happier in this very cemetery in his home village. Avigdor then pointed out that their plots had been reserved for them in the cemetery of 'HaShomer' in Tivon and that this was where they both belonged with their old colleagues and friends when the time came…

"Besides that," Avigdor reminded Alexander, "as well as being in the shade, the air over there under the pines is much fresher from the western winds and smells sweeter."

To this Alexander could offer no further argument and both seriously nodded to each other in general agreement that indeed the cool and well-aired burial spot on the far side of the valley under the pines would be the most comfortable and honourable final resting place for them both.

When their time came, I know that Avigdor was taken across the valley to the pine-scented cemetery of the 'old guards'. Our dear friend Alexander sadly died in the 1980s shortly after our return to England. We believe he remained true to his original intentions and was buried in Ramat Yishai where most of his family were living and where Yudit, his stalwart and loving companion of a lifetime, was to join him some years later under the blazing sun and the winter rains on the bare hillside of their beloved village.

I know less about Avigdor but can believe that in his young days he had been a very fine young man. He was Caucasian, tall, straight and broad with blue eyes and being an expert horseman must have attracted young ladies by the score. We understood that he had remained a bachelor for a long time until one day when he met a Yemenite girl called Shulamit. At the time she was a very promising young singer famous for her folksongs. She had a beautiful voice and she fell in love with Avigdor, who in turn had finally met a woman whose sensual charms held him spellbound. He married her. After their marriage, however, Avigdor insisted that she stop her singing career as he was mightily afraid she would attract too many younger men through the power and seductive quality of her voice. That is what he said, although he failed to mention that she was also very attractive whether she was singing or not with a fine figure, oval face, beautiful dark brown, almond shaped eyes and shiny long black hair. More to the point she was considerably younger than her husband.

Arni had cause on one occasion to visit them in their stone house along our street and Avigdor's wife had answered the door. He was very impressed with her still beautiful face despite by then being well into her fifties.

The couple had a son and a daughter and the quiet Avigdor had along the way acquired quite a lot of land in Ramat Yishai. Much of the valley below us where he grew watermelons belonged to him. Having been a guard before Independence he had learned to speak fluent Arabic and after 1948 was known to have been in various partnerships with the Bedouin. His reputation for being fierce but fair enabled him to act as middle man in various deals which involved him meeting with the Bedouin in places to which most Israelis had no safe access. He was also a crack shot and one way and another, but mostly from his business with the tribesmen, he earned a lot of money with which to buy the land he accumulated.

His younger wife sadly died some time before him. On Avigdor's death his son inherited the land for which he applied for change of usage from agricultural to building at a time when Ramat Yishai was moving into a new era of development. The younger generation were facing different challenges in a very different political and technological environment and for them property development deals would take the place of land cultivation as a way to make an easier living.

Avigdor lived until well into his eighties and my husband learned of his fate only in 1995 when he came into contact with Avigdor's accountant who had been in the army with Arni at one stage. Apparently the *old guardsman*, living on his own, started to develop pains which did not decrease and after suffering for some time he had sought medical advice. He was given tests and told finally that he had an incurable cancer. On receipt of that news he came home, took out his hand pistol, went into his garden and shot himself, leaving no message for anyone. Avigdor, like his friend Alexander, was a good and courageous man. He remained solitary and strong to the end.

✦

Mordecai Son of Jaacov &
the Family Kirschenbaum ...
Builders United!

Mordecai, a man of middle years, was one of the Ramat Yishai old
school, scratching a living, we thought, from a little of this and a
little of that. He rented land on a short lease from a local farming
community and would cultivate this with a small tractor and drill
and other bits of equipment which he kept in a shed near the
house. He would sow and reap different crops in different seasons
or maybe keep the land for a year or two for a better turnover. To
supplement this existence he also kept a flock of milking sheep in
Ramat Yishai, which was by then quite an unusual sight in our fast
developing village. But there were one or two other smallholders
left like him such as Pinye with his single milking cow and our
neighbour Muscal who reared a couple of calves for veal next door,
which desperately upset me though 'other countries, other ways…'
as they say.

Mordecai's flock of sheep was quite substantial, probably nearly
a hundred woolly heads and he would lead them to any grazing he
could find around the village on land not under lease and buy in
feed when this dried up in May to October. This uncultivated land
he had occasionally to share with the Bedouin and their goats,
who were not an uncommon sight across the road from our house
during the winter months.

One day the man approached my husband, took him by the arm and said, "Engineer, I want to build a house here," and pointed to his plot.

"So, what do you want," Arni enquired.

"I want two bays at the ground floor for shops and living accommodation above." The engineer was surprised if not shocked at Mordecai's rather grand designs.

Arni produced some drawings according to his client's requirements with two bays of about four and a half meters across and six meters deep, making a substantial building of just over nine meters wide and two storeys high. Drawings were presented to the council, permission given and the work went ahead with the driving of piles into the ground for substantial foundations at six meters, a costly concern all together.

While this work was in progress Arni received a call from Mordecai asking him to go to the site. The client then said that his wife was pregnant again (*Maazel Tov!*) and he had decided to build on another two bays. The connection between these matters escaped Arni, unless Mordecai was thinking of building an annexe to keep his wife 'at bay' to allay further conception, but Arni reminded Mordecai that he had only received permission to build the two bays and in any case his land did not extend far enough for further additions without compromising the statutory width for a vehicular entrance to the building from the road.

"Never mind, you just carry on," he told Arni without the least hesitation or change of expression and added, "and then I want to extend the flat upstairs and to build another storey above that."

Arni remembers smiling indulgently at the time for it does not do to exhibit professional or other indignation before a client, especially out of doors on a building site in a small village, but having left the scene of the conversation he did not go beyond his brief for the original building and did not produce any further drawings for alterations or extensions which he knew would contravene rules.

If approached about progress in the matter, Arni decided to tell Mordecai to look for another engineer without adding 'someone with a more flexible approach'. But why blame the sheep farmer? Perhaps he had '*friends at court*' and surely numbers of substantial building works would get built 'by default' in Ramat Yishai before the last building plot was covered and if not by our *poor* sheep farmer and his kith or kin then by others with an eye to the main chance and good contacts. What we did learn on this occasion was never to judge even a part-time farmer by his mucky boots and old felt hat, 'where there's muck....'

The Kirschenbaum family had originated in Rumania and this meant, by general and prejudiced consent of others from different backgrounds, a certain dexterity with property, either their own or that of other people. Of course this was simply an old prejudice based rather on a need to feel superior than on any reliable evidence....

The parents had come to Israel from Rumania around 1949 and brought with them four children, two boys and two girls. They grew up in Ramat Yishai with a reputation for succeeding one way or another....often the other! Old man Kirschenbaum, like a certain predecessor called Marks in Manchester, started with a barrow. This he would take to market piled high with produce and soon was able to purchase a proper cart with four wheels and a horse. On this cart he could pile a good number of crates of fresh fruit and vegetables which he sold at all the local villages. As the sons grew up they developed an equally keen zeal for buying and selling and the family did well enough for them to invest in one lorry and later another and so on until they were running a successful haulage business. By this time they were chiefly contracted to building merchants and for the collection and delivery of agricultural equipment. The daughters married in due course and their husbands joined the expanding Kirschenbaum business, which now boasted four men at its helm, six or seven lorries and some hired labour.

The brains behind the business belonged to the eldest Kirschenbaum son who had purchased the first lorry and had great plans for the future. It came to his knowledge that council plans were afoot to build a number of starter homes in the village with three small rooms, a kitchenette and a shower room. There were to be about sixteen of these new semi-detached, single storey houses, eight buildings per plot. Word went out that the council were looking for building contractors and despite little if any direct experience in this area the eldest son registered himself as a contractor, got all the necessary paperwork and presented himself to the council with total confidence and a winning assurance that it would be cheaper and more efficient to employ an 'on the spot' contractor from the village. He was told to put in a tender and no doubt with the help of those in the know was able to produce a viable set of figures. The council offered him the work despite being aware that his business was haulage, for such was the pride and touching faith, perhaps, in keeping business in the community. As it happened, opposite the council development plot there was another vacant plot for sale which the Kirschenbaums promptly bought.

The council buildings began apace and at the same time a building of precisely the same design and dimensions began to emerge on the Kirschenbaum plot across the road. That is to say that on the completion of a double unit on the council plot, a cottage of equal size sprang up on the family plot in place of a single dwelling for which permission had been granted. Naturally, while erecting their own building our contractors already had the architect's plan, the engineer's advice, all the professional information they needed for the council work, not to mention materials delivered to site.

As the council buildings progressed, the contractors applied for permission to build another so called 'single' dwelling on their plot. Permission was strangely granted without too much ado and this new house was raised on pillars a few feet above the original and next to it, well actually attached to it. So this eventually became part of a large split level house upon which yet another storey was later placed. Thus, like Topsy, the Kirschenbaum dwelling grew and grew to quite large proportions without, it seemed, official visits or condemnation so that one day the family could finally boast they had arrived ~ with probably the largest, if a-centric, house in the village. *Chutzpah* had triumphed over normal council constraints and the worst idiosyncracies of planners, who at the oddest times can pretend to 'see no evil, hear no evil, speak no evil' while acting out laws unto themselves and making absolutely no sense whatever to the average homeowner and his applications. A global condition I fear.

Some time after the tenancy occupation of the council housing, the two married Kirschenbaum daughters bought from the council the semi-detached units opposite the brother's large house. They had been living there a little while when we first came to the village. Having learned that Goren was a structural engineer, one of the daughters asked Arni to call around to her bungalow to investigate a problem of water penetration. After Arni had checked various features and possible sources of this infiltration he concluded, without knowing the background history, that the place had been poorly constructed without sufficient materials. The lady looked at him very sternly, stating that this was impossible while explaining that her brother had been the main contractor. She dismissed my husband with no intention of paying for the consultation.

We later heard that Arni was the third engineer who had been invited to inspect the property. It was also gossiped that Arni's report and conclusions had finally caused a bit of a family uproar. Some remedial work was undertaken by the brothers and as soon as possible both sisters sold their ex-council semis to an unwitting buyer for a good price.

It was some time later that Arni learned more about the council building work from a story that leaked out at a party held by Arie, our right-wing Herut man and husband to the second lady mayor. The booze had been flowing and Kirschenbaum boasting about how he had built his large house opposite the council bungalows. He proudly stated that during the building process he had found a use for 'left over' council materials for his own building. That is to say he personally ordered and paid for around half of what he needed for himself. The other half, or a good percentage, was simply 'extra' material from the council work. He had, it seemed, been able to keep within reason any little increases in costs as work progressed without attracting undue attention. He laughingly told his admirers that the council had no reason to complain as he had not taken more for himself than he had left for them; *chutzpah* indeed! From haulage of one kind to haulage of another it seemed! Or perhaps it was just an idle boast, who knows?

Arni had reason to meet the eldest son professionally some while later when he asked him to get involved with property he'd bought in a nearby town. Obviously there had been no hard feelings harboured against him since the earlier encounter with the sister. Perhaps his findings had proved that he was indeed an engineer who knew his stuff. The place he visited had been a small bungalow, like the starter homes in our village, which the brother Kirschenbaum had converted after purchase for use as an office, though without registering change of usage from private to commercial. Mr. Kirschenbaum required Arni's services to draw up plans for an additional storey on top of the existing building.

"And what about change of usage to the ground floor area?" Arni innocently enquired.

"That's no matter" was the prospective client's answer. "What I need is permission to build on, not permission for change of usage of an existing building."

So Arni went ahead and produced site extension plans for the regional council who immediately picked up on the fact that consent had never been requested or given for changing the original building from a dwelling to an office. Well you can't win them all and we understood later the owner had to pay somebody something by way of compensation or punishment for ignoring the rules but permission was granted for a dwelling extension over the office.

One wonders how long that extension remained a dwelling and by how much Kirschenbaum was in pocket by paying the council retrospectively, as it were, for change of usage. There had to be something in it for him. My feeling is you have to be properly 'equipped' to angle in the pools of power where local or regional councils are concerned and my husband never had the fishing rods or bait for that sport. He was far more likely to fall in the lake than get anything out of it.

Ramat Yishai was of course no different from anywhere else in this respect. Councils, planners, the righteous and the unrighteous abound in every community in the world and whether we envy or get annoyed at those who get away with it seems a waste of energy which would be far better spent enjoying a real day's angling under a willow by a river sparkling in the sun.

Christmas with the Cablan

In our third year in Ramat Yishai, Arni was building for us a highly individualised, family house on columns of nearly two and a half meters. For one half of the building, facing south, a man-made heap of earth gently sloped up from the garden enveloping the columns to a wall dividing the front and back halves of the building. This earthy mound afforded entrance to the living area through a pair of large French doors and was known jokingly around the village as *tel Goren*, or Goren's hill. From the north-facing rear of the structure you could see through the exposed pillars to the dividing wall and the steps to the main entrance door on the side at the back. The shaded half under the pillars at ground level would be used for hanging the washing and parking the car.

There were other features of our personally designed house, on a piece of land near the central crossroads, which made it stand out as being unlike any other building in the village. We had terra-cotta, Marseilles half-pipe tiles to a pitched roof with dormers in it above the staircase and bedrooms at the rear, most unusual then in Israel. The living area opposite was octagonal with a flat roof entered from a turning on the stairs and surrounded by a wrought-iron balustrade, which like the staircase had been designed by myself and executed by the village blacksmith. A few discreet lamps were to be installed at intervals around the balustrade, tilted from floor level to cast a soft light over the tiled area where we might sit in the evening to enjoy the long, lovely view down the Jezreel valley with its twinkling lights from the scattered settlements.

On the east side *'But, soft! what light from yonder window breaks?'* we had a pretty, curved, wrought-iron Juliet balcony to the main bedroom and wooden shutters on the windows. Before it was finished and could be named it was already called *bet anglit* 'the English house'. But to achieve our architectural wishes we were dependent upon our contractor, or *cablan*, who was a charming Christian Arab from Nazareth, Said Besharat.

Arni and Said became friends and fortunately Said proved extremely patient in dealing with all of our weird whims and wishes, even to the point of knocking out blocks to redesign a window already in place. I had wanted the high, arched window on the turn of the staircase to be tall enough to frame a wonderful, curvy cyprus tree in an adjacent garden.

Somehow the window had been built sixty centimeters short of the design height so that as you walked up the stairs the head of the tree at the half landing was missing from view. The fact that the tree might grow taller or that the neighbour might cut it down at some stage did not occur to me in my architectural enthusiasm. For the time being the window on the staircase framed a real life picture, a Van Gogh of a deep blue-green, wavy *cupressus* that could rock wildly in the wind, as his trees did, and change colour as the light changed, as his paintings would. The arch was the feature which took some time and cost to re-instate but it was done to satisfy my mad whims, despite my husband's annoyance.

By December of 1975 the new house was well on its way and my parents were coming to visit us for Christmas. Said, knowing that Arni's wife and family were not Jewish, requested us all to join his family at his home in Nazareth to celebrate Christmas Eve. Midnight Mass would be relayed on TV from the Church of the Annunciation in the town centre, as well as TV film of scenes of the festivities from St. Peter's Square in Rome. All this would be flashing quietly at us when we sat to eat at our host's table alongside his extended family; his father, brothers and in-laws.

The women, including Said's wife, mother, daughters, sisters and brothers' wives would remain discreetly in the background and serve at table. My mother and I were to be the only women sitting with the men.

We had been talking with our neighbour, Alexander Shoshani, of the intended visit and he asked to come along with us, which was perfectly in order and especially as we were very fond of him and knew that he enjoyed a party with the odd dram or two. We had arranged for the children to be looked after and the five of us piled into our small old Saab, with Arni driving and my father beside him. We climbed up towards Nazareth at dusk looking forward to a special occasion. Indeed we were made very welcome in Said's large house, which they had gradually built over a number of years as funding became available.

The rooms were tall, the floors attractively tiled and there was colourful patterned tiling on the walls and many other decorative features. The spacious rooms were at least twice the size of any of ours and the house was built near the top of a steep maze of streets densely occupied on the very hilly, rocky ground of the old Arabic town. Said's father, in the traditional Arabic tunic, was sitting cross-legged on a cushion on the floor with a bubbling hookah and a pot of coffee on a little stove beside him. Alexander joined him and remained talking with him for the rest of the evening, downing the Scotch and sharing the hookah and coffee. They were soon deep in conversation, heads nodding, hands dramatically orchestrating emphasis to their words.

The table was laden with good things to eat; tasty *meze*, chicken, lamb, rice, wonderful dishes of spicy mixtures, followed by fruits, including succulent fresh figs, and sweetmeats and finally the rich, dark and sweet Turkish coffee known as *botz* in Hebrew, or 'mud'. Throughout the meal, bottles of every kind of alcohol were passed around, especially whisky which Said's brother, next to me, drank liberally. Arni was sitting on his other side by my parents who needed some translations as English was not the predominant language. There was a good mixture of Arabic and Hebrew and I knew enough of the latter to manage quite well with Said's brother. Being a woman, I was not offered the whisky but had a little wine and a lot of fruit juice. Arni was having difficulty saying 'no' to the spirits with his manly pride at stake so his glass was continually being filled, though he normally drank very little.

As midnight approached we were a very merry crowd indeed and the conversation veered towards the state of the world as we glanced at the screen of the large television beaming down on us from a bracketed perch high on the wall. We heard the Christian message of love and hope being loudly proclaimed to the crowds in both Rome and Nazareth. The clock struck midnight, glasses were raised and through genuine laughter and tears we unanimously agreed that Jew and Arab were brothers, we were all brothers and there was no reason on earth why we should not remain brothers for ever. All we had to do was to love one another. Love was our toast. We knew we had no personal reasons for discord and every reason to get along together and make a safer, better world for our children, as indeed we were all trying to do. To adopt negative and bitter attitudes in the face of current opportunity would be unreasonable and stupid. We hugged each other with, I believe, a real longing for the sort of world about which we shared a common dream, along with most other human beings.

If, as they say, *in vino veritas*, then each man was speaking a deeper truth than he dared to acknowledge or express when completely sober and beset by the politics of distrust, greed, chicanery or even measured goodwill aimed at ensuring that the rich keep their wealth and the poor do not become a nuisance in attempting to share those riches.

We all politely ignored the problem of *'whose land is it anyway?'*. That special night we were common folk sharing a very good standard of living in global terms, with a belief in higher education for our children, girls and boys, and a knowledge that despite differences in culture, background and religion, life would be easier to navigate for everyone in this 'land of milk and honey' in teaching and disseminating mutual respect and tolerance and forgiveness for the sins of the forbears. What we needed was a clean sheet and wise governance. Glasses were raised again to that.

Arni, who by this time was looking decidedly tired and hazy, embraced everyone around him as my father and mother, who had been sincerely moved by the goodwill and hospitality of our hosts and the whole occasion, suggested we take our leave. Alexander was still sitting on the floor near his friend and looking mellow, if not rather sad. I was not sure why that should be and put it down to the highly emotional nature he had no doubt inherited from his Russian ancestry, but that, we later learned, was only part of the story.

My husband handed me the keys and asked me to drive us home. After falling into the back of the car with my mother and Alexander squeezed in beside him, he promptly fell asleep. Having no precise idea of how we had arrived at the house through the maze of alleys, I looked up the street and noticed that a road was running along the boundary of the town with open ground on one side and a bright moon in a clear sky alive with stars above it. I headed up the alley to the perimeter road, turned left, which I hoped was the right direction, and started a rough descent on the outskirts of the town until I met a main road with which I was familiar and made for home. The two Israelis in the car who knew the landscape inside out, were beyond giving me any help and indeed the one was snoring loudly next to my mother, who nevertheless remained buoyant and very cheerful.

Turning into the land in front of our house in the early hours of the morning, we woke the sleeping man. A body can react badly from being suddenly shaken from deep slumber and my husband promptly dashed off into the dark area of tall pine trees and was sick. Alexander, who hoped his wife Yudit would be in bed and asleep next door and not wake up upon his entry, sneaked quietly off. I had gathered on the way home between snatches of softly sung, lyrical Russian love songs, that Said's father was known to Alexander but in concentrating on my driving, only half hearing what he was saying, it was a day or so later before Arni filled in the details. These he had learned as the two men conversed after rising in the early morning, as was their habit, to moisten the land at the bottom of our gardens before continuing their toiletries indoors.

Before and after Independence in 1948, Alexander had belonged, as was previously mentioned, to a group of 'guardians' who, like lawmen of the Wild West, had policed the areas around the Jewish farming communities in the Galilee and our district on horseback. The men were not uniformed but suitably dressed to saddle up, carried rifles and were employed to maintain order and prevent theft, guerilla activities and so on. One story we heard was that Alexander had a beautiful white horse at the time he married Yudit in the 1930's and that following the marriage ceremony he had carried her off on this white stallion into the night. Well…he was romantic enough to do that, and in any case he had no other form of transport, so why not make a get-away from the guests in the quickest and most familiar manner. Yudit was a real woman by any man's standard and I'm sure she was quite up to leaping into the saddle behind him and spending a fearless, first night of marriage under the stars, had that been the plan.

As a member of *Hashomer* sometime before or during the Independence war, Alexander had received orders to go to an Arab village close to Moshav Nahalal nearby and clear it and raze it to the ground. It was suspected of being a centre of dissidence and terrorist activities. Alexander knew the village well and was extremely unhappy with these orders but had to assume that others had intelligence that he could neither know nor verify. He put off the job for as long as he dared but finally went in with his guards and quietly but firmly ordered the inhabitants to leave before destroying their homes. The only shots fired were in the air. This had remained on his conscience and in his memory until this Christmas Eve when he had unexpectedly asked to join us for the celebrations in Said's home. He was unaware at that point that the old man sitting on the floor with his hookah would turn out to be the headsman he knew from the village he had destroyed so many years ago.

Strangely, the two men had never encountered one another in the intervening years. A circle was about to be completed. Alexander and the older man talked all evening of the events of that day and the way of the world. What had happened to the other villagers, where had they gone, where were they now? It was true that Alexander had looked sad and I do remember seeing him weep a little. These two men were now in their late sixties. The elder Besharat had survived and his sons had done well and the past was the past. Explanations were given, some truths were exchanged. With the old Christian Nazarene sharing his hookah with Alexander, who in turn confessed his deep feelings and regrets, our friend felt that something of the sin visited upon him by orders from above had been cleansed at the heart of its guilt, drifting gently away with the sadness of their shared past in the cooled blue smoke enveloping them both before dissolving on the air.

There was a strange irony in the fact that none of the rest of us, who were talking so enthusiastically about the desirability of brotherhood, were aware that a genuine act of forgiving and forgetting was taking place at that very moment in the same room. It had not been a light crime, people's lives had been altered for ever, other people had needed protection and the full truth would never be known but it had happened a long time ago and time had finally provided a merciful moment for healing, perhaps for both men.

To carry around an unforgiving spirit is as heavy a burden as to carry an unforgiven sin. The opportunity to throw off both burdens leaves a lightness in their place which can only be described as real joy, tinged though it may be with the sadness that gives it birth. That night we were indeed celebrating a birth intended to bring joy to the world and in one tiny corner of the globe called Nazareth, it did just that.

✦

Sausage & Smash!

Our house building was going on apace but that sometimes entailed as much re-building as new building since some of our workmen seemed unable to read the plans or preferred to exercise their own imaginations. The master-builder was not always on site, having to earn a living for his family. His main contractor and foreman, Said, was also occasionally absent without leave.

To repair some of the oversights, Arni virtually knocked himself out during one hot August week in 1976 helping his Arab labourers to put matters right. This began with drilling through a concrete block thirty centimeters thick and high to loosen it in its place above a window opening. This opening was not the right height and had been designed with an arched top but constructed with a square one. The hall walls also needed knocking out and replacing and an arch formed, as designed, over the opening into the living room from the kitchen-diner and into the living room from the hall. Arab architecture is famous for its lovely arches but I suppose our builders had got used to doing nothing so fancy for their 'squarer' Jewish clients. There were also adjustments to be made to the bathroom wall.

All this hacking out and building up and arching-over took place despite Arni having done his nightguard for the village between 1am and 5am on the last day of that arduous week. After a brief nap, he was at it again by six o'clock that morning because time was limited. The next day he was off to the Reserves for a month with only weekend leave, when his workers would also be absent.

The re-constructions were finally completed and the master overdone. Having four small children screaming around the house since nursery closed at 2pm, I suppose this wife did not fully understand why, at supper time, she had to put up with a fifth male shouting all over the place as soon as he got home. Poor man! Dinner was served but was not long on the table. A plate of hot sausages in brine ascended towards the ceiling, the lighter sausages descending a little less quickly than the plate as they glanced off the body on the way down, the plate naturally smashing on reaching the floor. The conjuror was showered with the boiling brine and a minute or two later cold compresses were being applied to his bare shoulders as he discussed a property conversion with some clients, who had unexpectedly turned up just too late to enjoy the whole show. I cannot now remember exactly what explanations were given for the application of the compresses but I have absolutely no doubt that they were magnificently inventive.

Following this folksy scene, it occurred to me that people who live in hot climates should not work, or overwork. Or perhaps the true moral of the tale suggested that some born in hot climates should avoid attaching themselves to others born in cold climates. If unavoidable, through the natural heat of desire, I wondered if the offspring of that union might, as they grew up, be terribly torn between a desire to scream and maintain a stoical silence ~ as if life were not complex enough without that.

But there were some compensations for our harassed provider working in his own office on his own plot of land where the house was being built under his nose but not always under his watchful eye. Number one compensation was provided when Arni employed a draughtswoman, 38 – 24 – 36, who kept him occupied … or rather whom he kept occupied and who was proving to be more than worth her pay.

Micki, no mouse I assure you, was quick, efficient and very pretty. What more could a pressure-ridden businessman desire, unless it were two of the same model? But for a busy man, one was enough! Well, our artistic draughtswoman who was married to a handsome fellow, certainly speeded up the work process and Arni was doing so well that he told me he was seriously thinking about cutting down on the architecture and taking up a partnership in a mushroom growing venture. "Well, if it mushrooms like your architecture," I dared to quip, "why not?"

I have never believed in questioning a man's capacity for imaginative invention or spontaneous fancy if it's headed in a financial direction and since I believed that mushrooms were grown in cool, dark places, I could also dream that such an environment might help to keep Arni's temperature down. But I had a feeling that this fancy, unlike his natural fancy for a beautiful and dutiful draughtswoman, was passing. And so it proved. But Micki, too, soon moved to more challenging work leaving us only with a pen and ink self portrait which Arni was able to pin up in his office.

From all this you may gather that being an *ola hadasha* had its playful side. Life may have been difficult at times but never dull. On this occasion, however, a respite was in sight as our energetic Major Goren was detailed to drive the army to desperation for a whole month from August to September on Reserve service, so that they too might fully enjoy the *shalom* that followed. My dear husband was, I know, reading my thoughts at that time but equally happily guzzling down a cool ripe water melon to compensate for the burning brine and binned sausages … which he had already forgotten.

Living in a precarious marital democracy, as we were, the Major told me that he was looking forward to donning his khaki and taking respite in the ascetic company of his fellow males. Were four sons really not enough? Maybe I should have hied myself to a nunnery a long time ere that!

Those in the astrological know, might realise by now that my husband was born a true Aries and I with my sun sign in Scorpio, fire and water. This is also a thought provoking starry match when you consider that the ram attacks with the head down and the scorpion with the tail up and over, thus never the twain shall meet eye to eye. Since, however, we are told that love vanquishes all, I would like to believe that peaceful co-existence can and will prevail some day, somewhere between us and the stars ... when all the wars are over.

✦

The Desert Bedouin

While on his month's Reserve Service, Arni had a few days leave at the old Nabataean city of Shivta in the Negev desert, where despite drought during most of the year, the peoples of that ancient civilization found ways to cultivate the land around their city with a natural technology.

The problem of irrigation was solved by taking stones over the dry period out of the wadis, the deep ravines and water courses between cliffs, and piling them up ready to ring around large areas of land in which would be caught the huge amounts of water from flash floods. These floods from the sudden great downpours of the first winter rains on the high areas above and beyond the parched desert, would slide off the hard dry surfaces they first hit but nevertheless pick up topsoil. When the floods reached the edge of the high cliffs the muddy water, with tremendous force, would be funneled down the wadis, rising to a height of up to thirty meters before bursting and spreading over the desert plain. There it would be trapped temporarily in the large stone-ringed areas, depositing its topsoil before being absorbed into the desert ground. That would have been a sight worth seeing.

The floods over, the considerable top soil would then be tilled and immediately planted with vineyards and vegetables before surface water could evaporate. Further natural conservation of water was continually achieved. The desert nights are very cold in relation to the dry heat of the day and combined with the effect of the damp, strong prevailing winds from the Mediterranean Sea the condensation at night is extremely high. The Ancients also knew how to make use of this moisture. Around their trees they would pile more stones from the wadis and the heavy dew that formed on the cold stones at night would slowly percolate downwards to keep the trees watered. For the Nabataeans, originally a nomadic Arab tribe who settled to form their own State around 300 B.C.E. and who were powerful traders for several centuries, the desert flowered.

Today the same desert area is inhabited by their descendents, the Bedouin, wandering from place to place with their goat and camel herds, having no desire to stop and catch the rain and making no attempt at cultivation. On his short leave Arni observed these fascinating people, who in the summer don't even bother to erect their tents. Babies were placed under sacking held up on four poles. Often he saw large herds of up to a hundred camels wandering in this desert with no sign whatsoever of a Bedouin herdsman except on one occasion when Arni noticed a little girl, not much more than five or six years of age, quite alone with a big herd of camels. She spent the day with them, walking about underneath one large, pregnant female camel to keep in the shade and with no sight or sound of other Bedouin within miles. You could be sure, however, that if so much or so few as one camel went missing in the night a delegation would be sure to arrive in Beer Sheva on the following day to complain of theft to the local authorities.

Arni told me how the army lost quite a lot of gear to the silent Bedouin but only certain objects. When half-trucks are riding at night over very rough ground in the desert it is not uncommon for some of the contents to be occasionally spilled out. The following day soldiers would be sent back over the area to recover whatever they could that had gone missing. It would seem that the Bedouin were smart enough never to pick up arms for which they could get into serious trouble. What they liked were refillable shell casings made of copper. Other casings were made of an alloy looking like silver. The copper would disappear while the alloy casings remained untouched.

You never saw a Bedouin with anything more innocuous than a stick but should some feud arise between families, they would appear armed to the teeth to settle it. The Israelis never found where the Bedouin hid their arms' cache in the vast desert areas but it took these nomads no time at all to become fighting fit and ready for the fray.

The Tale of the Transatlantic Sofa

An American lady and her husband, so we were told, appeared one day in Ramat Yishai in the 1950s having bought a very small property standing on a large plot along our road. Before anyone could say *Maazel Tov*, builders had arrived and started extending the little place at a great rate and it was understood without proper planning permission. Our new immigrants were fresh to the ways of earlier immigrants looking to make a fast buck in the land of *chutzpah and honey*. The builders, it turned out later, were relatively new to that game and with decidedly less than the modest level of expertise necessary to undertake sound building works. Within fifteen years the entire house had cracked in the most salient places, leaving it truly unsound for dwelling. However, with the re-building nearing completion at that time, the few villagers regularly watching the progress of the works were surprised to see a lorry arriving from the port of Haifa stacked full of antique furniture shipped from a previous home in the United States.

Everyone then understood that this lady and her husband must have been important and wealthy members of a Jewish community somewhere in the United States but had obviously decided to leave all that behind to live as good Zionists in the new State of Israel in the basic settlement that was Ramat Yishai. That, at any rate, was the accepted interpretation of events. And indeed the American couple lived there quietly and rather parsimoniously for something close to twenty years. Both had died in the one or two years before we arrived in 1973.

The delivery of the lovely furniture had been an eye-opener for most of the villagers who had never seen anything like that before. Indeed very few of them had any memories of such grandeur. But the new immigrants lived simply enough and it was only when the old lady was left alone after the death of her husband, visited occasionally by one other equally elderly lady from the village, that thoughts of the furniture returned to the minds of village neighbours. What, they wondered, would happen to the house and its contents when the owner died as there appeared to be no children living in Israel, if indeed there were any offspring anywhere else in the world, or other relations. So the day on which it was rumoured that the elderly widow might indeed die was the day on which the word went around that she should be visited.

Whether or not our American lady, like Bouboulina in *Zorba the Greek*, had finally closed her eyes on this wicked world before the doors of her house burst open and the window shutters were flung wide, remains apocryphal. The fact was that, while blessing her as they passed by the bed on which her old body had been carefully attended to and lay stretched out under a sheet, most of the visiting 'mourners' were as busy as a quiet visitation of vultures, snatching at all the interesting contents of that solemn place. By the time the doctor and coroner arrived to indeed pronounce the lady dead the house was virtually empty of its contents. These had been smuggled away to other houses in Ramat Yishai where they would no doubt have been kept in the dark for a suitable time, recognising both the statutory mourning period for the passing of a good Jewish neighbour and the passing of any other interested parties who might be responsible under the law for the property, now vacant and cracking badly.

Before launching into the transatlantic sofa, so to speak, it should be stated that the curse of our American lady, alive or dead when the final visitation took place, remained alive. Or that is to say the woodworm remained alive. It would appear the immigrants from the New World had not taken into account the need to apply a certain lotion, known as Rentokil in England, to kill woodworm which loves boring holes into fine, or even less fine, wooden furniture. Consequently, and unbeknown to the *thieving magpies,* much of the furniture 'rescued' from the American lady's home, the sofa being one exception, had already been invaded by worms, many of them dead but alas not all.

Within a couple of years of 'storing' this antique furniture in new homes, not only were the owners coping with its dusty disintegration but in some cases with their own furniture being ravaged by the pest. Of course one has to allow for exaggeration and the situation may not have been as dire as gossip suggested. In many cases preventative measures would probably have saved both antiques and newer furniture with which they came into contact. But as the curse would have it the 'furniture removers' were also unaware of the efficacy of Rentokil and chose instead 'to toss out the baby with the bathwater' making a bonfire of everything infected. So from time to time the village would be lit up with such bonfires and the additional curses of the cursed. The sofa, however, on inspection by its new inheritors was indeed free of wormholes and was saved for a different future. If this was not the curse reversed then it was pure karma reflecting, one hopes, the good deeds in a previous life of the present owners or owners to be! This is where our personal involvement in the story takes shape.

It so happened that a charming Yemeni family, the Yanai's, living three doors away next to the Maman's called my husband in when the married daughter living with her mother decided she would like Arni to draw up a house design for herself, her airforce husband and their tiny twin girls.

The grandmother, Miriam, felt that this extended family of hers needed more room than she could offer and especially so as one of the small rooms was made smaller by the area taken up with a magnificent, large mahogany sofa. This sofa remained shrouded in a sheet for its own safety and to discourage all her grandchildren from playing on it and wrecking it but it was shown to Arni with pride.

228

The fact was that the sofa was regarded with some awe so that few had sat on it since it had been installed at a time which happened to co-incide with the death of the American lady along the street, a matter discreetly ignored. The sprung seating of the sofa, covered in thick green upholstery, was in good order, as was the lovely carved and curving mahogany back frame and the eight carved feet which supported the four-seater with its two wide cushions and buttoned arms. It was a handsome piece indeed, dating back perhaps to the 1860s or '70s.

When Arni came to present the daughter with a bill for his architectural design, which had met with family approval, the young mother was somewhat embarrassed for she had only managed to save the money she already owed and had promised to her mother Miriam for some considerable time, a sum which Miriam badly needed for the purchase of a new set of false teeth. Skilled dentistry in Israel cost then, as it does today, a lot of money.

So Arni's client was torn between paying him and paying her mother. It was Miriam who came to the rescue. She had suffered for long enough with her poor dentures which neither cut nor chewed well and hurt her mouth. Going without dentures was more than her pride could bear and she was not in a position to make the purchase from her own meagre income. She mentioned the sofa that Arni had freely admired and asked him if he would be prepared to accept the sofa in lieu of payment in cash from her daughter. That would free up space in the house and enable her to use the money her daughter owed her to immediately purchase a new set of teeth. She was positively beaming with anticipation at this sensible and clever compromise.

Arni hardly needed to make a quick calculation to realise that he was probably the winner in such a bargain but suddenly had another idea as he really wanted the cash, or so he thought. He told Miriam that his sister-in-law in his ex-kibbutz was collecting antiques and would surely buy the sofa for the price of the dentures. Arni would organise the business.

Aliza was married to Arni's brother Yigal who was a member

of the kibbutz where they lived in a flat provided by the community. On her marriage to Yigal she had not accepted kibbutz membership as was the custom upon such alliances because she had a private income from rented property her immigrant mother from Latvia had left her when she died. On becoming a member, Aliza would be obliged to render or surrender this income to the kibbutz treasury, responsible for providing every member with all their communal living requirements. She had frequently been requested to change her status but to that time had refused to do so, holding on to her private money which she spent as she wished.

So with this interesting arrangement underway Aliza paid a flying visit, unbeknown to me, to look at the sofa and happily agreed the price. No money exchanged hands at that time but everyone was content with the proposition and Arni promised to sort out the collection, delivery and payment in due course. Miriam went straight off to get her new dentures.

To that point of the proceedings my dearly beloved had not discussed any of this business with me but before cash changed hands and delivery was made he imprudently told me about this clever deal, being unable to resist sharing a good story. He was dumbfounded when I exploded with indignation saying that although we'd intended to have three children that number had unexpectedly increased to four (the twins then barely a year old) and how could we possibly manage with just our little Victorian two-seater any longer. That charming sofa, which we had re-upholstered ourselves in gold brocade before leaving England, was greatly loved but rarely used, being too delicate to withstand our romping older boys aged six and four.

It seemed to me so fortunate Arni had been offered such a bargain on a piece of furniture we really needed. How could he think, without even consulting me, of selling the sofa to my sister-in-law for whom all things were provided in her communal life on the kibbutz? Not surprisingly, he was shocked and abashed by this impassioned outburst.

"The deal's already done," he replied as firmly as he could.

"Oh no it is not," I answered equally firmly, "leave it to me."

I went on the instant, leaving him with the kids, and rushed up to Miriam's house where I examined the sofa, with which I promptly fell in love, explaining how Arni had arranged the deal without telling me about it and how we had now decided that we needed the furniture for our own family. This would be perfectly acceptable in lieu of her daughter's cash. Miriam either way was set to get her new dentures but apparently fully understood how I felt and in any case we liked each other.

"That's a man all over," Miriam volunteered, "putting his wife last," and laughed heartily, her ample body shaking as she did so.

To save me embarrassment, Miriam offered to phone my sister-in-law and getting her straight away explained to Aliza that she was sorry but the sofa deal was off because the money had been found to pay Arni, adding, while winking at me, that this was a blessing because she really loved that sofa. Aliza accepted this explanation without much ado and it was then left to Miriam and me to decide how the sofa should be transported from her property, a few plots from ours, without any damage being done to it.

After I had returned home triumphant, Arni and another able-bodied neighbour were asked to find the largest wheelbarrow available anywhere along our street, which they did. They then securely fastened the sofa to the barrow and in a hands-on effort steered it carefully, under my watchful eyes, a hundred yards or so along the rough road to our house. At that point a decision had to be made regarding where it should be placed in the house. In truth there was not much space available but some could be made by shifting our little sofa into another room. Then I clasped my hands to my mouth with an inward gasp. The crew stared at me obviously wondering what next!

"Oh, my God," I whispered, "supposing Aliza comes to visit and finds the sofa sitting in our house?"

"Be sure your sins...." quoted Arni at me with a malicious smile.

At that point it was decided that the only place the sofa could be put out of sight until we moved again was in the roof space entered by the flat roof above the wash-house attached to the back of the property.

"How do we get it there?" Arni peevishly asked, thoroughly fed up with the machinations of women by this time.

"You're the engineer," was my prompt reply, "what about making a proper hoist with ropes?"

So at the end of a long day, ropes were gently placed around the well wrapped sofa and it was duly hoisted to its temporary roost in the roof space. As it happened from that day in 1976 to the day we left Ramat Yishai in 1977, a full twelve months, Aliza never paid us a single visit. The sofa, after being gently descended on its hoist at the appropriate time to be loaded into the container shipping our belongings back to England, has since been greatly admired and provided elegant comfort to the family and friends over three decades. I hasten to add that Aliza was told the full story a few years later, to absolve a twinge of conscience on my part and my sister-in-law neither remembered the incident nor showed the least interest in it. She had obviously moved on mentally immediately the deal was off and had filled her kibbutz flat with other furniture before she finally became a member of that institution.

There is, I think, a rather doubtful moral to this tale in which false teeth, sofas and sheer determination play a promising part but cannot entirely account for an accompanying sin of covetousness and the everlasting misunderstanding between husbands and wives.

Exploding Apricots

Our garden was a taste of Eden no matter how far west we were of Babylon. I remember counting around seventeen different fruit-bearing trees including almond, apricot, clementine, grapefruit, orange, peach, tangerine, lemon, pear, pomegranate, black and green olive, fig, grape, cumquat and prickly pear or *sabra*. The last named is the large cactus-like weed found all over the Mediterranean with extremely sharp prickles and tough fruit, after which native-born Israelis are nicknamed. *Eh bien!* ... as they say in France.

My greatest delight was to watch the huge apricot tree at the bottom of the garden when its starry flowers opened and blossomed to herald the arrival in good growing time of fruit of that amazing, sun-kissed, burnt orange. Every year our tree was laden and I would wait for that precise moment of ripening when the skin was baby soft and warm. To pick and bite into such a fruit burnished by the sun and smelling of all the goodness of all the fruit in the world was sheer, sensual heaven. No wonder Christina Rossetti's 'Laura' was so tempted by those horrid goblin fruit merchants. I thought of her as the juice ran down my chin, wondering how an innocent apricot or peach or pomegranate could be poetically presented as the source of sin. But dear me, how could I forget that first fruit, the apple...or indeed the woman who ate it, whose name is synonymously etched in our minds with original sin? Somehow it seems so easy to forget he who planted the tree… not to mention a snake in the grass and goblin men!

One day we had a visit from a Canadian neighbour from the other side of the village. This was Terry Raza who lived with his Algerian-born wife, Hagit, in a little *shikun* set in its quarter acre with a charming entrance and pergola covered in grapevines. Terry was a practical man, a retired engineer, who had last worked in a technical college in a nearby town but gave that up at the age of fifty-two to relax and enjoy life while thinking of the next thing to do. An inveterate pipe smoker, one of his hobbies was carving items such as smokers' pipes and walking sticks out of olive wood. These were people who had travelled widely around the world but had been settled for some years in the village with their children who were now grown up and no longer living at home. The couple were very genial company, interested in everything. Happily for me the house language was English so that we could share jokes, gossip on village politics and generally philosophise about life, enjoying each other's tales of the comic, curious and ridiculous.

Terry had noticed that our apricot tree was full to overflowing. What, he had asked, were we going to do with all that fruit? Frankly, I was so busy with the children and Arni so occupied with building up his small architectural business that the apricots had been left to their own devices. The house owner's canning equipment had been found on the property and Terry offered to help us pick and can the fruit and said he would be delighted to have a few cans from the process. We thought that was a splendid idea and my kitchen soon became a canning hive of industry.

The bags of apricots were turned out on the kitchen table and the cans filled with fruit and sugar-water and sealed. We put ten cans at a time into a sack and lowered it into an urn of boiling water which was brought back to the boil for some minutes. Sterilisation completed, the cans were withdrawn and cooled. Terry was director of operations and we did as we were told but it followed that there was quite a sticky mess to clear up and it was another job keeping the children out of it, so my time was cut out. We produced around a hundred and twenty cans, a single can working out at a quarter of the cost of a shop-bought tin of apricots and greatly superior in flavour. Having distributed a few among friends, Terry took his share away to store in his house while we placed ours in the dank, dark wash-house built onto the back of the property.

Later that same year, towards the end of September, we were invited to share a meal with Terry and Hagit. The grapes were beautifully ripe on their pergola and we had just popped inside the house to help bring out some appetising Algerian starters and good bottles of wine when a series of shots rang out very close, or that was how it seemed. I don't remember anybody panicking or jumping up and down although Terry did languidly reach for a substantial rifle propped in a corner of the living room.

It was only then that we smelled a strangely exotic, fruity smell from above and looked up to see a liquid oozing gently through some cracks in the very thin plaster work where this old prefab-ricated house had been creaking at the joints. Terry had been reluctant to tackle the D.I.Y required with more interesting things to do. Further startling shots occurred as the canned apricots our host had carefully stored exploded in the roof space under roofing with virtually no insulation and upon which the endless summer sun had relentlessly poured down. The contents of the cans had naturally fermented in the heat and the cans had expanded under the pressure and finally given way. The now recognisable smell of fermenting apricot assailed our noses as the juice ran down the walls of the room.

Wondering whether it was safe to enter the loft space amidst so much exploding metal, we left the men to deal with that side of the business while the two wives, in retaliation against the unex-pected invasion, shifted furniture and pictures and attacked the walls with buckets of soapy water.

We were later able to laugh at this hapless accident which had left Terry feeling a little embarrassed at a certain lack of fore-thought. There was no single can of apricots that had not blown out in a 'canon' of explosions that night. We gladly brought over a number of tins from our cool store that had not suffered a similar fate. After all, how many tinned apricots can a family eat in a year, whether you stuff lamb with them or simply eat them with rice pudding and ice cream. And nothing, but nothing, as far as I was concerned, could possibly beat the taste of that first, fresh, 'forbidden fruit' from the tree.

Dr Peugeot & the Chinese Carpet

One day a new family arrived in our village. This was Dr. Peugeot with his wife and two young children. He was working in a town in the area and somehow rumours had already reached our nurses that for whatever reasons, true or conjectured, the doctor's medical reputation fell short of excellence. Dr Peugeot had come to Israel at some stage of his professional career from Iran and judging by his Hebrew was a relatively new immigrant. His credentials and practice, it appeared, had not enabled the doctor to find a long-term position anywhere since his arrival to the country. So he could perhaps have been described as a medical peripatetic at that stage. Despite the considerable experience of our two nurses who also had doctors they could call on in the area, the clinic administrators had agreed to offer a contract to Dr. Peugeot, requiring him for a few hours each week to attend patients either in the clinic or their homes, supplementing his work in a local hospital. The doctor was gently spoken and pleasant enough but I must now digress to set the scene for a couple of interesting tales involving this medical man.

There was an elderly man living in the village who did not appear to be working for his living but had commercial or other connections which kept him busy. He turned up one day in my husband's office near the village centre and told Arni that he had a fine Chinese carpet and wondered if he would be interested in buying it. Perhaps the old boy had learned along the grape vine

237

that our house was full of strange old English furniture and that we might therefore be the right people to approach.

All Arni knew about Chinese carpets was that the best of them were usually made of silk with a huge number of knots to the inch, very fine knotting that would excel the Afghan and could excel the Persian carpets. Only an oriental carpet expert could really judge quality and Arni was not even faintly schooled in the subject, despite having once had a Jewish client in London who had shown him over his oriental carpet warehouse and persuaded him two buy a couple of Afghan rugs at a knock-down price, he'd said. Though these had been colourful with traditional patterns they were not quality, simply what we could afford at the time.

Arni agreed to go the man's house to look at the carpet and was suitably impressed with its silky texture and beautiful colours. It was about two by one and a half meters and most attractive in shades of blue and cream. My husband asked the man for his price, which seemed reasonable, so they haggled a little on the final money before sealing the deal with a handshake. Since my husband did not have the cash on him, and the man only wanted cash, Arni said he would drop it in and pick up the rug at the end of the week, which was amicably agreed. A couple of days later Arni turned up at the man's house cash in hand only to be told that the carpet had been sold to our new Dr. Peugeot. Asked why he had reneged on the deal, the old man simply said that the doctor had offered him the money on the spot and he couldn't resist it ... after all, *a bird in the hand*... he'd commented, spreading his hands in a familiar gesture. Well, every language no doubt has a translation for that, modern Hebrew no exception! Arni and I were naturally disappointed and upset at not only losing the purchase but also with the double dealing. So what can you do?

A few weeks later my husband took to his bed with a bout of influenza accompanied by a touch of bronchitis and felt ill enough to call on the services of our new medicine man who now, wittingly or not, had a Chinese carpet which should have been gracing our bedroom. In his vulnerable state Arni felt it best to leave that subject alone. So our doctor came in and sat by the bedside, checked the temperature, took his stethoscope to Arni's chest, looked down his throat, listened to his raw coughing and pronounced that he should take aspirin, stay in bed for a few days and drink plenty of hot lemon tea. Standard procedure. He then leaned nearer to his patient saying that he needed some advice from him. Needless to say Arni hardly felt well enough to indulge in business but with running eyes and a chesty cough offered to listen to him.

Dr. Peugeot pulled his chair closer to the bed and explained to Arni that he was involved in a land deal for which he needed professional drawings and planning. Arni struggled to sit up while the doctor kindly plumped up his pillow. Through his wheezing breath my husband asked the doctor to give him the details. At this point the good doctor did no more than take out a cigarette case, light a cigarette, without asking whether the patient minded his smoking, especially in the bedroom, and started to talk for all the world as though it were an everyday office consultation.

Arni was not and had never been a smoker, so you can imagine the effect of being in such close proximity to a chain smoker, as the Doctor turned out to be, while he was suffering from 'flu and with a chest inflamed with an infection. The fact that Arni started coughing badly did nothing to deter the doctor in his smoking and my husband was either too foolish, ill or taken aback to ask the man to stop blowing smoke his face. Perhaps the doctor felt he had done his doctoring and now was visiting the engineer, sick patient or no.

The story followed that Dr. Peugeot had once or twice been called out to an old man living down our street, a widower who was quite incapacitated, in need of frequent attention and generally in very poor health. The old boy had a daughter who visited fairly often but could not come every day. During the most recent visit he had told the doctor that he wished to organize the division of his half-acre plot into five building plots, for which he would need change of usage and planning permission. He then said that he required Dr. Peugeot to visit him twice a day and look after his health and ensure that he got all the medical treatment he needed for as long as he lived and for this he was prepared to give one of the plots to the doctor. Such a gift would be legally incorporated in his will and the solicitor briefed to assure the doctor that this legal bequest had been completed.

The sick man was obviously not just content to organise one building plot to attract the services of the doctor but saw the sudden profit he might accrue by dividing his entire vacant plot for housing development. Probably this plan helped to give him a new lease of life. The development of private and State land for building plots in the village was a new departure, with the local council and its aspiring Secretary happily realising that providing more homes for new immigrants might finally make the original purpose of these plots as smallholdings a thing of the past. This presented a huge opportunity for making money for private land-owners, State registered leaseholders and indeed anybody in the area concerned with building development and its auxiliary trades.

The doctor was naturally very interested in the proposition put to him and asked Arni if he could draw up requisite architectural plans for the five plots to present to the local council for planning permission. Only on permission being granted for the full development would the Doctor be happy to assure the landowner of his devoted medical service until *death them do part*. Arni was sworn to secrecy concerning the proposed deal and until today had treated it with total confidentiality, discussing the matter at the time only with me.

My husband assured Dr. Peugeot, coughing loudly in the process, that as soon as he had fully recovered he would meet him on the site. Never was he happier to see a doctor leave his house. When I entered the smoke-ridden room, I was bursting with indignation and opened every door and window throughout the house to get a circulation of fresh air again, insisting my husband lie down temporarily on one of the children's rather uncomfortable bunk beds. It took several hours to clear the house, let alone the bedroom, of the exhalation of that pernicious weed and several days for Arni's chest to recover from the shock. He vowed that never again would he allow himself to be trapped in a confined space with our new doctor, discussing matters more important to Dr. Peugeot than his patient's health.

I ruefully suggested, in double ire, that if Arni's services were so dearly required, he should receive not only the fee that would come from the old boy but also the gift of a certain Chinese carpet, recently arrived in the doctor's possession by less than an honest route. While hugely enjoying the idea of such circular commerce, Arni could not somehow bring himself to that level of bartering out of pure professional pride. Women, it has to be agreed upon, can be very sharp in the market place in the presence of double dealing and especially when there is something dear to their hearts to be won ~ or this woman at any rate.

On his full recovery Arni did meet Dr. Peugeot on site at the old man's property and drew up the requisite plans, got the site registered and put all the necessary papers before the council. These were passed within a few months, the rubber stamp given, the will made up and the old man attended to twice daily by either the doctor or a nurse swiftly organized for that purpose. Arni received his fee from the owner for his work and everybody was more or less happy.

Doctor Peugeot's happiness could only have been increased when six months later the old man died, despite the daily ministerings, and the doctor became the new owner of one of the five building plots. We never learned whether or not he built his own house on the plot or simply sold it on, as we left the village shortly after that. Either way it had been a very financially lucky and painless stroke indeed for the new doctor. The old man in his turn may well have winged his way to heaven or hell with a satisfied smile on his face. There is only one pleasure that can exceed the dreaming up of a clever piece of business .... seeing the dream become a successful commercial reality. Surely on this occasion at least, when the love of money had paid out reassuringly 'healthy' dividends, even death must have lost some of its sting.

The Judas Tree

I have been thinking lately about what it means to be Jewish and have come to the conclusion that the burden of being a member of God's 'chosen race' resides in the definition of that concept. Its descendents through the Jewish birth mother who accept its qualitative implications must automatically find themselves uniquely separated from other races, other people. By the same definition Judaism does not inherently proselytize ~ is not seeking to convert outsiders, which would strictly be a contradiction in terms. You belong or you do not. The 'club' is theoretically exclusive and that can be culturally provocative. But one can see how that powerful belief in being God's 'chosen people' was the strongest link in maintaining a cohesive sense of identity for displaced Jews of the diaspora across the world who had, for over 2500 years after the Babylonian exile until the birth of modern Israel, no permanent geographical sense of place to unite them. Historic Jerusalem and its Temple destroyed around 580 B.C.E. and again in 70 C.E. was, until 1948, a magnetic vision rather than a physical home.

There must also be an extraordinary power and strength within an ancient monotheistic religion which can retain its ideological integrity after giving birth to Christianity and heralding Islam from its own religious roots. But this can only add to a deeper historical sense of isolation for Jews and Judaism. In opposition resides the inclusiveness of Christianity and Islam seeking and gaining converts across centuries, creating strength in numbers as well as religious faith, each stemming from the one and same Judaic base.

Whether the notion of being a 'chosen people' came from the mind of the Almighty, as the sacred texts suggest, or was developed mystically and intellectually from earliest times to shield a people from their own peculiar destiny, is a question of faith rather than debate. The fact remains that there is probably no other 'race' until today that has deliberately attempted to avoid, rather successfully over millennia, assimilation and integration into adopted cultures to the point of losing that singular identity.

A race of scattered people, however, who developed a self-sustaining, survival mode from systematic, concentrated learning while living in ghettos, instead of owning and accumulating land, a practice from which they were excluded, gave rise to a different kind of power which was not debilitated by constant warfare. It bred outstanding intellectual acumen, producing financiers, philosophers, intellectuals and artists of the highest calibre world-wide as well as ranks of ordinary folk. That kind of recognisable success may be widely admired but with its roots in a racial exclu-siveness across history has also sadly bred, out of dependency even, envy and ultimately neurosis and fear leading to the worst genocide. The notional yet tangibly physical fact of being separate, the 'chosen race', over time and across geographical boundaries has resulted in constant persecution. That, to my mind, is the inescap-able burden of being Jewish.

This suddenly brings to mind two people in Ramat Yishai whom I may have subconsciously avoided mentioning but whom I must finally acknowledge out of love and sorrow.

Adella came regularly to our village. She was a lovely lady, kind but timid, fairly tall and slim and a little angular. Her hazel eyes smiled gently at you with care from a thin face, lined and sallow. Her hair had been brown but was now wispy and greying. Adella was probably in her early sixties and she wore quiet, nondescript clothes than had a post-war look to them. She was neither shabby nor elegant, just ordinary. Hebrew was obviously not the language with which she felt most comfortable. She spoke German to me, although my school German had largely been forgotten. I had to guess at some of what she said but somehow we understood one another. We laughed and chatted together. She spoke quietly, loved the children and had offered to come once a week on a Tuesday morning to give me a hand in the home from simple kindness, especially after the twins were born.

Adella knew how to make pasta. Did she have some Italian blood? I don't know, but she was a wonderful cook and her pasta was out of this world. I had never seen pasta hand-made before and since I cannot claim any Italian connections, I was only familiar with the far inferior products you buy in packets from the shops. One day Adella gave me a lesson in making *tagliatelle* with eggs and flour. It seemed to me quite a complicated process before being rolled out super soft and cut evenly in long strips. When ready it was tossed into boiling, salted water. It took little time to cook and was delicious enough to eat while really hot simply coated in butter with a little seasoning. It needed no fiery tomato or other transforming sauces. Adella, quite rightly, was confident in her cooking although shy in most other aspects of her character.

My friend lived in Haifa but she had a friend whom she visited almost daily in Ramat Yishai and with whom she would sometimes stay overnight. I would see her trudging up our road in all weathers with a canvas bag full of shopping, having come by bus from Haifa. She walked the kilometre from the main road along our sparsely populated street to the last house overlooking the valley, one which had virtually disappeared behind a mass of undergrowth and mulberry trees. In fact her friend's house was so shrouded in overgrown shrubs that you barely noticed it, and besides that it gave off a gloomy air of hopelessness by suggesting that no-one wanted to take care of it. The only redeeming feature on the plot was a tree that stood in the corner nearest to the road, rising a little above the other trees. This was the Judas Tree which every Spring would be ablaze with deepest pink flowers, a canopy of splendour over a dark corner.

244

So the old stone house went unnoticed and indeed that was largely the fate of its owner, due basically to his own choice in the matter. Very occasionally he would pass by our house with his thin Malacca cane tapping against the uneven asphalt. I had no idea where he was going, perhaps to get the bus to Haifa as I'd never seen him in the centre of the village. I would catch a glimpse of him briefly beyond our front garden in a white homburg style hat and white jacket that had seen better days, his head down, eyes scanning the road with a kind of intensity which forbade any social intervention, even a quick 'Shalom'.

I do not know the name of the man, though surely it had been told to me. What I do remember is Adella's explanation of her connection with him and why he lived there alone and unwilling to be part of the community. As far as I knew, only Adella was allowed into his space. I am not sure how they met but perhaps it went back a long way and I believe he not only trusted her but, in as much as he was emotionally able, cared for her. But truly, it was Adella who cared for her friend. She cooked and washed and cleaned for him and was simply there to tend his needs. She soothed him in the darkest hours when he was woken by ghastly nightmares. Without her, he would no doubt have deteriorated mentally as well as physically far quicker than he did. On the other hand it might have been a blessing if death had called sooner.

So this crumpled old man, a neighbour to whom I had never spoken, was left in peace because that is what he wanted. One day while Adella was helping me in the kitchen she sketched out his shocking story with great compassion and no drama. Briefly he had come from Germany, where he had been a married man with three lovely young girls. He had survived the concentration camps and arrived in Israel after the war and bought the house in Ramat Yishai. At some point during his incarceration in a camp he was made one night to witness the brutal killing of his three daughters. The camp guards had held him, bound, while they machine-gunned the three young girls before his eyes as they called out to their father in their innocence and terror before slumping to the ground in pools of blood.

The Judas tree never gave me the same joy after I heard that terrifying story. It carried with it an overwhelming sense of betrayal epitomised in man's inhumanity to man. I would look at it and see only three lovely girls, falling softly like beautiful pink petals at Spring's ending.

It was in Spring 1977, and towards the end of our few years in the village, that I realised Adella had not called for a month or so. I did not know then, until I made enquiries, that her friend across the way had died for no funeral had taken place in Ramat Yishai. It appeared he had left Adella the house but she did not want to live in it. She visited me once more after that and we embraced with tender farewells. It had been a privilege to know her.

El Al & the Pregnant Mormon

This is a final tale about Adrienne Napper, my old friend around whom troubles blew even when there was no wind ~ a gentle-woman fired by some deep need to collect lame ducks, human or ornithological, and by so doing create for herself and those around her more problems than either they or she needed.

To be chronologically correct, this was not quite her final story but the last two events we witnessed are too painful to recall in detail; the one involving the near death of her daughter Cassie when medical incompetence following treatment of a tooth while she was in the army led to emergency hospitalisation due to the decimation of her white blood corpuscles at an alarming rate. The other event involved Adrienne, nearer sixty than fifty, going on a rally to Jerusalem and joining with a band of Jewish protesters wanting more land and less peace. They physically clashed with the police and military who waded in with batons and other weapons and the lady returned home bleeding and heavily bruised but not bowed. But let us return to more mundane family matters.

Adrienne lived on a very meagre budget indeed, making and mending to augment her basic income but she nevertheless kept her cupboards full of what she termed essentials. These included flour, oil, pastas, rice and cheap tinned foods, stored against the probability of having to live under siege when the last great war with the Arabs would find Israel with her back to the wall and Ramat Yishai surrounded by insurgents, Armageddon in the

247

offing. How our village was supposed to barricade itself against that possibility I failed to imagine, in its exposed position on an accessible promontory next to a main road to Nazareth, a major Arab town, or Haifa in the opposite direction with its considerable Arab population. One's mind boggles at the strange workings of another's. So Adrienne's poor patch of soil at the back of her little house was always planted with as many vegetables and fruit as might nevertheless survive for pickling or bottling and putting away against the evil day.

Adrienne had a daughter in England who had joined the Mormon faith, married a Mormon and at that time had four Mormon children with one on the way. She had decided to visit her mother with the kids but without her husband and had been enjoying being thoroughly spoiled and waited upon by not only her mother but also her young step-sister Cassie. Arni volunteered to give mother and children a short guided tour to various places of interest around our area as Adrienne had no vehicle.

After more than three weeks of considerable effort trying to feed and please the visitors, Adrienne admitted to me that she was worn out and would be quite glad when they all went home again. Apparently even picking up a tea-towel to dry the dishes was too much effort for this lady in her fifth month of pregnancy and resentment was growing fast in her half sister. I mention this only in the light of energy she later expended.

Finally the time came for Arni to take mother, daughter and children to the airport, after giving El Al twenty-four hours confirmation of their return journey on a particular flight to Manchester. They were told that seventy-two hours confirmation was required by El Al, as by all major airlines, whose officer added that they were working to rule and the family had been struck off the passenger list when not getting in touch within the specified time. This, of course, had left El Al the possibility of re-allocating the seats. El Al was in fact renowned for working an over-booking system and very often, so we were led to believe, had a queue of company men, their wives and children who were just waiting for such cancellations in order to fly out whenever their fancy or the company allowed them to do so for a short holiday, sometimes at the company's expense. The airline later went bankrupt, before being re-invented, but this did not help Adrienne's daughter at the time.

Both mother and daughter were anxious that the family get away on the original flight. So Arni decided to try his luck and drove his packed car to Lod airport. On arrival the daughter asked him what they should do. He suggested they brace themselves for a great battle. The lady went with her children to the Check-In and was immediately told their names were not on the passenger list for her flight. At this point Arni, a perfect Hebrew- speaking *Sabra*, stepped forward asking where he might find the main administrative offices. They were pointed in the right direction and he asked the daughter and her kids to follow him. Adrienne, who by now was looking white and wan, was deposited in a lounge, where he hoped she would not get into any trouble. What, the daughter asked, should she do if the company continued to be unco-operative. You must throw a fit, is what Arni suggested. Make as much noise as you like because in the Middle East no-one complains quietly.

They then entered a small office with about four desks at which three members of the management staff were seated. The visitors were ignored until Arni went to the nearest man and explained that he had with him this woman, heavily pregnant and with four children who needed to fly back today to Manchester on flight so and so. He added that they were being met at the airport by the husband for an ongoing journey of several hours further north by car. The husband could not be contacted for a change of plans. The man looked up and without asking for more than the names checked his latest passenger list on what was the company's fairly new computer system and naturally the family did not appear on it but their replacements did. Arni asked the manager to check the original list and the reply was that no such list was now operative. When they argued about this, the manager simply told the Mum that this was how things were done in Israel. Arni asked for the next option.

"Well," said the operative, "we might be able to arrange a flight for them within two to three days but after taking their names for stand-bys they would have to keep checking this up with the El Al office." The man turned his face away and got on with his job. This sounded like never-never to the mother and the children began to cry that they wanted to go home. At that point Arni turned his back to the El Al employee and nodded to his companion that it was time to make a fuss. So this woman started yelling and screaming in a way that even astounded him and could surely have won a BAFTA award. The children also started to yell more loudly at seeing their mother in such a state and suddenly she picked up a model of a Boeing 747 resting on the table and threw it against the wall so that it shattered with a noise that brought the room to the attention of other passengers in the area who could see straight into the glass-walled office.

The furious manager demanded the family stop breaking up his office and Arni assured him they would do so but at the same time he leaned heavily across the computer on the desk, pressing a jumble of keys to add to the general disruption. And indeed the machine started making all sorts of noises with paper spewing from the printer. Meanwhile the manager too had pressed bells to have the invaders repelled. Then Mum really came into her own and started on a further rampage, tearing posters from the wall with her children running after her screaming loudly. So everything was going according to plan and after two minutes two policemen arrived and the demented manager asked them to arrest everybody. One policeman informed the manager that he could not arrest a pregnant foreign national, we don't know why, and as for the children, they could hardly be counted at the speed they were tearing about.

It was not a pretty picture and by now quite an interested crowd had gathered to stare at the proceedings, voicing their own opinions as to what was happening and who were the victims. The manager then complained that Arni should be arrested because El Al's aeroplane had been smashed. Arni protested that no damage had been down to any plane, only to a model. There was then a noisy argument concerning the semantics of the matter, what had or had not been broken and naturally the question of over-booking was loudly aired. It became obvious even to the policemen trying to pacify the children that some kind of an impasse had been reached.

Meanwhile another employee, who had regained some composure following the initial shock of what was happening, was on the phone. He interrupted the argument with the manager and whispered something into his ear at which the man brusquely took the phone shouting "*Ma*", or "what!" as you would say in English. The policemen were still trying to calm mother and children when the manager above the din shouted that the plane was about to leave and would the female passenger and all her children present themselves instantly at the check-in for immediate departure to Manchester.

They left the office in all its mess and rushed with the pile of luggage for a quick departure on the original flight. Arni was not intercepted or arrested and in due course, having seen them all to the entrance to the departure lounge he returned to Adrienne, who though wondering where they had been was dozing and happily unaware on this occasion of anything but relief that her daughter and grandchildren, and one on the way had, after all, been allowed to travel as she had firmly believed they would.

"After all," she sweetly smiled at Arni, "we are in Israel here, home at last in the land in which we belong and for which we have waited so long." He nodded, grinning with the thought of the mayhem he had just left behind him but a few yards away. And indeed what need was there to abuse an innocent of her dreams while those dreams might last? Unfortunately his dreams that night were neither innocent nor quiet but when rest finally came and he was no longer besieged by children towering over him, wielding ten foot models of Boeing 747s, he slept the sleep of the dead.

Sheep May Safely Graze'...

It was fortunate that our own unexpected exit, from my point of view, from Israel was quieter, tidier and without undue incident save a change in schedule.

We had been phoned to say that instead of leaving at 11am we would be leaving at 6am from Jerusalem rather than Tel Aviv and would we please present ourselves at a certain bus stop where we would be picked up and taken to Jerusalem airport. Since we had never flown from Jerusalem before we were unaware that a Boeing 747 could not possibly take off from that tiny airstrip at an angle which could clear the mountain at the end of the short runway with a full passenger load.

The fact was that there was a commercial dispute in full swing between El Al and the charter company MAOF with which we were flying. The big boys had flexed their muscles to get the smaller competition out of the way and found some obscure union rules which proved MAOF could not officially take off from Tel Aviv. So to circumnavigate these rules MAOF was officially taking off for the flight to London from Jerusalem. For this they needed only a dozen passengers to board in Jerusalem for a five minute flight to Tel Aviv where those passengers would all change and get on the scheduled flight for the second leg of their journey at the original flight time and with all the other passengers who would not have been thus far inconvenienced. These details had not been shared with us.

You may imagine our surprise then at finding ourselves among fewer than six others who had been 'hand-picked' for this joy ride. On getting out of the 'mini-bus' at the silent and seemingly deserted airport we watched the sun rising lazily and hazily above the Jerusalem hills. No one was there to greet us as we entered the tiny airport building, hardly a terminal, but once inside a fellow approached and told us to sit and wait for attention in the waiting room. Well at least we'd been spared the usual airport crush, we thought. There was only one small plane we could see parked outside but suddenly a Boeing 747 cruised in and gently touched down. After being checked we strolled across to the plane on a concrete runway which had grass growing through the cracks and on which some few hundred yards away towards the end of it we noticed sheep were happily, if not safely on this occasion, grazing.

I suppose being a family of six made us the first target for getting numbers out of the way with less passenger reproach, despite the fact that we had to cope with four children, two of whom barely two years old. In a fight to the death, which MAOF lost, I'm afraid that was the least of the airline's concerns.

Since none of the selected handful of passengers for this unexpected early morning aerial view of Jerusalem from a jumbo jet had been informed of the planned change of planes, it was only when we asked the single steward on board what was happening that the situation was explained to us. By way of compensation we were given a voucher for a few lira and the list of duty free watches, pens and drawing pads etc., we might buy. When the children had eagerly made their choices, they were told "Sorry, dear, that's not available, that's not available and that's not available…" I don't believe they had anything on board, coffee included. To add insult to injury we had gone through a full security check at our 'rural' airport of embarkation before our baggage was loaded and on arriving in Tel Aviv, after being escorted by armed military police in a jeep from the plane across the tarmac to the airport entrance, we were simply dumped at Departures, with our luggage, to join the queue for another security check for the scheduled flight to London. It was May 1977.

Maybe Arni had a point in deciding that the '*aliyah*' for me was over. The 'going up' was now, liked a pierced balloon, definitely 'going down'. After a short holiday with my family in the Cotswolds, my husband intended to return to Israel to tidy up his business before driving Rosie once again, with no family or caravan in tow, back to the port to embark for Naples to return as quickly as the old girl would allow to England. But before this extraordinary 'flight from Israel' we had the memory of our last party still bubbling in our minds.

✦

The Last Party

Saying goodbye to good friends, possibly for always, is difficult. Leaving Ramat Yishai, and indeed the country, to return to England in 1977 was more than difficult. Leaving was considered by many of those good friends to be a moral dereliction of duty as well as personally sad, though most were polite enough not to press the point.

Israel in 1977, despite a sea change in its politics from fundamentally left to fundamentally right, was still subtly infused with the sense of *'the promised land come true'* or at least still surrounded by an aura of hope and spirit of possibility. It had only recently celebrated its 25th anniversary and, despite if not because of four wars fought from Independence forwards, surely the creative energy and drive was there to build on those shaky foundations a nation that could compromise, find a way to temper might with right. And this even beneath the great grey shadowy wings of international politics which consigned plain soldiers of the Middle East to playing bit parts in fight scenes of much larger dramas.... and losing their lives.

So leaving Israel was like leaving the threatened if not sinking ship. *Your Country Needs You* was still the heart-cry in those days and Arni more than I was naturally aware of this and desperately trying to avoid telling people of our plans to return to England. His excuse was that his clients would not feel the press to finalise payments if they knew he was leaving the country and we would therefore stand to lose more than we could financially afford. This knowledge had to be kept secret until the last moment possible.

Villages being what they are, somehow the word got out. We were, after all, obliged to sell our newly completed house, in which we had never lived, much to my chagrin ... so much imaginative and physical input and so little pleasurable return. Needless to say, the chap from a nearby town who wanted to buy the house knew somebody in the village and the word was leaked. Not the best way of breaking bad news. So we had to face the music. Our real reasons for returning to the U.K. were not fully understood by myself as it had been Arni's decision, based on his feelings about his work prospects, financial security and maybe some gut feeling that the children might be better off growing up in a land less beset by wars and political instability. I was morally, if not practically tested, a pacifist and he knew that all our boys would have to serve in the army or air-force for three years from the age of eighteen. Beyond that Arni was always an instinctive animal, always moved to spontaneous action brokering chance and change.

Our friends, having recovered from the moral disappointment to some degree, insisted we have a party, a final fling before turning our backs on four wonderful years of fellowship, affection and downright good neighbourliness. And they all turned up. The carpet was rolled back, the music played, there was good food on the table and the wine flowed.

These are bittersweet occasions in life when you laugh but want to cry. And we did not get off Scot free. Benny Shadman, a very handsome man of Persian origin, with fine features, shiny black hair falling across his forehead and wonderful, laughing brown-black eyes, who had been invalided out of the Yom Kippur débacle with a bullet through the lung, reminded us gently of the biblical words written into the Six Day War anthem 'Jerusalem the Golden' ...'if I should forsake you, Jerusalem, may my right hand waste away' and smiled at us wistfully. I understood he had to express that and remember opening my hands in a gesture of 'what can I say' … before painfully smiling back at him and turning away with a feeling of shame and a lump in my throat.

Danny Shoshani, the sea captain and psychiatrist son of our lovely neighbours Yudit and Alexander, was a man straight out of Tolstoy or Conrad and he asked me to dance with him. Danny was a big man in every respect. His English and his wit were honed and his deep bass voice issued from a large chest. He had the proud head of a lion, broad shoulders, a seaman's grand beard and the sharp blue eyes of his mother. I respected him and we had greatly enjoyed the Shoshani hospitality on several occasions. The *art of living* was central to Danny's philosophy and it involved generosity of mind and spirit.

Like so many large men Danny was very light on his feet. But he was not a captain for nothing. I was used to mooching around the floor with my husband for whom rhythm was missing a connecting link between ear and foot, which meant I generally had to shuffle us back into tempo. The naval captain was having none of that. 'Let go', he said, 'relax. I lead you follow'. And I did follow and what a dance that was. Hot and breathless after foxtrotting and quickstepping in close rhythmic harmony he laughed and said "You're learning" and added as a quick afterthought, "Pity you're leaving…. *at hevreman*" which very roughly translates as 'you're a good bloke…' That was for me one of the greatest compliments I have ever been paid.

And so it was that when all had said their final farewells and walked out into the night air and the door was closed behind the last and closest of our friends, we were too full up to speak. We held each other closely and that night lay in bed unable to sleep for a long while. My eyes were wide open, staring into the dark room, not thinking but feeling all those emotions of love and loss that are the stuff of life, the deep connecting tissue between human beings who are essentially joined and essentially alone.

257

Just a Thought ...

For years while my lovely sons were growing up they were faced with a handwritten quote stuck to the kitchen wall where we sat together to enjoy communal family meals. It was something Betsy Trotwood, in her inimitable Dickensian way, said to David Copperfield, her Trot. It was there because, short of the Ten Commandments which would have been as lacking in impact as a Victorian moral sampler, it encapsulated what I believe held all those values in a pithy and pertinent expression:

"Never," said my Aunt, "be mean in anything; never be false; never be cruel. Avoid those three vices, Trot, and I can always be hopeful of you."

Charles Dickens, *David Copperfield*

A Tale of Two Villages

A great deal of the Israeli and Palestinian sky has been lit in recent years with fire; sudden bursts of guns, bomb blasts, rocket explosions. Villages have been smashed and bulldozed and thousands of innocent people killed. In the last war in the Lebanon in summer 2006 young army reservists, like my nephew aged twenty-one, lost their lives unforgivably after an official United Nations cease-fire was ignored by Israel.

Ramat Yishai has grown apace leaving virtually no traces of its former untidy human progress during our time there over thirty years ago. That was when two feet were still planted on the old soil in which Ben Gurion had attempted to grow a new nation with something of a will for justice and peace to help water the young roots. But young hands even then were outstretched to a different, unknown future that offered security based on strength and economic prosperity, maintained and fortified with political money from a super-power thousands of miles away.

None of the children or youth of the 1970s could have known that twenty years on their Prime Minister Rabin would be assassinated, like Kennedy, by one of their own extremist people for even attempting a peaceful solution to the political problems of the region. Some of those youth would have been too young to be interested in or familiar with a General from the Israeli wars called Ariel Sharon and to realise that his dubious and bullying military past would be a very good reason to make sure he was

kept out of politics for the sake of Israel's future morally, culturally and politically, though many Israelis I know today would not
agree with this. Others, from the more liberal left like ourselves,
could not imagine such a man ever being given the reins of power.
Yassir Arafat's equally dictatorial, hardline attitude did not help
Israelis to decide to exclude Sharon from the Israeli political
arena. However, two wrong men do not make a right one.

Time and again it seems to me that the man effectively makes
the history rather than the other way around, whether in exhorta-
tions for peace like Ghandi or prosecuting wars like all dictators
from time immemorial. Napoleon was finally defeated but not
before changing the face of Europe. So although circumstances
breed leaders, this matters less historically it seems to me than
what they do in their time, especially when you consider events
for which they are personally responsible which can scar relations
between peoples for hundreds of years. We only have to look at
our own shores and the Irish problem to understand that.

I firmly believe that it is finally and seminally personal example
and commitment to all humankind which militates for good in
human history, as with Ghandi and Mandela. Their influence is
legend across all nations as with all those in the past who chose
to repudiate force or sacrifice their lives for a deep faith in a
higher path to any freedoms whether political, social, economic or
individual.

At the end of the day a man can reach only as high as he can
spiritually lift himself and sometimes only gains freedom in
giving it away. Such a man as Mandela grew in his thinking, his
faith and his stature in the solitude of the denial of his physical
freedom. This is a strange dialectical process to think about
which Solzhenitzin went some way to exemplify philosophically
in his wonderful book *One day in the life of Ivan Denisovitch'*.
Inspirational personal example, I believe, exceeds all ideology,
even that which prompted it.

The improbability, if not impossibility of any real or lasting
global justice in environments of basic social and economic

inequalities in nations and between nations is what we face. A genuine desire to address these inequalities, apparent to millions of us via instant film, the internet and other media, may breed a Ghandi or Mandela or the United Nations Organisation. At the same time those inequalities also create the breeding ground for envy, greed, vice, power-mongering, fear and corruption, creating war upon war and problems upon problems with which we have difficulty in catching up let alone dealing.

Equally, the laissez-faire cynicism and apathy bred of affluence, though understandable, is demoralising and we should be thankful for those minorities of concerned people everywhere who are prepared to stand up and be counted. It is they who offer the spiritual voice and moral strength without which no nation can consider itself half-way civilized.

I am aware that deeply complex problems of every sphere abound at the heart of all international relations and like the tip of the iceberg more truths are hidden than appear on the surface. We can never see or grasp the whole picture but occasionally justice should be seen to be done. For that reason alone I come to a particular, personal plea for two small villages in Israel and a lost way of life that I am privileged to enjoy, living today in my village in the peaceful heart of England. It is just one small example of how a stupid act of a single, over-zealous soldier involving the few can lead to years of injustice breeding bitterness amongst thousands.

In Israel, just inside the border with Lebanon, were two villages like Ramat Yishai called Ikrit and Bar-am. I imagine the same kind of people lived in them as lived in the village around which I have centred my tales. In Christmas with the Cablan I told of one Arab village that was razed without promise of a return and of the scars carried by two persons involved with the incident.

The difference with Ikrit and Bar-am was that following the 'evacuation' in 1948 of the Christian Arab villagers on the orders of a young officer, an Israeli Supreme Court Order in 1951 gave permission on judicial evidence for their return. The government of the day ignored this Order. In 1953 Israeli forces finished destroying those villages by razing all the houses to the ground but the Catholic church on top of the hill in Ikrit remained. Nearly fifty-five years later, with constant court cases overturned by successive government intervention and despite national and international demonstrations both personal and public, this sad business has not been settled. Neither the original villagers nor their descendants have been allowed to return to their land, nearly 6,500 acres, much of which has been annexed by Israeli agricultural communities with the rest of the previously cultivated land going wild so that today it is covered in scrub oak. Sharon's fear of demonstrating military weakness or culpability or of creating some kind of a precedent has become a sad indictment against subsequent governments with their Jewish settler policy in the Palestinian West Bank, not to mention the infamous Wall that will fall one day soon, I hope, with or without a Joshua to bring it down. All such walls and fences built on foundations of fear and ideological mistrust cannot last. In the end, as with the Berlin Wall, people power must bring them down. Peace has to be brokered on a level playing field.

Both Ikrit and Bar-am were inhabited by Christian Arabs to which the largely restored church and burial ground in Ikrit bear witness. The elderly scattered inhabitants, who found themselves in towns like Haifa or Acco or nearby villages barely two or three miles away, wanted to return home to die or at least to be buried in their own churchyard. Across the years the burial ground has been tended by Ibrahim Iassa aged sixty-seven. When there was no room left recently in a nearby Arab village cemetery, permission was not given to extend that cemetery but ironically government agreed that the Ikrit cemetery could be used instead. The dead don't walk, talk or farm!

There were about 400 villagers in Ikrit when it was evacuated and now, in 2005, there are only around 60 or so of the original inhabitants left but with the descendants of those 400 there are now 2000 'Ikritis' who have a judicial claim on their land. Although it is said that the Israeli moshavs have farmed only 10%

of the original land this is not correct as they have been continually expanding into the area, the government turning the rest of the land into National Park, bringing animals into it while the rightful owners are kept out. The unsigned, unnamed dirt road to the Ikrit site and its church was dug into trenches with heavy equipment one night by members of a local Israeli farming community. The word went out quickly and 'Ikrit' families from nearby villages appeared with hoes and other hand tools to fill up the road as quickly as it was being dug up. Before trouble could escalate the Military Police and Army arrived and re-instated the road. But any attempt by villagers to plant, put up a fence or a shack on four poles on the village site is quickly dealt with; plants, fences and makeshift shelters are immediately pulled up. Only one shelter ~ its walls carpets, its roof tin ~ is allowed to remain outside the church where two elderly villagers in turn act as caretakers of the church building, night and day.

As Askkar Marrouf, a villager evacuated aged nineteen and now in his seventies, said to me in October 2005, "Ikrit will remain long after me and my descendants have gone and long after all the words that have been spoken and written about it have been forgotten."

The church in Ikrit has become a symbol of both a legal and moral injustice and it would be foolish of any Israeli government to destroy it now or in the future, adding stupidly and without foundation to an ignominious chapter in Israel's short history.

I would not now wish to live in the Ramat Yishai of the new millennium but I would respect those who live there today and ask that the same respect be offered to the communities who were uprooted from Ikrit and Bar-am by allowing them and their descendents to return if that is what they wish. These Israeli citizens have never posed a threat to the State or come into conflict with the law and yet were forced to leave their homes in a time of war and see them destroyed in a time of peace. They received no compensation for their land. It is time for redress. I would ask this simply in the name of commonsense and common humanity even at a time when both would appear to be in short supply: a fair and generous gesture is never too late and might indeed create a precedent for more fair and generous gestures towards a more equitable and less bloody peace for everyone. An example is needed.

And on the final larger scene surely the need and wish for peace and goodwill in the hearts of ordinary men, women and children in the region has sometime to overcome the awful personal pain as well as the hate and intolerance of present minorities in growing numbers, both Israeli and Palestinian, who believe might is right, God is on their side alone and that force can hold down a mounting pressure forever. One has only to think of the volcano St. Helena.

Watching a world beset in recent times especially by huge natural disasters which have wiped out thousands of homes and people in the blink of an eye, life may seem cheap ~ but the one real way to make life cheap and meaningless is in killing, maiming, de-humanising our own kind. Volcanoes, tsounami, hurricanes are obviously beyond our control. Human nature it seems is also beyond our control, unless ...

✦

Afterthought

I have come to the belated conclusion that the only valid reason for writing this notebook of a momentary period in my life, apart from the pleasure in doing it, is because I like people. If you cannot find some sympathy for the people around you, the good, the bad and the in-betweens, where can you live? In remembering all those wonderfully ordinary or extraordinary individuals and places that were once a part of my life, I am simply hoping to share with readers that corner of this world's engrossing and endless tapestry of complex lives.

It has nevertheless been a strange personal experience dragging out of the mind details of a past life. In many ways it is like living that life all over again, in short time clips and without the exercise. It is also odd because the first person of whom you write no longer exists, indeed is hardly recognisable in thought, word or deed. Making links from that character to oneself is like trying, to little effect, to stick a shadow on its subject ~ the outline continually reforming in changing light, the inner content remaining dense and dark. I tend to live in the present, where else indeed, to which the easily forgotten past relates definitively but uncertainly. If the present attains impetus from the hope of a future perfect, then it surely derives energy from a sense of a past imperfect. Even as I scribble this I feel the present is my real home, solid environment, happy landing ~ and gone.

So, why have I visited that particular corner of the past? Well, apart from finding all people fascinating in their diversity and commonality, I think something from my distant historical past about which I have no knowledge may be responsible for an inexplicable interest, going well back to my youth, in Jewish people, their history and humour. It was pure chance that at some stage in my life a closer connection would be 'accidentally' forged through marriage. My interest in the Jewish race is neither academic nor sentimental, more a curious empathy. It presumably happens to others who develop an interest in the people of Arabia, India, China, South America, Scandinavia, Ireland or wherever. Who knows what genes are lurking in there just waiting to pop out?

What else may have been genetically handed down to me I can only describe as a marker indelibly printing in my brain or mind that being human is all that any of us can be, irrespective of race, religion, gender, time and space. This is the species to which I belong, for better or worse, even if I once was a fly. And this may explain why from an age when you can attach yourself to others, I variously and colourfully did so. By others I mean ...*the others*...those who are not in your cosy circle, from your safe home surrounds.

Today no effort is required to meet people from different backgrounds, I only have to walk down a street in any major town to be enveloped by cultural pluralism. But in the mid nineteen-fifties, aged seventeen, it was different. I joined the International Friendship League with its rooms somewhere in a large house in Hyde Park. For all I know that may have been a cover and hotbed for political shenanigans of the then popular intellectual 'left of left-wing' ~ the communists! I cared not, for I simply wanted to mix internationally and came to no harm, politically or otherwise as far as I know.

Soon afterwards I took a holiday job as cook on an International Farm Camp in Cambridgeshire. So to be involved on an international scene was then the call for me. Maybe that is why my first love was an Indian Sikh, my second love an Italian Catholic, my third love and first husband a French Communist and my fourth love and second husband an Israeli Jew.

I was not aware of deliberately choosing 'foreigners' as friends or lovers. Those relationships evolved naturally and hopefully I was as much a wild card choice for them! It matters not. That's how life happened for me and tends to go on happening in much the same way as I frequently and happily make new contacts with people at home and abroad.

Having admitted to my eclectic tastes, I must go further and say I really see very little difference between these and those as far as the human race goes. The cultures may vary but the sins are the same.

Additionally and increasingly, I understand that we all need markers, faiths, shibboleths to give our lives meaning but at the end of the day we all share the same failing planet in the same failing way; failing partly because we largely, of necessity, consider ourselves in charge of it. That is surely a joke. Our powerful planet earth is in charge of us, I think, or at least foresworn to pay us back in multiples for our muddled survival strategies which encourage us to behave so badly to each other and to a global environment on which we all depend.

If we believe that what is important about being human is a level of consciousness raising us above other living organisms on this earth, of which we are more or less aware and depend, it is natural to concede that such an amazingly ordered, 'infinite' and indecipherable universe, of which we are such an infinitesimal part, might be better understood than we understand it by some other 'intelligence', whomever, whatever. Some call that God, others Allah, Buddha or other names. I'd like that naming idea if we didn't make such a mess of it, so I prefer to call it 'Unknowable'.

Surely, in our humanity, we can try to remember to where all our markers, faiths, shibboleths are finally pointing ~ to the unknown, to mystery and ignorance. Whatever our beliefs, or unbeliefs, we all share that mystery and ignorance. I happen to believe we also share what we know but do not understand and crucially too often ignore ~ an unquestionable capacity for love.

April 2011

About the author

Maggie was born in London in 1937 and graduated from Oxford Brookes University in Art History in 2002, after a year studying anthropology with interest but no outcome. Across life Maggie has been employed in the music industry in the U.K. and Australia and finally spent six years with the BBC TV News at Alexandra Palace and TV Centre working as news typist, teleprompt operator and producer's secretary. In 1970 she married an Israeli engineer and in 1973 emigrated with two sons to Israel, arriving in time for the Yom Kippur War. On her return to the U.K. in 1977 with husband and four sons, she edited, with monthly editorials, a local magazine resulting in 'Monthly Letters from Middle England, 1980 – 2000'. Maggie's first love is poetry with her first anthology 'Hunchback & Clown', 1990. Since then she has produced with her composer son, Dan, and actor friend, Sheila Probert, a hand-crafted book of poems with CD illustrating the beautiful etchings of the extraordinary master printer, Michael Fell ~ 'A Simple Easter' is due out shortly. A new illustrated book of poetry 'Sighing through Grasses' is also coming out later this year. A more recent excursion in writing has been in exhibition catalogue essays for the amazing, New York abstract artist, Jeffrey Kroll, his latest show at the Saatchi Gallery in June 2011. Maggie lives on the edge of the Cotswolds, enjoying her family, garden, music and continuing to write whatever she fancies.